THE COLLECTED POEMS OF
KENNETH PATCHEN

BY KENNETH PATCHEN

THE
COLLECTED
POEMS
OF
KENNETH
PATCHEN

A NEW DIRECTIONS BOOK

FOR MIRIAM

CONTENTS

Poems from

from *Before the Brave* (1936)

"Let Us Have Madness Openly"

Let us have madness openly, O men
Of my generation. Let us follow
The footsteps of this slaughtered age:
See it trail across Time's dim land
Into the closed house of eternity
With the noise that dying has,
With the face that dead things wear—
                              nor ever say

We wanted more; we looked to find
An open door, an utter deed of love,
Transforming day's evil darkness;
                    but
We found extended hell and fog
Upon the earth, and within the head
A rotting bog of lean huge graves.

Among Ourselves and with All Nations

Chiefly I prize this loss of patience, deep
In riot-days around us; these swollen
Times propel the future forward: tear
Alike my friends and turn about my foes.
I think not every lesson learned
          is
Full of welcome; weeds in suburban streets;
Stalking gangs who fire at sight; and ghosts
Marked with print of million moving feet;
—You guess the answer, gather courage:

Wash your linen on the wires of storm
       and song
Advertising no shadow hope or unemployed regrets
              take care
These withered times prepare no turkish-bath
Of comradeship or endless singing in the square:

The fight goes on, goes out, goes in—
We cannot loiter though legions repeat
The final word of the final orator.
This time is wrong. The fact is law, not tactical.

That We Here Highly Resolve

Offer no borrowed proof or energy; the dust
Does not despair of reaching will as well
As crippled goats and false delight. For faith
Is not of desolated moments, or care
Of millions faked by praise or belly-rubbing.
Chains and sickles have an equal base:
The mind behind the hand confirms belief.

Hold out for no heaven; accept no hell—
What use a perfect plan too soon, a lesser one
Too late. Invent no floods or fires.
Give solid laughing eyes to those
Who would defeat these gains by kiss, or blow.

Be generous to generations who had nothing
To take, or give. O be willing to wait no longer.
Build men, not creeds; seed not soil—
O raise the standards out of reach.

new men new world new life

When in the Course of Human Events

Turn out the lights around the statues.
Unlock the vaults of unhewn stone; put down
An order for new men. Place high the value
Of those others: do not forget what they have done.
Do not destroy. They build a world we could not use;
They planned a course that ended in disaster.
Their time is up. The curtain's down. We take power.
We're sorry they left so little. We wonder
If any will say of us: Do not forget. Do not destroy.
We wonder if they will mean it as much as we do now.
Turn out the lights around the statues.
What do you think the dead will wear next year?

It Is for Us the Living

Now I commend this body to this earth.
Soon to know the swamps and suns
Shall burn it out or lead it quite away.
Eager: O fathers, how can you hear
            with any heart at all
(So laughing: so wise in nowise being hunted, hunting)
How can you hear of journeys taken through your world?
Do you think to stay the tramp of history's feet? (no land:
        no flag: no past) O should we die in tents
Of anger fouled by ghosts? Do we require blueprints
Of the hand holding knives at our throats? Do we need
More light to see our blood upon your lordly ground?
Do you think we'd buy salvation in the stark market-places
Where we ourselves were sold? Do we know another guilt
        than waiting? and should
You meet us (no land: no flag: no past)
We shall not smother in the wild sobbing heat of it.

3

The Last Full Measure of Devotion

I think the deed was richer than the dying.

They are no more by death than those
Who die beneath a trolley's wheels
Or take it in the ring for fame or money:
We will no martyrs or legends.

We can't get there by taxicab or sentiment.
The road is sterner than pride.
This is not a dedication to sudden understanding.

They too are craftsmen whose fingers close
Over careful triggers, whose targets we are.

Set up machine guns over the stale bellyaching of our books

Thus Far So Nobly Advanced

Give us the grace to be men
With heads and hearts above the fall of power
Come to us.

Give us the courage to take
Another's failure. Give us wisdom; give us love
To know that scarcely all can see the quiet war
That points to victory of discipline and honor.

Give us less of scorn.
O give us time to guard the winnings
From the winners. O give us words that shrug
Giant shoulders at the false display of poetry
That does not show the pilgrim far before the brave.

We Mutually Pledge to Each Other

I claim no tide can wrest from us
What good we are; nor country proud
Of lovers' Spring can gain parade
Of less than continents, to make us glad.

There is nothing to admire in birds
That do not fly; there is nothing to regret
In scholars trained on charms and dazed
To see us die. We come alone
Though millions nod to see us go.
We have so much to do
And lightning's slow to strike so many.

We have not long: our plays are few.
Can we convince in better speech? Yes, guns are loud
And history has place for orators not quite so proud.

We Hold These Truths to Be Self-evident

Let the loud men grow louder, weak weaker.
Grave brides foster motherhood: even church
Is better than long use of hate. There is
Adventure enough on earth . . . sky chattering
        on million feathered tongues
Hundreds of years from this moment. O comrades
What will they have killed? The hawk? The plunge
Of divers clean in sea? The private music
        of her voice? Shadow under leaves?
O save the station of men standing
Looking through the fresh eyes of their sons
With reason that nothing dies by will of man
Save man's capacity to *be* when words are stale . . . not done.

Prayer Not to Go to Paradise with the Asses

Marshal the quaint barren fogbeats in harbors
left by wings of those whose mansioned lonely
powers rode a hermit's riderless hurricane into
the dark-fretted eyes of the Golden City:
on, through fervent dreams and crystal worth
through the bellowing brainlike splendor, and
spirit's girth like dandelions growing
         bestowing
April's promise under skies of dust: where
growing hard they tipped the barrel marked
God and found the little fish of memory
          a crusted
monument in the fairest head of Man.
Lover: Siren: Advance: Survivor:
     through pretty hoops all fast in honor
O captive dainty words denoting massive
          glory
glory squashed in the hinge of a history
as dread and lovely
as bonfires burning in the breast of a dove
whose head adorns a penny-dreadful; whose heart
beats in fascist tread of marching feet and seas
    now rolling
over the grave of the fretful forgotten brave.

1933

The World Will Little Note

At least we cannot live to see it all; no comfort
Rests in this. Yet, this record is not empty of flags;
Is left the private curve of living like the others
Whom we loved; is left our duty to the earth.

We have this history we make: it is not theirs
As money; it is not theirs as goods or change—

It is as an eternal conscience to speed the task.
It is as an admiring mother with a natural child.
It is as the homely kettle to spend its steam.
It is as the growing body of a normal tree.
It is as sympathy and love can make a place for it.

O not the drill and brazen energy of singing.
We shall reach a stand and cause for fighting.
O we should be the hunter in the hall of eternity.

1935

The guilt of man does not defer the sun.
The sky sends out no S.O.S., the rivers
Reconcile the valley-seed to villages
Removed from priestly murders in our streets
Flowers ask no mercy, needing none,
Though stained by blood of pickets.
The lynch-tree sends out its shoots
Above the stripped slain body of the Negro.
And the stars witness only the horror of space.

Like perspective give to us: perform
No wailing over wooden days, that
Take an acid, either way.
This is a winter time too recent cold
For the burst of spring in our veins,
In our view.
There is nothing to decide: or kill.
Guard against the treachery of heart:
It is the head that signs your will.

A lot of men and armies stand to take
no chances with the prisoner Goddamn
them standing there near the bars watch their fingers
flex their eyes proud their legs firm their earth this
time next year last year a hundred years from now
they think it's all ours belongs to us we've got
you where we want for nothing

                              any painter
can't paint any carpenter can't build any
doctor can't cure any man can't say how deep
it goes inside to watch to stand dumb
in the streets of their cities and know
that your head's crummy your feet drip blood
that your belly rots your life is shot
                                        your days
are spent in two-bit flops because of them
because they get away with murder away
with everything we are or ever were come
to think of it

                    Goddamn them standing on
the cover of our world their heavy boots grinding
into our faces their ropes about our necks their guns
shut your mouth you bastard where do you live
what are you doing here look out
look out we don't know anything about that but
I'll tell you where we live and what we're doing here
tomorrow maybe I'll tell you then I'll tell you
when your guard is down when the thing breaks
I'll tell you all you want to know come to
think of it

I'm not too starved to want food
not too homeless to want a home not too dumb
to answer questions come to think of it
                            it'll take a hell
of a lot more than you've got to stop what's
going on deep inside us when it starts out
when it starts wheels going worlds growing
and any man can live on earth when we're through with it.

The Magic Car

O splendid to reach a craft and creed:
                            smoke
Selling sky the fingers of this florid ruin;
Our foggy cities slain in silence, joy's
Commencement stilled in commerce willing
Wars and death—out there is signal,
            neighbor, friend and love;
Out there is land of power, river's pulse
And sprucer weight of mountains; there is wealth
Of lovers; the will of glory; stress
And plowing fight to dream and win
The Car, the way: the scope of Peoples' clan.

We enter the fields of New: our famished images
Crack. What is glory? what is dream? Only
Swing above the echo's currency; the Dismal Swamp
Controls not day nor coward's dark. Endure
This action: pay out those pools of self
                            and hear
On peaks above possession, the factory
Of time merry in the sterner making of an earth
Which is the Car we build in you and all you are.

We Leave You Pleasure

We leave you pleasure in the earth:
Burnt grass in the sun; waters'
Body, lovely in the waste of years,
Having no wings for us;
The stellar vast wonder in the sky;
      the furniture
Of Space shattered within the heart;
The cynical image of smoke
      curling up
From homes we never had.

We leave you seas upon parched shores;
The iron twist in vines
Over our graves: the deafening sound
Of silence over everything.
Turn from the rebel body: here;
The crude question of the grass;
The spirit's face bleary
With sightlessness. It is enough.
We leave you.

Letter to the Old Men

What have you left for us to say to you?
What have you done that we can praise?

You stand on the ice of our hatred; your faces
Are turned to the wall. *You have not long.*
It is quite late for anger: we have not time
To forgive you. Where can you turn?
Our searchlights rake the streets of sight. O vision
Is in having power like the morning star,

Like weather in new world of stellar joy;
Is in having the power to be what you are
On earth where all is change with reason. O elaborately
Sightless old men in cathedrals of decay:
Death is the bitter goat in your gardens
        the traveler come
Like a wonderful lion in dream of redemption
To take you away. What have you left for us?
Our frontiers are all guarded; the day's work's begun.
The heroes flee your prisons; the sick approach the sun.
Our welcome is for others: your graves are ready,
        waiting . . . and pity
Can feed on the stone. For time and love
Are our ancestors, these, and these alone.

Demonstration

I thought your face as lovely
As mind knows silence in mansions
Read about, so slowly real and long ago:

Here words are pigeon-toed schoolboys
        lisping
Through the halls of sunny love on earth
For at the moment, and sudden,
While kissing you,
The sound of a crowd in the street
Gave the kisses double homes
And the press of your lips was a toast
To the torch which they carried,
Was a flame tossing above the shoulders
Of an unloosed wonder where are no words,
        like hairy dreams, to squat
Above the wild sweet grave of our honor.

History Is a Throne and a Gate

(an exercise in statement)

I walked to the edge of you, looked over

calmly serenely

it is not usual that music should have this body
it is not well that shadow should singe the sun
it is not time to tell you of what I saw has done

and often now, it seems

and this moment's muscles divide me down
to the road called forever and sceneless days are wound

All the Day

Because we have no type of earth for everyone;
Because we hold against all sign of pride
In men whose wakened love endures not long,
        not well; because our joy is mixed
Of valley-peace of mountainous pain, we bar
No singing shiver in slighter use of all we know.

Our likeness designs no further war,
No element of disaster; and yet the orbit
Of all things begins in us. We walk
In self, confined in pressure's share
In crumbling world—the pleasure gone,
The rooms reserved for "bird" and "flame"
Untenanted; the heart now counts the piggish hair
        on childhood's "loveliness."

Our world is hollow under guise of heaviness.
We leave the homely grief; are left
An agony that builds to save itself.

While the birds make music

All else is shallow storm: the shadow strength,
The pigmy strapped in harness of despair—
Because your shape is shaped *without*
This peopled solitude must build in self one everywhere.

A Letter to Those Who Are about to Die

You were the last to love America; too grim
Are the hours of waiting, too new are the names
On the map of this geography: for more
Than all the truth which drums and flags deny,
For more than all that we can tell or feel or do
Is told, is felt, is done, in this: about to die.

You were the first to love America; as men
Love the mother who leaves them, as kinsmen
Falling in feuds respect the draw of a blood
That has made of wilderness a reasonable earth.
You were the victims of a synthetic tradition
Of love, you who should have hated their healing from birth.

You can be the first and last forever to love
This country: you whose lives are empty of living;
Whose bodies already are bargained for and bleeding . . .
           O vow
To alter nothing of living but life in our time,
To plant the dynamite of hate in all our love and seeding
O to build and break and march and climb and climb.

The Ladder

Whether my day is day for you
Or light on other plane in other eyes,
Is not renunciatory measure of speech.
Men on little shelves of occupation
Must find another shelf, another day,
When houses are put in order; you will not
Get near the pigeonholes of what they've been.
Coming then to place of bodies: not cities,
Not plans, or greater age, new culture,
Can alter the system of being a man.
Stay near to that. We've had enough
Of games; enough of pressing selves
Along the grooves of epic dishonesty.

Revolution is not career as making
Coffee is career. It is the ladder;
The mountain is man.
Save the mountain.
Ladders are useful in their use.

Night Has Been as Beautiful as Virginia

This ends: entering the show of silence:
Voices gone: the outposts of glory given
Bare to stillness. Traps are sprung on day;
Corpse sprawls free, is spared a second's
Grace—blunted by dark the trees
Draw back, like ghostly badgers given
Homes whose profile needs a brighter earth,
        then, as we watch,
Like collapsible drinking-cups, they lunge
At space, in full gulp getting the first star.

Through hours, intent on fields within ourselves;
Exploring maps that lead from womb
To will of being here where every flower closed,
Where every use of light goes late to memory
And goal awaits tomorrow's massive towns

We hear the dark curve of eternity go coughing down the hills
No bird could stay this dangerous bough, no singing
Equal this

Our shield shall bear divorce of time and bring
O bring, as we watch in this dark
   like dawn
O bring proclaim the pity shock this hunger's timeless game.

The Firing

O seal the shining! this stillness binds the stars
In ageless shell of space. Permit no caricature
Of puny hare betrayed by moon; no sober
Music's beeless hive;
   O give
Blow for blow and back to fellow-back
The driving shine of quiet mind . . .
In end, the starry scream is uniform disaster.
This weasel-rage of generated murder
Is wilder stand for peaceful verse;
The utter bird our skies cannot withstand.

I watch this paper-record's woven sound:
The pageantry of rustless guns the planted horror—
   I hate
This boy's siege on witless Troy: this Helen's epic
   soulless noise.

This Man Was Your Brother

(footnote for newsreel)

How white how calm the hours are
I still have time
    the body of living beats in my hand
schemeless
    like a garden of voices in the sky
                       what
crucified   mounts a creatured stair
soldiers   gentlemen soldiers'
boots have made it crimson there
soldiers flay the earth with music   woman
shriek I said and cry I said and say   his name
    is not the rush of flesh to hold
    when soldiers place
the long far distance over the flight and song of him
ponderous eyes move in the silent face
his mouth is strained with stretching crazy roots
we like the sound I said the sight I said of boots of boots
    I said I still have time

A Letter on the Use of Machine Guns at Weddings

Like the soldier, like the sailor, like the bib and tuck
    and bailer,
like the corner where we loiter, like the congressman
    and lawyer,
like the cop on the hill, like the lead in weary Will,
like the kittens in the water, like the names on Hearst's blotter,
like the guys and dames who laugh and chatter,
like the boys and girls who don't matter,
like the preacher and the Pope, like the punks who
    dish the dope,

like the hungry singing Home on the Range,
like Father Coughlin acting like Red Grange,
like the grumble of the tuba, like the sugar war in Cuba,
like the bill-collectors, like the Law-respecters,
like the pimps and prostitutes, like Mickey Mouse
     and Puss-in-Boots,
like the churches and the jails, like Astor's hounds and quails,
she's like you like her, now don't you try to spike her,
she's the nuts, she's a mile of Camel butts,
she's honey in the money, she's my pearl,
what am I offered for being alive and willing to marry the girl?
though her insides rumble and her joints are out of whack,
let's give her a whirl, why grumble or try to draw back?
though her hair is false and her teeth are yellow,
let's get chummy, let's all get a break. For what's a fellow
got at stake, for what's a guy to do
who hasn't the guts to deal with sluts, guys like me and you.

The Other Side: The Green Home

The earth is near tonight; O slow
within that wonder, turning
mouth to mine, the million laws of world
forgotten, love: this is the solid level goal
of all we seek forever, the gate ajar . . .
the timbers of the self give way
          slow: our posture
stays the strain a moment
more, explodes in flashing panic
          then, fails
the rebel wounds of wanting O peace
in spite of death our empty star assumes
its place in sky.
We shall ascend again within that wonder, love.

17

The Mechanical Heart

I have no answer, time or will, to answer those
Who fear defeat of mind in casting heart aside.
I hold as guest no literature of feeling:
Strain, story, swerve of faulty hands,
No final stab of hunger. I heed
In fuller part that thing we are when quiet,
Unconfused by motion, unconfessed of comrade-love,
When quick to call the millions monkeys whose eyes
Reflect the sanity of a Santa Claus stuck in a chimney
    much too big for him—
When cool to easy trick and cosy task
Of sorting out the middle class, the muddled case,
The Word in flesh, the crawling wart and Fathers' curse.
    I have no answer, time or will
To question what truth I know. We need
So little proof: no house is ever started at the roof.

Nocturne for the Heirs of Light

Acknowledge last this human peace:
Summer patient holds precisely duplicates of chords and tides
That overcast by time, relax their magic late or soon
To those whose noonfilled faces blend
The autumn's coming blight, the willful waxen spring . . .
The faltering heart is held by creature ease in orbiting
    frames of earth.

So like the sagging flood of light the dazzling shine of fire
On these hills whose phantom helpless flowers blossom
In the fuselage of this Tennessee flow of death and dark
                  constricted
Like pale fruitless orchards on the roaring slope of despair

18

Or like our own chase ribbed by death's atomic street
By waves of doubt issuing the wound's riding power
The final road the plight of eyes grown hard
Believe me if all those endearing young charms
                                        girls and gasmasks

But we go back. We know the nature of the lie.
We know no feckless later leaf shall rivet sky
            O faltering heart the magic hill shall shine in human
Face the awful valley send a child!
Belief in Winter's iron music turn the lands of home to Spring.

Having Been Near

My quality is such as common things
Decide: the lack or amplitude of air;
Ribs' placement; heart's strength; belly's
Load—how can I create a goal
Beyond confessional speech in this?

The way of special sight? acquiescence
To wild brakes upon the doleful belly-gas:
Having charity like lizard's tongue
Within the head's starblanched crying?

Or should I stretch a single wire
Quite through the spirit's snobbery,
Hanging from it, in qualified display,
The graphs of love's scant honor: lungs,
Star-hunger, bird's cry, flowers,
The "moving," "drawing near," "coming
On;" enormous wings in steaming hash
Of sun, night, rivers,
And the loveful "having been."

There's a Train Leaving Soon

I want no easy light to lift my eyes.
Conversation in cells is rich as words
Arranged to pin imagination, spinning
Loose as death's more lenient glove.

Call to me at end of operation: when love
Sewn into the breastwork of this sky,
When lanced of greed and hate and fear,
When lost of anger, envy's vivid eye
Gone blind and black, when all is clear—
Your way to me—call: and I shall try to answer back.

Loyalty Is the Life You Are

I shall be with you when hollow faces
on Time's screen stare at you leaning forward
leaving no distance from here to Berlin or Rome
leaving no roses under the wheels of the traitors
or hate's tractors tearing up earth Goodbye to golden
technique of grain till attack the landscape background
of fists police bombs till staged a comeback being
our eyes are the eyes at your windows gentlemen
our hands are the hands at the latches of your doors
stopped horsing around with the fascist whores I tell
you I shall be with you stopped toying with them
with the mind spirit god or what have you
or I to gain and I think the strain is good gentlemen
for us the pity we felt with the goat to be shot
in the drinking place of our sorrow
        our frightful
white lives laid bare to the clever photography
which armies employ with men cheap gas masks cost money.

Note for a Diary

I

I want no wonder's cloud or church to wake me.
O let us come
We are so long away: the apple orchards on the slope
Of vivid hill; the glint of wind in sunny trees
Along the lake, its water cold and bodies clean
Their shape in break of it . . .
          diving. Girls whose simple naked laughing
Give to clothes and green paths gaining country roads;
Your great hand! I listen now the turn the lastly earth.
But ever that sky should fall from delicate heights
And the lean slicing wings should fill all sleep of creatures here
It is this time we wish no wonder; knowing ends
Are break of growth and breath; knowing no circumstance
Of danger can stay the daring of the circling bird: the summer
Heart of time within this place. The gloss-trees of corn,
That crawl across the windows of this cottage, are story
Growing into us: the soil and seed of fate is now
The engine WE nor any love or hour's shadow glory gain
Shall learn from "one" the lesson's voice and Day, O let us come.

II

And at the closing awful calm
When voices give muffled praise whose meaning
Cannot matter to the rest: "How has the anger worn?
How deep how pure these wells?" Out of
          the careless crumbled West of nation
And of man, the heart will climb a little way
In slogans, sand and ease . . . O hollow
The weakling's heaven the birthright of the fool
Whose folly is the common botch the pitch of human's speech:
O let us come
                       include
This argument this hour's blade and creed its closing awful calm.

Country Excursion

Now this remains: the thunder stopped;
the stubborn sky grown thick,
all clumsy, holding back
and we
in silence, running, as though
on padded drums; hitting nothing,
no sound and something singing
close and hard and all around
    us, like
sudden angles loosed in wind-murdered hair.
Not laughing now, against some reason
    running, not followed
and earth   ·
this field is dry and water needs
while drools a frivolous sky: this nasty
waiting being everything in one, a civil
war in perfect check
and then

                         the rain!

It all remains: endured the shelter, and through
the limbs and leaves of chosen tree
we heard that coaxing, that definite clean.

My Generation Reading the Newspapers

We must be slow and delicate; return
the policeman's stare with some esteem,
remember this is not a shadow play
of doves and geese but this is now
the time to write it down, record the words—
I mean we should have left some pride

of youth and not forget the destiny of men
who say goodbye to the wives and homes
they've read about at breakfast in a restaurant:
"My love."—without regret or bitterness
obtain the measure of the stride we make,
the latest song has chosen a theme of love
delivering us from all evil—destroy . . . ?
why no . . . this too is fanciful . . . funny how
hard it is to be slow and delicate in this,
this thing of framing words to mark this grave
I mean nothing short of blood in every street
on earth can fitly voice the loss of these.

A Letter to the Inventors of a Tradition

How do you know what effigy of self
This radiance has willed? Headlights hold
Not wheels to rail nor find the aerial sight
Of South-living cities too cruel for bulbs
Whose duty rests in human eye within the cabs
Of cattle-trains; there is a mixed resemblance
To fields of war in this: man the maker, unmade . . .
Like the name I called, O like the answer
                              never come.

I cannot think the earth is greater now
That dwarfs have set it high: each tree
A throne, each river roof to greater past.
Of all the blown wild pines of yesterday's
Power; in all the humble soft skies kneeling
              on the motherbreast of the Mississippi
There is no leisure, no earnest loss nor rest
Save in the name I called, save in the answer
                              never come.

Dostoyevsky

Was pain within you then—a grinning thing
The world could strike; releasing hell to plow
Your features with—before the accidental coil
Of days had brought Siberia; before your need
To find a passage out had brought you
Torture in the famine of a traitor's love.

How seared the wasteland of your sight:
How well you knew the horror
In the beggar's eye; the eyes that leaned
Against the fabric of your exile
And drew you back to drown with them
In troubled lands where masks have shown
A tattered front and fungusteeth
Are seen at work on pleading thick faces.

And when ambition had brought
The hollow stint of words to light
What arms, what words were kind to you?
            Retreat was yours, I think, in going
Fully out . . . deep into the universe of self:
Where faithless women prepare no hurt
            or healing, but lift
Their arms in shadowed bitterness to hold
At last the shells of I and I am this
You leave to them; where hungry men move through
The huge and tender brain to file themselves away
In harsher ledgers of despair.

And if you felt a rebel's sense of shame
In using eyes so strained above the pigmy's day, outside
Recorded areas of breeding and dying—
Your range of love like flowering water
In a desert place eludes their simple pity.

A Letter to the Liberals

It's not enough
That doom shall find us whole of hate
And terror; valid ruin admires devotion
Growing out of wonder that it lived
At all. Can we admire and will the sport of clowns
Performing in their tents, enclosed
            from us
By shock of finding now that we
Have other things to do? For after all
The truth is out, the hour breaks, the bridges
Fall, the dams give way; our time's
At hand. We know the voices, the clumsy faces:
"Almighty ghost, have us. Almighty God, save us."

We bring no boxed solution; our flags
Stream out for use, not trumpet-masses.

I'm tired of all they say: "How do you say 'worker'?
Make it ring?" Near the run-down factory
The hills still climb to cloud and silence,
Birds singing, their notes no whorish alphabet
Or key to foreign trade; the horizon,
Indolent and shifting as men or tides,
Has scars and wonderment unchanged by general strikes.

Submit no more. They said the wind would polish names
And thunder clear the quiet streets: I saw them smile
I knew they lied
Spies aware of danger grasp for guns
Not straws: be noble and be true
Your whiter cloaks provide a better sight on you.

A Letter to the Young Men

When the days grow teeth at last and games
Are over; when sunset stills our eyes and search
Is done, the ways all blocked, the wind's
Majestic house gone slack to the crush
Of quarreling planes in all their blue skies;
When bayonets are dearer than sunflowers
In all the stalls of earth; when your country
Needs you asking Why do naked good bodies
Go up like stale rockets O proud bloody flowers
Growing in History's garden Break it
Up young men   their guns are pointed
At you are pointed at all the mad flaming
Grandeur which killers can never make die.

Leaflet (One)

The speaking mouth's a hearse of wasted days
and in the swamps they track him down they cut
him up they make a mess of him and in the streets
we run for cover · they're opening fire they're opening
mouths to laugh and laughter has a bell to ring
an even politician-sleep from the I-said-a-dirty-word
ritual of living · even now they're ganging up on us
run like hell run into the speaking mouth · you crazy
bitch keep your cards down out of sight

but what of those who cannot speak? who fail to laugh?
ladies' lovely garments are the clouds and music
blew her nose · the snot was eaten by the poor my god
to thee to this · someone
tell that woman not to show her cards tell her to come
up to the Hotel Nacional · come out to see the bull

get his   in all the world   golgotha   (the crazy
woman with the pampered paunch do you know the one?)
I scarcely know the name of any they shot
without this rage · without I know they shoot to get
us all to kill the gentle silent men because
they ask to live · they ask alone to live.

Tell her to come out and hear the band play Dixie
at the hour of our death while the fleet waits
in the harbor · color of horror: confetti acts
as wine in Cuban waters and the bright little Christs
flit through the crowds into the church bearing
tidings of great joy to the fat woman
in penthouse—paradise · while we wait   speak?   laugh?
They raise
                their glasses, rifles, grenades, their jeweled
hands and take another card another life another Omaha
another sack in another river another knife in another
back · my dear · these dreadful strikes   and we
fear no hear no see no evil being dead being alive in death.

There must be time · turn your eyes away shall we
see the murdered peace the cheated hope the fire
flickered out the Negro dead (the sun is kind and wise)
your friend shot through the mouth the flame
stilled the gang storming the jail while the wounded
stir the dust with maimed hands · while we wait · the sun
is kind to us in motorcar and diningroom · do not
lose heart O the day is good to us the poets in the papers
say   amen unto you a child is butchered but Gloria's
got a million
                loving her tonight for every baby born
in Cuba, its father long in jail · sleep, baby, sleep
your mother sold herself to England · baby, sleep
they raped her with a battleship · my baby sleep · what
time is it? We watch the well-dressed man leaning

propped against the doorway
                              dead · we took his watch
his purse; we stabbed him with a borrowed knife · once
upon a time upon a time · sunlight destroys the shadow
where we stand · What fraud is this? what place
is this? his eyes stir · there was there was · We're on
the spot   jeweled hand: another card
please.

The prisoners see planes over Havana, slim as girls
against the night and stars · from their cells
they hear the chatter of machine guns · rumble
of heavy trucks along the street.   They do not ask
for cigarettes: they call to the guard: what time
is it? Even the doomed can wait a little longer · even
the condemned can lift their arms a final hanging car
geared to ride the world on the wires of our bodies.
We stumble against the hand reaching for another card
we are gray, color of decayed dreams and starved children.
What is the price of sugar? we view the work
of high-powered rifles on the screen · "Machado
has withdrawn." We flee the theater knowing
they'll get us · they'll get us everyone
                              When
will you give an answer? shall we go down like rabbits
in an iron wood with the dead dripping their rotten sleep
into our throats? silver tassels on the casket · gold
filling from the teeth of thieves dug glistening
from their graves and the word was the wind honest
to God it was Suddenly we knew nothing of words
could save us · we knew the man across the street would
come for us we knew whose hand supplied the card
bidding a final trump   once upon a time once
when I am through with orators when we are through when we
begin there must be time   there must be Now.

28

Leaflet (Two)

"The powers of the blood, unbroken bodily forces, resume their ancient lordship. The air-man, type of the modern warrior of the Faustian world, stalks with cynical laughter over the ruins of the Reichstag. Out of the night of history, old shadows are appearing . . . The figure of the Leader —comes out into the stark day . . . the grim serenity of Mussolini, the harsh force of Hitler. And behind them stride the eternal *condottieri*—the gallant, vivid Balbo, the ruthless Goering."

W. E. D. ALLEN
Former Member British Parliament

High over the graves of our comrades, banked
sharp on the barn-waste of sky, where groans
of prisoners and sobbing of women, cannot be heard,
the easy drive of humble pistons bears
the Warrior Hero home:
      honor to him. Honor and heaps
of bloody earth to those whose deaths he did.
Bitter clear the waters echo voices closed
in them; barren-green the meadowgrass . . .
black and muddy trenches goad
the beautiful, raped bodies of boys . . .
Oh land alive with hypocrites and harlots:
hang wreaths upon the butchered West.
And the orator blew into his hands, pulling
a pamphlet "Pledge of Peace" from out his pocket,
he neatly shot a thousand pacifists and two nations.
      While, overhead
the bombing plane made music all that day
bringing Hitler back from Italy
for Mussolini had a bug about the British fleet
as thick as motor oil all up and down the Mediterranean Sea.
"I shall respect your wishes, sir," he said,
"My hands are clean of Austria." But
"the powers of the blood" got little Dollfuss
and the "unbroken bodily forces" wiped

out another brood of ugly ducks:
      (O grim serenity the gallant vivid pop!)
    Schleicher and Röhm, Karl Ernst
    and Heines   this great hand stark as eternity
O gain: the shadows opening
                like skulls like flowers
opening hand!

    Down, down, the plane
clears trees, buildings; fondles earth in massive style
to release a ridiculous mustache,
the man, scrambling
    after, into the Kroll Opera House . . .
the Warrior Bold now greets the perfect smile
     "over the ruins of the Reichstag":
ranks of troops, the battalions of police, and
his friends. "My friends, I wish to explain . . ."
        like skulls like flowers
             opening hand

and all the time and all the time
for all time
we know our enemies.

Poem in the Form of a Letter: to Lauro de Bosis

Fire and wings, De Bosis, soaring above
Rome and Mussolini into the night
in a clear flame over the cities
    and the waters; into the hands
    of those who walk with heads high
    down lanes of men through the jeers
    and bayonets. Head, quick and laurelscarred
    from the trodden dust into the ages

while motors drone in prayer   our father
which art Mussolini fascist airmen take off
in pursuit chanting
hail and hallowed be thy name from loss
of sleep   the blood warm
drenching an appleblossom-sleep
through the skull
                    the spiders of death
welling into the throat   machine guns
exultantly thy kingdom come
over the poet's head bent in a moment.
Hand releasing the stick, releasing the fall
and the flight releasing thy will be done
with zoom upward not to go down
and the blank thud for an instant through sleep
being all over on earth as it is in Italy.
See, high in the empty air power and glory forever
iron fist plunging into the throat
words bubbling through the fingers
power and raving vision glory
in the cockpit with hunger of the moth
for the star   slaughtered cities wrapping
themselves in acid of the words tongue
in the mangled cheek falling falling
sweeping away all barriers from the earth
burning flesh and flower's bloom   blood
liberated from the useless bone-plates
tunneling down
message to the corn and grapes
                    crippled wings
telling the story of the salesman and the farmer's
daughter to the torch hovering near
the wreckage
asking
who is to pick me up   who is this one
to lift me up for the love of God what

did happen and lift me from the broken wheels
and torn silk teeth jutting redly in the fire
ankles of the countryside boasting pus
and old scabs
and nobody telling me
give us our daily bread telling me amen.

Huge serene head in the dust reading the book
                of an American poet
who wrote of the old old beauty fleeing Minos
on to the sun and Athens lost falling
into the sea Icarian unattainable with wax
and gasoline onward in flight leaving nothing
Ariadne fifteen hundred years before Christ
Erigone and Phaedra
                hear O my fathers
thunderous feet marching through my dust
in Grecian tunics lion skins and field tanks
submarines   through the barbed wire lily strewn
skulls floating grinning eye sockets draining
gas and tainted beef   Diktynna-britomart
and the dancers in the chorus trailing necklaces
through the guts on the granite altars
splashing the faces of the poor in Marseilles
and in Trenton New Jersey swords spears
Big Berthas and the rain and the drought
beggars strolling into the museum lobby
trying to peer into the gloom inside
where are the dead and the instruments of death.
O Mother of God when you have seen the ruin
of wings put out over all you are and hope to be
when they lower vision into your eye's void
of seeing   can you go back to celebrate
the strength of knowing faith and charity
beloved . . . God, the dark of wonder in the alley

sunset roses or perhaps the swastika
    tattooed on the belly of president McKinley
doing
    a two forward one back pause and around
    and about and a one and a two and a swing
from the tree
    hands clawing for breath you bastard
    you nigger having a little party
    up to the house tomorrow night
    only the best people
    on to the sun Apollo and the wheat exchange
    looking up from the book serenely smiling
in Italy   hand reaching forth
    an American hand to the head
    in the dust smiling smiling.

This then is the story of my death
    listen O my countrymen
the seasons moving on in a cycle
    of night and of death
are surely moving in the pulse of the earth
a better race of men are surely moving
and the risings up and comings forth
are to be pure and new on the streams
    and the hills of the earth
we should love but cannot love being as we are
heads serene in the dust
since that which is ours does not belong to us
    evil hand releasing
Shelley and de Bosis and the night coming on
with the curve of the earth we are not lost
who have never known a path
we are not wise who are flabby with our wisdom
    hovering near the wreckage
we are not brave to lean our elbows smugly

33

on the strength of a few words   not telling us
what did happen to the farmer's daughter
being lost unwise and cowards   my country
with the seasons moving the weeds
        above our graves
forgive us our misgivings as we forgive those
who mislead us
        for all is not well
and lead us not blindly into a new death
but deliver us from all   O my countrymen
this then is the story of my death.

When we stand narrow in the maw of eternity
        our bodies at rest pretending nothing
                the long reach of root and grass denied of nothing
        when the cities and the waters move on
without us   savage in the heads of other men
then it will be time to think no more of speaking
to the King   or to the people   but now our cause
        a mystery like the vision of good stars
        supported by the head in wonder-skies
is thrilling through the heart   and power
of the stars of the vision's blood is yours
to use.
        The fences of the ocean's shore
        the chill hands of the dynamo
every power known to function in this time
what are they as power O Comrades
compared to the driving wheels of our purpose
compared to the iron worlds of strength
our every step is loosing on the restive earth.
Power is in brotherhood
O *who is this one to lift me up being all over the earth*

Power is in living clean before our love
has written what we are
on every distant corner of Tomorrow's sky.

This Early Day

Before the braces give, the cripple eased to earth;
Before barrage and barricade emerge
      us
Conquerors of time and men, or leave us
Models for a better maker, propellers of a surer motion,
Masters in a stricter sense . . . alive or dead;
Before the casual trucks tear up the farms
Whose yield we saw deflect to smoke and mortgage;
Before the cables under submarines announce
The latest prices paid betrayers and priests;
Before the heavy anger of the howitzers levels
The factories and freighters; before the super-super
Gas gets the robot-pilot, thereby
Alleviating any technical flaw in ground defense
      or spoiling the Ph. D. of any relativity;
Before the streets are cleared; before the firing starts;
Before danger, or victory's danger . . .

Before . . . how are we lost?
We are that thing for which we fight.
We are the deepest task of centuries; lucky
To stand where we stand, hardy
To weather all they can give who have taken
The every weight of a more hopeless war
      since the day we were born. O we are not
Afraid of wounds we've always had. O death
Is a minor thing to those who've never lived.

After the braces give; after the cripple
      is eased to earth
In my house the stars accumulate.

Ark: Angelus: Anvil

We do not bargain for delight; vitality
Of book and bugle has nerve enough outside
The crying holy stars of self: despoiled
Of growing round a sounder base, we launch
Despair—its steeples churches chiming

Lizard-joy O justification of jurors
Condemned by thieves. The unaccounting criminal
Flower world and town
Father work and time
                              are
Floating clear above the wreck are fully
Steeped in joy's relief: jests relighted
Swinging rise of dream the cape of sun
                              this
April's thumb points well to sound of snapping strings
And glaring ghosts are straight in heart the fury found.

We do not affirm delight: would you
Have the signature of sun itself to stay the dawn?
This enterprise is earnest balloonful flowering
Of brain and all the wonder blowing good like grain.

We Must Be Slow

For you and I are bathed in silence:
Here where the country all about
Is quiet; asleep in the softness
Of this evening star, sparkling
On the wrist of night. The village lights,
Like ancient bards at prayer, come

Gently to us over fields of growing corn
And docile sheep. We'd like belonging
Here, where sleep is not of city-kind,
Where sleep is full and light and close
As outline of a leaf in glass of tea; but
Knowledge in the heart of each of us
Has painted rotten eyes within
The head: we have no choice: we see
All weeping things and gaudy days
Upon this humble earth, blending
Taxis' horns and giant despair
With every landscape, here, or anywhere.

Fields of Earth

The press reports the enemy in power: the solo
Flyers comb the countryside for volunteers
Demanding first in deeds. Not words or dying themes
Of flag or wooden guns can save us now.
We lose no ground by right of number;
Who are the area of time, a legion whose skill
Is best put forth by order of a public bond
In blood we've lost on every field of earth and sea.

In this, control
The eyes reversed from paper war
The eyes reserved to will no narrow savior's
Indignation or decay . . .

                              let others
Block the private gain of surface passion:
Our task is not to clean the padded cells
Or heal volcanic pity. We shall live
In no cathedral: our country is the careless star in man.

A Letter on Liberty

How hasten? hearten? O morning star and
morning paper hold and help O evening
star and rival party number numb
and spell our names our like our lucklessness
nor dawn nor dim shall solve shall slaughter
us O heart the agent and the anger hold
and help they wheel the sullen guns into our rooms
and rots this sunny wilderness now love
now lease these fallen flung to number
numb and touch not teach that dawn
is share of dark the scrawl of grief
the scowl of grass and did and do the final fort
of dirty weather hastens heartens O bright
bastards bitches babies our like into our rooms
our lucklessness observed obscured
these rack the silken guts within the tombs
of men who needed more than exercise and excrement of words

Class of 1934

Say something, man, say something before the nations and
        the people;
tell them your story tell them the earth is a bitch gone crazy.
Explain the joke the shadow-days explain the troops and guns
              get down on your knees young men   What happened
to your girl? remember that night in the hills? the moon
        the stars
her face her lips   bloodily   What did you promise? what
        did you do?
              gentlemen I offer two dollars I offer bread and a blue
dress with puffed sleeves   *Once the weight and fate of Europe
hung*   her eyes were bright and dreamful larger than life

when they
cut her down (stop it kill him swing it sister swing it over
the limb of a tall tree where they can't get honeysuckle
    good night
God will guide you a gull will take you home) when they took
the automatic out of her hand when they met her on the street
            offering two dollars

Sin can never taint you now with the rocketflare the scream white
and holy eyeballs crimson shot with fire O mongrel froth of cities
being blasted to bits O vulgar little men operating beautiful in-
struments
        bringing the blue restless sky down into their eyes not
seeing not knowing not caring O my god my god where did they
go   better to die better to feel that all wisdom science and mastery
have been turned against you that they notice you and kill you
(with the newspaper here on the desk beside me   .

        tell them Joe tell them Ed tell them I read about
        pale-green bells in a beautiful book having the face
of a happy man on its cover) better to die while heavy
    guns shake
the earth and it's all big and clear   save us from
    the peace between
wars   Fool fool every man's at war who's hungry
    and hunted whether
in Omaha or Tokyo here they come. Here they come Look out
they mean business they mean an end to standing in rain waiting
    for freights out of Toledo and Detroit Did we ever make
a town? a porterhouse? we were always just this side
    of getting anything
or anywhere
        Down on our luck down on your knees O villages of
terror and the soft slow ping of a 32 and the sure happy grind of
teeth in the head of a picket shot down in San Francisco. Chinese
children have little faces and the sky over China is blue as gun-

smoke as lovely as memory of good food   beardless boys
        in the Nineteenth Route Army love flowers and taffy
they wonder at the joke but they do not laugh multitudes harvest
rice and the bombing planes sound like bees   *O thou that dwell'st
in the heavens high Above you stars and within you sky*   mad
after spotless lilies   5:5:3: 1.75: 1.75:   British American Japa-
nese
            French Italian battleships cruisers submarines torpedo-
boats *There were ninety and nine* listening to the man on the
radio Death Death
the retail price on cotton wheat and corn was
            Down on your knees
shells grenades bunting legs bayonets arms

more than two dollars   offers a chance
                                We present gas
                                Hitler offers
                                Death Death
steel helmets parade before the cells they twist his arms his testicles
Do you believe? Do you believe?
                        This is
the strain the eternal strain the Lord of all things loves Billy bully
Billy Hearst   barbed wire a crown of homos sharpshooters
                        "though
I cannot be a soldier, I can encourage them by dying"   Shanghai's
Big Sword Corps proves the cheering   1929 October 24 in every
pot a chicken a pot in every belly Morgan Hoover Mussolini   come
to bury them not to   Down on your knees   Palazzo Venezia
watch the stairs I'm coming up Watch that guy in the gray suit
thou dearest Augustine all is gone gone gone. What did they
say when you told them   *Where bright angel feet have trod*
They said O.
            We don't want much we want everything and the sun
            withers the grass in the parks From our benches we can
            see the stone faces of well-fed politicians we can hear
            the doors close in Packards we can smell the perfume

                            40

of fat bitches with poodles   we can leave our benches we cannot
leave what they have done to us   we can stand up Christ we can
stand up in their highest building and we won't have room for all
the standing up we need   we've been under We've been nothing
We've been around too long they can't take us in They haven't
got a jail stout enough to hold us
                                    they haven't
            got a leg to stand on   Fool fool   just across the street
            over those windows see their hard faces curl of cigarette
            smoke above the machine guns   we're in the line of fire
            they knock down good dough keeping us in line keep-
            ing us off Are they afraid are they sleeping less?
                        You're damn tootin' but he said we don't
            want much We want everything. A hundred million of
                        us coming
up those stairs in Spain in Mexico in India   O Father Abraham
puny business men reading newspapers thinking to tell us
            down on your knees!
                        Brothers! Brothers!
our hands in the sky in the sea in the earth making things grow
shut off the power shut off the power bridges roads tunnels trolleys
our factories our farms   What's the answer?   when you're down
on your knees with your mouth stuffed with worn-out views? lazy
bastards without the courage to see the deepringing beauty left to
us without the guts or heart to march in millions keeping step
with all that's gone before   making it live making it ours   O
huge epic time men
            up from your knees your books your prisoncots Avenge
your girl your youth   make them pay
                        where it hurts O earth
lovely tonight because of hope and stars and love
                        because of millions ready
to break the back of this muddle-born world
Young men
We must not fail.
We cannot fail.

The Stranger

He needs the antiseptic of the sunlight: neither
Mine's damp nor mill's noise can still for him
The eyeless straps and belts of natural energy:
The lamps and whistles of the void, the coreless
Energy of vast and loyal seas . . . for him
The union's foreman and the scab are one
In filthless destiny. The witness does the crime,
The noble deed . . . for him, the knitted heart,
                    the sexless bee,
Are real, are pulse of chance, are pain of rot.

How can he take a mind not his? how can he
Flood a world whose wonder is the desert of himself?

Hand across your hand: he is the ray of dark
To bright the camps whose men are bluster's riding light.
He is the shallow seeking depth, an obsolete like poet's lark.

Farewell to the Bluewoman*

The bitter veins reject the dream, dismiss the fire,
Betray the whetted mange. O shine
In shadow, holy myth. (Tattered hands
Extend forgotten myths forever.) For some
                    we'll count the stars as beads for thee!

I come for thee not as flesh but as night
Thy lover, folding heart with foam in heat
To strain a prayer with veils: great heart that zooms
In pain, O we in distant trust are spared no beat.

* This poem is included in this place because of the immediate message to
be found in the title (though no proper application derives from the poem
itself); and for an extended reason, my motivation is one of sentiment . . .
that sentiment which one feels for his earliest efforts.

What climbs the deep aloft from thee . . . 'tis thee!
Thy coasting thighs have room
To span the "what is not" with now, "must be."
What though the swarming fleets are crying doom,
Thy nursing sheets in softness cover them;
Or cast the bodies forth in righteous phlegm
    . . . Bluewoman prone in ecstasy . . .
They loved, they breathed, they hoped . . . our scorn, O sea.
All blurred in sullen sleep
Strange eyes are skating steep
    unwitness to
The leprous scud streaming in the charge
Of slithering green plate
Upon the dripping lips   O pistoned glory-barge
Thy tears are spilled in love to dash a pygmy gate.
    Dark sweetness weaving
Dynamos of lily and the rose; the architecture
Of sleep, what eye has truly followed it
And told one plan, one path revealed
    of shepherd-feet
That tend what flocks in pastures there.
    Ave maiden
Thy frantic voice is pitched to rot the heart.
Endless shadow strain . . . moist warm hair . . .
For you no birth, no death: a terrible driving
That drives the driven with the driver.

She moves in pride and nothingness.
O maiden-myth, thy burnished arms
    are more beautiful than death
    is beautiful. O foam-voice
    why doubt? it shall ever be
Not lonely.
Behold the flashing bride in her plight
I come for thee not as flesh but as night.
From petty loves of bone and gold we haunt thy bed.
O harlot sea, thy gift is real, and every bead is said.

The Bluewoman has passed the outer post.
Disconsolate ankles range a countless ghost
As with a lovely sweep she smooths her hair
She does not know that I am sleeping there.
      I rest.
          Ora pro nobis.
She deftly comforts me.
Never thy cruelty, O kinetsea
          beautiful must be
Coasting in thy blueness sleep sleep.

Pick Up the Evening Paper

What is it we want: not battleships
Or hand-grenades to haunt the marshy fog
Of memory; swinging lights and snowflake
Fires taking station in the quarter where
Is Shakespeare's head—a hopeless smile
Upon the face, now shifted out of memory
And swinging down
          against this market-ruin
With only sight of hellshaped charity
Written blearily over the toad-fouled wreckage
Of world when children we loved.

What is it we want: pick up the evening paper.
Have we support? time? this is no quiet
          darkness blowing down
                    O pattern of time
In cardboard in shirt of black and brown O pardon doubt
Now sound of storming lovely lead now crumble fall now
          smashing to
Hell all doubt. The underdog has found his fleas has eaten all.

Joe Hill Listens to the Praying

Look at the steady rifles, Joe.
It's all over now . . . "Murder, first degree,"
The jury said. It's too late now
To go back. Listen Joe, the chaplain is reading:

Lord Jesus Christ who didst
So mercifully promise heaven
To the thief that humbly confessed
His injustice
     throw back your head
Joe; remember that song of yours
We used to sing in jails all over
These Benighted States . . . tell it to him:
"I'll introduce to you
A man that is a credit to our Red, White
and Blue,
His head is made of lumber and solid as
a rock;
He is a Christian Father and his name is
Mr. Block."
      Remember, Joe—
"You take the cake,
You make me ache,
Tie a rock on your block and jump
in the lake,
Kindly do that for Liberty's sake."

Behold me, I beseech Thee, with
The same eyes of mercy that
      on the other
Hand we're driftin' into Jungles
From Kansas to the coast, wrapped

45

round brake beams on a thousand
freights; San Joaquin and Omaha
brush under the wheels—"God made the summer
for the hobo and the bummer"—we've been
everywhere, seen everything.
Winning the West for the good citizens;
Driving golden spikes into the U.P.;
Harvest hands, lumbermen drifting—
        now Iowa, now Oregon—
God, how clean the sky; the lovely wine
Of coffee in a can. This land
        is our lover. How greenly beautiful
Her hair; her great pure breasts
        that are
The Rockies on a day of mist and rain.

We love this land of corn and cotton,
        Virginia and Ohio, sleeping on
With our love, with our love—
O burst of Alabama loveliness, sleeping on
In the strength of our love; O Mississippi flowing
Through our nights, a giant mother.

Pardon, and in the end
                How green is her hair,
        how pure are her breasts; the little farms
        nuzzling into her flanks
        drawing forth life, big rich life
Under the deep chant of her skies
And rivers—but we, we're driftin'
Into trouble from Kansas to the coast, clapped
        into the stink and rot of country jails
        and clubbed by dicks and cops
Because we didn't give a damn—
                        remember Joe
How little we cared, how we sang

46

the nights away in their filthy jails;
                                        and how, when
We got wind of a guy called Marx
            we sang less, just talked
And talked. "Blanket-stiffs" we were
But we could talk, they couldn't jail us
For that—but they did—
                        remember Joe
Of my life be strengthened
                        One Big Union:
            our convention in Chi; the Red Cards,
            leaflets; sleeping in the parks,
            the Boul' Mich; "wobblies" now, cheering
            the guys that spoke our lingo, singing
            down the others. "Hear that train blow,
Boys, hear that train blow."

Now confessing my crimes, I may obtain

Millions of stars, Joe—millions of miles

                        Remember Vincent St. John
In the Goldfield strike; the timid little squirt
            with the funny voice, getting onto the platform
            and slinging words at us that rolled
            down our chins and into our hearts,
            like boulders hell-bent down a mountain side.
And Orchard, angel of peace
            —with a stick of dynamite in either hand.
            Pettibone and Moyer: "The strike
Is your weapon, to hell with politics."
                        Big Bill—remember him—
At Boise—great red eye rolling like a lame bull's
            through the furniture and men
            of the courtroom—"This bastard,
His Honor."

47

Yeah!
Hobo Convention:
(Millions of stars, Joe—millions of miles.)
"Hallelujah, I'm a bum,
Hallelujah, I'm a bum." His Honor,
            the sonofabitch!
One Big Strike, Lawrence, Mass.—
            23,000 strong, from every neck
            of every woods in America, 23,000,
Joe, remember. "We don't need
            a leader. We'll fix things up
            among ourselves."
"Blackie" Ford and "Double-nose" Suhr in
Wheatland—"I.W.W.'s don't destroy
            property"—and they got life. "I've counted
The stars, boys, counted a million of these prison bars."
            Yeah!
            San Diego, soap boxes,
Hundreds of them! And always
            their jail shutting out the sky,
            the clean rhythm of the wheels
            on a fast freight; disinfectant getting
            into the lung-pits, spitting blood
But singing—Christ, how we sang,
                        remember the singing
Joe, One Big Union,
                  One Big
                        hope to be
With Thee

What do they matter, Joe, these massed rifles—
They can't reach the towns, the skies, the songs,
            that now are part of more
            than any of us—we were
The homeless, the drifters, but our songs
            had hair and blood on them.

There are no soap boxes in the sky.
We won't eat pie, now, or ever
        when we die,
                but Joe
We had something they didn't have:
        our love for these States
        was real and deep;
                to be with Thee
In heaven. Amen.
                (How steady are
the rifles.) We had slept
        naked on this earth on the coldest nights
        listening to the words of a guy named Freedom.
Let them burn us, hang us, shoot us,
                        Joe Hill,
For at the last we had what it takes
        to make songs with.

A World Whose Sun Retreats
before the Brave

The greater light is set, my love; our fitful lamp
Has lost its station, has left its little meaning, blame.
Magnificent the harvest; the heart that mocked at camp
And followers has learned another language, name.
Those see the glory better, love, whose world in dying
Cleaned the man in them; upon the rotten waters, bread
They cast, returned; within the scope of self their trying
Clogged the earth with words—these new use fists instead.

What matter what is done to us: the manner counts
For little: things we say are said in newer tone,
Their message fails to set a style for murder, calls,
And calling, cancels use for heirs. This is the time

For us to live. Our sons shall find their private guide
As hostile to the fathers as ever we our own.
We know the plow of change is turning public good
Into a soil of harder stamp, into a flower of stone.

Get up before the sun, O love, the hills of heaven
Lean upon your face; the glens and gullies shimmer
In their blue; the ground and sky are growing heavy
With press of light; all talk is stilled, all time is summer.
Far out, beyond this common scene and country of words,
The dam breaks; we try to stem the flood, the silver wonder.
Standing close together, new, our heads are split by birds
Returning home to the silent lands of our wilderness.

Who were the property of every dunce and prophet,
Of every gust of wind, of every goutish giant on earth,
Are come now to claim ourselves and the profit
Of an ownership which has been our own since birth.
We are not cool: our hate has made us wise, not clever.
Beloved, listen, the stirring of life from the grave—
The heart breaks with the groan and the grind of a lever
Which lifts a world whose very sun retreats before the brave.

from *First Will & Testament* (1939)

"As Frothing Wounds of Roses"

for Miriam

As frothing wounds of roses
Harry summer over a wintry sea,
So does thy very strangeness
Bring me ever nearer thee

As the cry of the bird-torn wind
Hastens the heart beyond its usual need,
So shalt thy dear loveliness,
Upon the forlorn unrest of my cold will,
Be as that snowy stain the roses bleed

O as flaming wounds of roses
Marry summer to the most wintry sea,
So does thy very woman's separateness
Bring me ever nearer thee

Poem

Feeling chilled in that cold country
and having no fuel at all to light a fire
this deliberate man assailed his own shell with flame
and as he stood there, burning—
shivering men passed, muttering "He is a great fool"
but he answered them quietly, saying
"I am warm now and it shall never again be dark"

Dying, he turned his face from death
and there were commemorative cities built and destroyed
on the spot where the man himself had never stood

A SMALL BUT BRILLIANT FIRE BLAZED IN THE GRATE, on either side of which stood a large and roomy easy-chair; a white mongrel with well-filled stomach lay dozing on the rug: the little table in the center of the room was laid for dinner, and when an old woman bore in a hissing beefsteak, and a young girl simultaneously emerged from the shadows with a foaming jug of beer in one hand and a decanter of brown sherry in the other, I rather felt as if I had landed well on my feet, and established myself in comfortable quarters indeed

All this quiet sweeping round us on the earth's edge
Where we lie counting the night's white nipples, and
I go over to you and you come over to me—let us talk
About pleasant things—listen, the sea has his own wet dream,
Houses hold the real thing, Jenny nudges Joe and her wagon
Is fixed, see it roll; blame nobody, partner, but get yours
For she is the Daughter of God
As Christ the Son; don't blame the dickey-bird, brother,
Don't try to get your hooks on death's black geegee, but
Set up your house somewhere and take care of your own tootsie
For she is about all there is
And the times are plenty tough; let us get together now, brother,
You can kick my teeth out, sure, but let's chew the old rag first,
Because I know a couple numbers that aren't in your book
And the armies can do it better than you can anyhow, so
Let us get down to some things we like, maybe a glass or two
And a neat trick giving you that straight-up look; then let them
Bring on their cannon and iron sugar, brother, for all the flags
In all the world won't make a fatherland out of a butcher shop

And the guy who tries to tell the clock what time it is, will
Walk right up to Capitalism and start bleating about Democracy.
When the teakettle says sit down and nibble your country 'tis
Because it looks like you're a dead pigeon anyway
The war goes
> standing in a trench and showing your old lady's
> picture to the boys, letting them lamp her bubbies
> and then getting right down to thinking about
> your garden, "The apple trees must be in bud now,
> mates" and somewhere a lark spoils somebody's hat
> and war is pretty damn sad but we're all mighty
> brave fellows, "Let's see, little Stinker must be
> two by now, mates, Oh he'll be proud of his daddy"
> and somebody says how do you do it? remote control?
> we're going on our fourth annum, soldier
> and you go into town and the women level it right down
When the chamberpot says you will leave something
That shall be forever America and you hope the Crummiest Party
Looks into it
> lying still with your noggin twenty feet away,
> an arm in France, a leg in England,
> a toe in Belgium and a finger in Democracy's pie
When the pick and shovel tell you that this is everyman's land
And REVOLUTION bites the hand that feeds you to the guns.

*AVARICE AND AMBITION ONLY WERE THE
FIRST BUILDERS OF TOWNS AND FOUNDERS
OF EMPIRE; They said, go to, let us build us a city
and a tower whose top may reach unto Heaven, and
let us make us a name, lest we be scattered abroad
upon the face of the whole earth (Genesis XI: 4).
What was the beginning of this city? What was it*

but a concourse of thieves, and a sanctuary of crimi-
nals? It was justly named by the augury of no less
than twelve vultures, and the founder cemented his
walls with the steaming blood of his only brother.
Not unlike to this was the beginning even of the first
town in the world, and such is the original sin of
most cities: Their actual increase daily with their age
and growth; the more people, the more wicked all of
them; everyone brings in his part to inflame the con-
tagion, which becomes at last so universal and so
strong, that no precepts can be sufficient preserva-
tives, nor anything secure our safety, but flight from
among the infected. To spread our own disease

They scatter me from church to gutter.
They smear their doings over my hands.
I am lifted out of wombs
And never put back anywhere . . .
I look up from the grass and down from the cathedral.
They honor me with the stuff of dogs.
They place my body down and fill themselves.
I smile from the confessional and frown on the battlemount.
They offer me their wives
And kill my firstborn . . .
I am grown in their hovels like a vegetable that can be eaten.

They won't wash off my dirt.
They put me in parades and distribute pieces of my corpse.
They honor me with statues and seal me in the hardening
    mold.
I could never build a man
And I have come here to worship . . .

I have only this one wreath.
There is only one grave anywhere.

I am standing open.
You must not lower your eyes.

I want them all to know me.
I want my breath to go over them.
They should withhold nothing from me.
I am a respecter of dirt.
This is your house, you say. Then show
Yourself! I have not been on earth
Long enough to know about you. This
Collection of ills and organs means nothing
To me. Everybody gets a whack at them.
Tell me what you do inside there. I want
All your pain. I want to walk around where
You are. There is no war between us.

And every now and again somebody sneaks up and
Boots the hell out of you
But I could never build one of these curious things
And I have come here because of that simplicity

Is it so very dark in there, brothers?
Does it hurt all the time?
Does it rain without any end at all?
Are the same monsters in your streets?
Why have you nailed up your doors, brothers?
And every now and again something looks down and
Smears the doings of God over our murderous hands

I should like to pray now if I can stay out of a trench to do it
There is no war between us, brothers.
There is only one war anywhere.

He Thought of Mad Ellen's Ravings
and of the Wretched Skeleton on the Rock

It's more than a hundred years now . . .
That yellow hair, the white throat, the witching thighs
Gone! Left to rot in the wind and blue-assed water.
Tell me about your cities, your flame-footed ships,
Your proud maps and monkey dung; tell me of conquest,
Tell me how the blacks tugged your fat around
I don't want to hear it. I want to see her face again
I want to tell her not to be afraid. God! I don't want this
I want to hear her voice. I want to take her into my arms
I don't want to fight their wars. I don't want to kill anyone
And I don't want anyone to kill me. I don't want people
To come smelling round me like dogs with their damn tricks.

There's a huge house on the sand
And every day the gardener's dog should water
The munitions maker who lives there

Fires burn in a few places . . .
Ellen's wanton beauty . . . lost in the black water

Have you heard the mad fiddles?
Jig it, Death; slap it round, God.
I love the wikgirl, the sly moodus,
The stinking honker; make mine
You, O grinning angel, my gregbird,
Luklove, higbard, no holds barred babe.
Turtle in the bough and waterhawk hello.

Here rixnag, hi piphog, riding the bubsea,
Reeling like a soplad after this dohgal.
Hark my hundipper, pimpgetter whole.
Smear it up, Death; knock it down, Godie-Boy.

Tell me about the legend that can never die.
Were there proud songs? was there singing?
Christ! I don't want this. I want to hear her voice
I want her arms to go round me and the sea howling
        at another coast—
With all the lost dreams of men watching us and not crying

Flames hollow the face of our humble song

Fall of the Evening Star

Speak softly; sun going down
Out of sight. Come near me now.

Dear dying fall of wings as birds
Complain against the gathering dark . . .

Exaggerate the green blood in grass;
The music of leaves scraping space;

Multiply the stillness by one sound;
By one syllable of your name . . .

And all that is little is soon giant,
All that is rare grows in common beauty

To rest with my mouth on your mouth
As somewhere a stars falls

And the earth takes it softly, in natural love . . .
Exactly as we take each other . . . and go to sleep.

BEHOLD, ONE OF SEVERAL LITTLE CHRISTS,
with a curiously haunted ugly face, crouched beneath the first and the last, embracing you in its horrible arms, blowing its fetid breath in your face and using fearful threats of death and of judgment

Their war-boots said big shots to the plank floor.
I am the timorous mouse, brother mortal, take aim
at my wee brown eye and you will hit William T. God.
Bring her in Leather Face said: he is my leader, a strong boy
And the dirt of many marches is on his soul; swarms
     of camp fires
In the bush-country, lions like bastard druids, telling us
To come out and give them a taste, and the dust and the sand
When the water is gone and you wonder what you are
     there for,
Not believing the stuff about flags after you have seen
     a man dance
Rope-necked on a dirty platform and the pretty girls yelling
     like mad
Moving their thighs as though Death were coming
     into them too.
I am the crafty Caesar and my baby sister shall one day
be whore to all the world, tastefully gowned in your guts.
Beautiful my heart said when I saw her.
She was very young and everything good was in her face.
I could have been Christ if she had touched me.
Nail her to the door my leader said and they put knives
Through her hands and knives through her feet, but
I did not turn my face away
I am a singer of songs and there is no one
Listening now
Flame of all the world, honor of the wounded tiger,
There is something that has not been said,

There is something that cannot be said,
To The Word which is the girl who hangs here,
To the one upon whom her eyes now are
For her pain, for her innocence, for her pigeon-mouthed death
That coos and trills over the fogsweet deeps of her flesh,
For those who killed her and for the strange planet
     of her dying,
For all the mockery of the just and for the battlements of salt
That man has against the howling dark
There is nothing, there is no voice, no quiet hand,
There is the sneer of the bat and the gull's fang,
There is a lobster beating his breast and singing,
Yea, singing, I am the answer to your prayer, sugar,
I am the one to come to your window in the first
     stinking sweat
Of night and I shall bed thee down in star-manure,
A pot of green paint for thy Jerusalem, believe me,
Babe, till the seas gang gok my rod shall comfort thee
I am of the first thing and of the last thing
Mine is the face in your dream
Mine is the body beside you in the night
Why isn't she dead grumbled the leader
It was getting later than the night had room for
And the lanterns were beginning to look silly
(Birds pleading with something out in the swamp)
Our faces hunched over our brains like tight pods.
We looked again at the maps and a little stream of her blood
Had made a river that we had no fit equipment to cross
And her hand had fallen over the city that we hoped to take
Her hair went over us praying here all of us not the least
Nor the greatest not the pure alone but those who are
     most bent
On murder the evil more than the good over the lost
     and the hunted
Over the gambler and the bitch followed by the whole
     human pack

THE QUEER CLIENT AND THE FOREST-INN, *how at midnight he heard the sound of footsteps and a beautiful woman came to his bed*

We were a band of kids willing to learn something.
Beth said I bet the old guy would go for me.
Tim put it to him square but he rattled his head no.
Guess we don't eat. It was on the ass of dark, rain
Down our necks and getting cold. I am looking
At all of you, I am the one to judge, I want only peace.
Children, prepare me a way, make me to sleep now.
Shut up, grandpa, we told him, what could you do
With a girl anyway? Beth was still clean after
Two months of selling herself for us and we were proud.
The bastards. The dirty rotten bastards. Let me get
My hands on the bignoise of all this. Like dicks on a stiff
We made for the light in the house, our fists saying
Let us in. Shaking water on their clean floor like dogs.
These children are hungry the old gent said. I'll pay
For everything. Beth whispered you can have it for nothing.
I want peace and I am the only one to judge. We said sure
But let's eat first. The innkeeper had two wolves on a chain
And they watched us with tortured eyes, their faces bloody
With kicks. A fourth degree. Christ! I like to be warm,
I like to be somewhere nice, food inside me, light
On Beth's face, bed waiting, I want Beth, nobody else
In all the world can ever have her. Call us early, whiskers said.
The wolves had fallen asleep with open puzzled eyes, like pits.

It is the middle hour of the night.
I am a proud man out of my time.
God, if there be a God, prepare the way
That men may find peace on this earth.
Beth tiptoed in and said move over
The old boy's muttering in his beard

And I wanted to be good to him. Be good
To me, Beth, for the world that seems so various
Is neither here nor there, so let us lay us
Like a hugging-rug while ignorant armies
Clash around in the mud.

*SHE HAD CONCEALED HIM IN A DEEP DARK
CAVE, hewn far in the rock, to which she alone knew
the entrance on the world, and so treacherous and
uncertain was the descent that the law-givers and the
villagers passed over his head in the clear fields above,
content to allow him such safety as he had*

Going to bed
And when we have done
Lying quietly together in the dark

Warm houses stand within us
Sleepy angels smile in doorways
Little jewelled horses jolt by without sound
Everyone is rich and no one has money
I can love you Thank God I can love you
All that can happen to us is not known to the guns

   Are you awake darling?
   Do not fall asleep yet
To sleep now would seem a way to die so easily
And death is something which poems must be about

But the way our bodies were wings
Flying in and out of each other . . .

The Fox

Because the snow is deep
Without spot that white falling through white air

Because she limps a little—bleeds
Where they shot her

Because hunters have guns
And dogs have hangmen's legs

Because I'd like to take her in my arms
And tend her wound

Because she can't afford to die
Killing the young in her belly

I don't know what to say of a soldier's dying
Because there are no proportions in death.

You May All Go Home Now

The light was gaunt and crawly;
like a hideous worm, fat and dirty,
it crept over the faces of those women.

Two men from the city, two men with pads
of expensive paper—with expensive minds,
no doubt—came to check the job, to write
on the pads with even, careful hand.

The sky, like a peasant in a blue shirt,
put down white hands on the weeping crowd;
it was full morning: when people are shot.

Black were the rifles; long as death;
fat as a priest. A fly, bothered, no doubt,
because the soldiers drooled tobacco,
was buzzing about their shiny boots.
Its wings were little points of flat light.

And, yes, to be accurate, to be fair,
the snow made it hard to stand;
that is, the socks of the riflemen
were worn badly, though their boots shone.
The peasants, of course, had no shoes at all.
It can be supposed that this was noted.

A very tiny child, thinking that soon
somebody would begin to dance, brought
first one little hand up, then the other;
but no one smiled, and some were crying.
She lowered her hands as lids on dead eyes.
The woodshawk sighted a helpless sparrow.
Its assassin's face was a field of lifted grass.

But two men with pads were impatient.
Notice how strangely doll-like their hands are.
It was somehow comforting to see a large ring
on the middle finger of the shorter man: like being
able to say "You may all go home now."
Not only because the women will be shot . . .

A queer thing happened. At exactly the moment
when the soldiers were to fire; just as the hawk
hurtled down, drawing a mile-high hawk there,
God! I mean when it dove for the sparrow,
to kill it; just when all seemed over, hopeless,
and done—exactly then, the poor women, huddling,
in shawls, miserable, terribly gentle, like children,
were shot. And the sparrow was killed under great claws.

Creation

Wherever the dead are, there they are and
Nothing more. But you and I can expect
To see angels in the meadowgrass that look
Like cows—
And wherever we are is paradise
    in furnished room without bath and
    six flights up
Is all God! We read
To one another, loving the sound of s's
Slipping-up on the t's and much is good
Enough to raise hair on our heads, like
    Rilke and Owen.

Any person who loves another person,
Wherever in the world, is with us in this room—
    even though there are battlefields.

The Hangman's Great Hands

And all that is this day . . .
The boy with cap slung over what had been a face . . .
Somehow the cop will sleep tonight, will make love
    to his wife . . .
Anger won't help. I was born angry.
Angry that my father was being burnt alive in the mills;
Angry that none of us knew anything but filth and poverty.
Angry because I was that very one somebody was supposed
To be fighting for
Turn him over; take a good look at his face . . .
Somebody is going to see that face for a long time.

I wash his hands that in the brightness they will shine.

64

We have a parent called the earth.
To be these buds and trees; this tameless bird
Within the ground; this season's act upon the fields of Man.
To be equal to the littlest thing alive,
While all the swarming stars move silent through
The merest flower . . . but the fog of guns . . .
The face with all the draining future left blank . . .
Those smug saints, whether of church or Stalin,
Can get off the back of my people, and stay off.
Somebody is supposed to be fighting for somebody . . .
And Lenin is terribly silent, terribly silent and dead.

November 1937

The Poor Child with the Hooked Hands

He leads me into much that is sorrow
For his name might have been mine

He comes like a dead thing giving
Pennies that I would place upon the eyes
Of those who live in private horror
And all the rooms in them haunted by war

He calls for a lovely woman to take him
To arms where the tired may lean as though home
Were a woman's arms about him and it never dark or lonely

Because his hands are hooked and ugly
And someone will surely want to put nails through them
As though there were any wood to hold the hell of him
Who had been a wilderness where something very beautiful
Got lost and wandered away as beautiful things always do

65

BUT THE IMAGES OF HIS FORMER DREAMS
STILL HAUNTED HIM, and their hideous phantoms
were more powerfully renewed: again he heard the
awful singing of death, but unsung by mortals, being
pealed through earth up to the high heaven by
throngs of the viewless and the mighty: again he
heard the wailing of the millions for some remem-
bered sin, and the wrath and the hatred of a world
was rushing in on him

Hasten to your own gun, to your own star, to your own tribe.
Hurry while the light lasts, while still you need someone;
I don't trust this quiet, I don't like that grave over there.

Is it only death that bothers you?
So many have done it, brother.
So many have turned up their poor toes.

Is it only war that blackens you?
So many have gone there, brother.
So many have taken that boney grin.

Is it only blood that sickens you?
So many have bathed in it, brother.
So many are standing knee-deep there now.

Is it only God that heartens you?
So many have gone blind, brother.
So many have put their eyes in His cunning hock.

Is it only Man that frightens you?
So many have been fooled, brother.
So many hold that key, and that beautiful lock.

Hasten to your own kind, to your own dream, to your own land;
Hurry while there is still someone to go with you there . . .

*AS SHE WAS THUS ALONE IN THE CLEAR
MOONLIGHT, standing between rock and sky, and
scarcely seeming to touch the earth, her dark locks
and loose garments scattered by the wind, she looked
like some giant spirit of the older time, preparing to
ascend into the mighty cloud which singly hung from
this poor heaven*

so when she lay beside me
sleep's town went round her
and wondering children pressed against the high windows
of the room where we had been

so when she lay beside me
a voice, reminded of an old fashion:
   "What are they saying?
   of the planets and the turtles?
   of the woodsman and the bee?"
but we were too proud to answer, too tired to care about designs
   "of tents and books and swords and birds"

thus does the circle pull upon itself
and all the gadding angels draw us in

until I can join her in that soft town where the bells
split apples on their tongues
and bring sleep down like a fish's shadow.

AND WHAT WITH THE BLUNDERS, what with the real humor of the address, the end is sure to be attained, that of roarous fun in the roused hamlet or mountain village which pours forth its whole population in a swarm round the amorous orator, down to the baby that can but just toddle and the curs that join in the clamor, mad with ecstasy at the novelty of some noise besides that of trees and the horrible clamor of the grass

We talked of things but all the time we wanted each other
and finally we were silent and I knelt above your body

a closing of eyes
and falling unfalteringly
over a warm pure country and something crying

when I was a child things being hurt made me sorry
for them but it seemed the way men and women did
and we had not made the world

coming into it crying
(I wanted so not to hurt you)
and going out of it like a sudden pouring of salt

later, being tired and overflowing with tenderness
girl's body to boy's body lying there and wondering what it
      had been
we got to our feet very quietly so that they would not waken
but we felt their shy sorrowful look on us as we left them alone
      there

.   .   .   .   .   .

All things are one thing to the earth
rayless as a blind leper Blake lies with everyman
and the fat lord sleeps beside his bastard at last
and it doesn't matter, it doesn't mean what we think it does
for we two will never lie there
we shall not be there when death reaches out his sparkling hands

there are so many little dyings that it doesn't matter which of
      them is death.

To Whom It May Concern

It is as though three forms move on a road
And the road is mankind

The first is a woman whose long hair covers thieves
And cities and whom men take like turbans around them
Because it is dark and cold in the places where they
      will be killed

There is no betrayal in the human face.
Time's fin, hoof, wing, and fang struggle there
And the battlefields and cathedrals appear
   and the stare of the broken Christ
Is the second form, a pathway for children and plows

It is as though a star could weep and we could hold it
     in our arms
And somehow tell everyone *This is what they have done*

But there would be that other presence on the road
What the Irishmen of '16 called The Revolution
And proudly stood in that cold morning and went to her.

THOUGH I HAD MUCH MORE TO SAY (for the life of man is so short that it allows not time enough to speak against a tyrant); yet because I had a mind to hear how my strange adversary would behave himself upon this subject, and to give even the devil (as they say) his due, and fair play in a disputation, I stopped here, and expected (not without some fear) that he should have broken into a violent passion in behalf of his favorite; but he, on the contrary, very calmly, and with the dove-like innocency of a serpent that was not yet warmed enough to sting, started to read from his latest treatise called How to get ahead of the other fellow

It was to our interest to be quiet.
We realized the danger.

So-and-so said the troops would move up,
But they didn't come.
The heavy fellows were beginning to get the range.
I knew then that we couldn't last the night.

Perhaps you have seen our naked bodies
In carvings of their most beautiful cathedrals.

We played Black Jack and I won seventy cents.
Wild ducks going over at dusk got our ammunition.
An empty rifle is about as much good as a used grave.

We heard the iron breath of a plane going over
And I had to look twice at my cards.
It made its dirt up ahead somewhere.

Have I neglected anything?
Yes, a shower of stars
Folded round us
Falling like white moss from an imperial wall.

Boxers Hit Harder When Women Are Around

The sleeping face folds down over this human country
And a battle crackles through the fat, blue air above us.

Rock-a-bye poor ladies, the world was ever cruel and wrong . . .
And while you sleep, be sure your sons will make a mess
    of something.

Ho! ho! my hovering leopard. Ho! my hungry dogs . . .
Inspect my savage house;
Here the moth-bladed light stabs at fake, lancing remote lies.

Do they stir in their troubled sleep?
Somebody will always look out for my poor ladies . . .
Rock-a-bye my darlings, the world won't always be wrong.

The sleeping face folds down over the broken harlot
Who stands behind the plow unshakeable,
Bewildered as all the bells in the world thunder
Against the castles where chained tigers await
The tread of the Huntsman from whose hand they will feed,
From whose desperate heart will flower a manflame honor.

Who fights the gunclan will wear hard gloves and come out
    fighting . . .
And it won't seem so lonesome when the lights are all on.

ı'd ıııke to die like this . . .
with the dark fingers of the water
closing and unclosing over these sleepy lights
and a sad bell somewhere murmuring good night.

And a girl would stand beside me,
her hair lifted out like a hand against my face;
and I'd say "I'm going to die now."

And she'd answer "All the guns are still:
for men have learned to love one another."

Then a star would nose the water, like a weary gull
which had flown a long way and come at last to rest.

And, when I'd lift my face to look on the God
I had found for myself,
the girl would say "You're not going to die."

And she'd not mean me at all.

The Character of Love Seen as a Search for the Lost

You, the woman; I, the man; this, the world:
And each is the work of all.

There is the muffled step in the snow; the stranger;
The crippled wren; the nun; the dancer; the Jesus-wing
Over the walkers in the village; and there are
Many beautiful arms about us and the things we know.

72

See how those stars tramp over heaven on their sticks
Of ancient light: with what simplicity that blue
Takes eternity into the quiet cave of God, where Caesar
And Socrates, like primitive paintings on a wall,
Look, with idiot eyes, on the world where we two are.

You, the sought for; I, the seeker; this, the search:
And each is the mission of all.

For greatness is only the drayhorse that coaxes
The built cart out; and where we go is reason.
But genius is an enormous littleness, a trickling
Of heart that covers alike the hare and the hunter.

How smoothly, like the sleep of a flower, love,
The grassy wind moves over night's tense meadow:
See how the great wooden eyes of the forest
Stare upon the architecture of our innocence.

You, the village; I, the stranger; this, the road:
And each is the work of all.

Then, not that man do more, or stop pity; but that he be
Wider in living; that all his cities fly a clean flag . . .
We have been alone too long, love; it is terribly late
For the pierced feet on the water and we must not die now.

Have you wondered why all the windows in heaven were broken?
Have you seen the homeless in the open grave of God's hand?
Do you want to acquaint the larks with the fatuous music of war?

There is the muffled step in the snow; the stranger;
The crippled wren; the nun; the dancer; the Jesus-wing
Over the walkers in the village; and there are
Many desperate arms about us and the things we know.

Next year the grave grass will cover us.
We stand now, and laugh;
Watching the girls go by;
Betting on slow horses; drinking cheap gin.
We have nothing to do; nowhere to go; nobody.

Last year was a year ago; nothing more.
We weren't younger then; nor older now.

We manage to have the look that young men have;
We feel nothing behind our faces, one way or other.

We shall probably not be quite dead when we die.
We were never anything all the way; not even soldiers.

We are the insulted, brother, the desolate boys.
Sleepwalkers in a dark and terrible land,
Where solitude is a dirty knife at our throats.
Cold stars watch us, chum,
Cold stars and the whores.

Poem Written after Reading Certain Poets Sired by the English School and Bitched by the C. P.

What are you doing today, brother?

Where is your face that no one sees it?
Where is your death that no one dies it?

Just so the soft girl goes into the bed of the dollar
And love comes like sour to milk

Under the sharp leaves
In the lean shadows
Kiss now your home-grown Judas
Beneath the bleeding root
Above the rotten branch
Kindles the evening star of anger

Even as the lovely girl is thrown from the bed of the dollar
And death comes like sour to milk
The originating brow of poetry
Made to squat like an epilogue at the beginning of a fool's play.

The State of the Nation

Understand that they were sitting just inside the door
At a little table with two full beers and two empties.
There were a few dozen people moving around, killing
Time and getting tight because nothing meant anything
Anymore
Somebody looked at a girl and somebody said
              Great things doing in Spain
But she didn't even look up, not so much as half an eye.
Then Jack picked up his beer and Nellie her beer
And their legs ground together under the table.
Somebody looked at the clock and somebody said
              Great things doing in Russia
A cop and two whores came in and he bought only two drinks
Because one of them had syphilis

No one knew just why it happened or whether
It would happen ever again on this fretful earth
But Jack picked up his beer again and Nellie her beer again
And, as though at signal, a little man hurried in,
Crossed to the bar and said Hello Steve to the barkeeper.

The Soldier and the Star

Rifle goes up:
Does what a rifle does.

Star is very beautiful:
Doing what a star does.

Tell them, O Sleeper, that some
Were slain at the start of the slaughter.

Tell them, O Sleeper, that sleet and rain
Are falling on those poor riderless heads.

Tell them, O Sleeper, that pitiful hands float on the water . . .
Hands that shall reach icily into their warm beds.

All the Bright Foam of Talk

Followed by garrulous hunters, the soft children grovel
Down the valley of sleep . . . so gentle . . . shining . . . but
Not singing
Never singing . . . it is the midnight of sense . . . mind's
Desolate cave

The decayed clock booms out in puffs of sound
That stagger like drunken apes through the streets,
Fingering the paint-stripped houses and the wood
Where death has flung all things beautiful

Watch the fantastic eyelid of that lark
How enormously lovely . . . hooded like an invisible engine
    and pulling earth's lustful plow right through the lark

The children do not remember the slow step of the mules
As they descended the hills lost in the snow
Knowing that there was no room in the inn
Where death has flung all things beautiful

There is laggard talk on the islands
Clatter of spoons as people stuff their bones
Mating in the slums and cheap movies
Fine hands folded over the tin cross where man tosses

There is no track before me, no light in the inn
At all . . . no fiery map nor singing . . . I cannot join the past
Who can never see as the lark does and think even in sleep

I Can't Understand! I Can't Understand!

I have food for my children in the cart.
But it is bogged in mud and its wheels won't turn.

My feet are cold and wet and the wind tugs at my poor coat.
It is an awful night to be helpless and far from home.

My wife worries; my children cry for supper.
It is not well to have no friend.
It is not well to have no friend.

The great hawk of death strides out of the woods
And looks at me with wondering eyes.

It is not well to have no friend in the world tonight.

Won't you help me lift my cart?

The millions who love you will help you.

The Deer and the Snake

The deer is humble, lovely as God made her
I watched her eyes and think of wonder owned

These strange priests enter the cathedral of woods
And seven Marys clean their hands to woo her

Foot lifted, dagger-sharp—her ears
Poised to their points like a leaf's head

But the snake strikes, in a velvet arc
Of murderous speed—assassin beautiful

As mountain water at which a fawn drank
Stand there, forever, while poison works

While I stand counting the arms of your Cross
Thinking that many Christs could hang there, crying.

Fifth Dimension

We walked under cliffs where the Upward and Downward are—
        under the rolling silence of the hairy stars
        hearing the jabber of tufted voices
    and seeing the splayfooted couples grappling
        on the rigid shelves
O Karahana, how those faces stared down!

We gave them trinkets of sea and air:
The tall girl whose motion was the sun's;
Choice screens of hammered brass. A fine golden shepherd dog
    from Wales

and great bowls of naked glass to stand beside wise,
    tortured harts
  all hornless and gentler than dictators.

Sitting, they and we, on the hot sand twisting our fingers
Miserably, like X and Z over a pot of stale tea
And the gulls diving ad infinitum dropping themselves
Down on the little pennies of fish with their wet squeals.

At night the caverns crawl with smooth sex
       breathing pitifully like a bearded child
       under the gasping noise of the hooded sky

And the human dream! the gritty, scurrying lashes
Over the dead eyes

The secret of any murder may be found simply
By getting together enough fingers to make a hand
And seeing if it can hold a gun.

In Memory of Kathleen

How pitiful is her sleep.
Now her clear breath is still.

There is nothing falling tonight,
Bird or man,
As dear as she.

Nowhere that she should go
Without me. None but my calling.

O nothing but the cold cry of the snow.

I NEVER HAD ANY OTHER DESIRE SO STRONG,
and so like to covetousness, as that one which I have
had always, that I might be master at last of a small
house and a contenting woman, with moderate con-
veniences joined to them, and, living there and with
her to love, dedicate the remainder of my life only to
the culture of myself; for though I have made the
first and the hardest step to it by abandoning all am-
bitions and hopes in this world and by retiring from
the noise of all blowhards and blatsofts, yet I stick
still in the inn of a hired house, among human weeds
and rubbish, and without that pleasantest work of
man, the improvement of something which we call
(not very properly, but yet we call) our own. If you
look at my hands you will see that if I knew where
to go I could build a road that would take me there

I sit in my window with a tommy gun across my knees.
When they lift their heads I shall let them have it.

They are eating supper now, laughing together, feeding
Choice bits of food to their young son; they can't get
Away with that. They have no right to insult me.

Down in the street a young girl speaks to an old bastard;
He puts his hand on her breast and neither will go hungry.
Two kids get in a fight and the smaller goes down.

Across the way they are preparing for bed.
The wife has long hair, colored like my mother's.

Now they are tucking the baby in, bending over him.

The woman crosses to lower the blind.

Our eyes meet for a wonderful moment.

And I think of the legend of the frog who loved a Queen: there are twelve different versions; the first by a little boy who hated candles; the second by a racehorse named Too Far To Carry; the third by a whore in Massillon, Ohio; the fourth by a gang of kids who lined up a middle-aged woman whose hubby was a straw hat salesman; the fifth by a cop who once held the lightweight title in Our Navy; the sixth by Spinoza; the seventh by Jesus Christ; the eighth by Villon; the ninth by the rivers Delaware, Mahoning, and Charles; the tenth by a Negro barber in Carson City, Nevada; the eleventh by a thunderstorm which broke up a trying picnic; the twelfth by a blind clown who did the Dance of the Swords for Ringling Bros. The stories are all alike in one respect, however: the frog will be primping himself, wetting his coat and spreading his toes wide, when, in clouds of dust, his ears hearing the silver talk of the harness, her face there almost to touch, his Queen and all the rest of it, clatters her carriage by, the right front wheel and the right rear wheel going over the poor little bastard, scrench! As a matter of record, I have seen this happen myself; why, one time I even heard it from the uncomfortable victim himself. It had been a glorious day, one of those that froth at the mouth a bit, getting their bright spittle over all of us. I shay, Quincy, I said, that being his name, you must be off your nut old fellow, how come you think you can make such a ritzy dame? He stirred uneasily, his fat eyes alive with sorrow (They certainly cook up some quaint murders in these parts. I can remember the time a friend of mine was picked off by a steel fan in the mills back home; it cut him all to hell but the rolls didn't stop and nobody missed eating at the proper time. I was seventeen and the nightshift was pretty hard to take. Not much later I got in on my first strike. I never had to read books to know where I belong. Fellow named Scanlon

I can stop here or I can go on; just mention the riot act and you've got it. Not all cops wear blue clothes.

But I won't go back. That's the funny thing about getting a swat in the puss; one does not relish it. How many smart guys shooting off their traps about the "working class" ever got off their tails long enough for somebody to plant a good one? That's why they can sell out whenever the wind blows; they think it's some kind of game like chess; they'll louse it up every time. It's Am-ER-ica the BEE-U-T-ful now: isn't that a honey of a way to fight Nationalism [Fascism]? Have you smoked a Liberty Bond lately? Have you a little gaypayoo agent in your home?) then his face broke into a grin, scattering it around. There must be some mistake, he said, you see every story that gets anywhere must have a hero; at which I chimed in impatiently, go on, you dope, don't tell me that you are not good enough for her; indeed, says he, giggling slyly, I am much too good for any of you, saying which, and preening himself, he tongued out beautifully, snaring a large bluebottle fly that had bothered my family for several generations. Yet the legend itself has many surprising features: I remember once being forced to put up for the night in a cheap hotel in a little Georgia town; my repast was satisfactory to a point, but after several hours in the hard bed, finding sleep elusive, I understood myself the prey of an overwhelming hunger; never one to succumb easily, it was the effort of a moment to gain the kitchen, rancid odors guiding my footsteps in flawless precision; normally I should not have experienced surprise at the sight which greeted me, but I was a trifle on the wobbly side; don't tell me, I said, but isn't that my own dear love stretched out there, so wan etcetera, her poor sightless eyes staring up reproachfully? and isn't that a train wreck in which two hundred souls perished, their horribly mangled bodies dripping scarlet horror? Lord love us, look at all the disconnected limbs floating hereabouts, like bloody feathers at that—and all the eyes are talking and all the hair are moving and all the tongue are in all the cheek, just so, Sweatfoot, I'll take a ham sandwich. But *I*

will follow mine enemies and overtake them, neither will I
again till I have destroyed them the graybeards spend most of
their time in the bosoms of deep wells, making their drab old
wind at the stars. It is more than unusual to write about anything
now. Hours of each day I pass in the work of perfecting a little
racket which is designed to interest spinsters and schoolmarms of
either sex. Tomorrow I have an appointment to visit a certain
well-known poet whose work is done altogether under the influ-
ence of large checks from his mama who never quite went to bed
with him. All his poems begin with x. This time I am not going
to give in without a struggle MYSTERY SURROUNDS DEATH OF
SNAKEYE MACGROAK
in your hat then
Letsch poool hour shtuff and beegin ovah againe
He was born in a beer keg on a boat headed for Havaner
Third day out it rained, fourth day out it snowed
He met his wife in a movie house on Thoid Avernew
Walk up to me and belch she said, why you big ape
Then the little one came, Horseface, Imer goner hav ah bahby
Mister and Missus Dimwit are proud to ernounce
The boith of a dater, lbs. 6, hands 2, legs 2, brains 0
All the old work-monkeys to the house and a handsome brawl
While the phonograph shaid I was going through the park
    one day

Do you see what I see? that when the kid got the flu
And drifted off leaving the whisky and the dirty towels
Above the cracked sink

This is the evening of two-fisted prayer.
The next version of the legend is in no other hands but your own.

My old man pads down in his long nightgown to lock up.
An angry fist of black smoke clutches at the air over the mills.

83

Religion Is That I Love You

As time will turn our bodies straight
In single sleep, the hunger fed, heart broken
Like a bottle used by thieves

Beloved, as so late our mouths meet, leaning
Our faces close, eyes closed
Out there

Outside this window where branches toss
In soft wind, where birds move sudden wings
Within that lame air, love, we are dying

Let us watch that sleep come, put our fingers
Through the breath falling from us

Living, we can love though dying comes near
It is its desperate singing that we must not hear

It is that we cling together, not dying near each other now

Niobe

Dear queen and mother—what do the archers now!
Proud men of Thebes—look! what shameful command
Unleashes their shafts? No usual quarry draws their aim!
—Look! as you are a mother first, then a queen—
It is your sons caught out in that merciless rain!
Remark your eldest, how his trim young fingers
Clutch at the quivering shaft; ah, the humble boy,
The beautiful train of his body as it greets death.
Death isn't horrible, is it? Perhaps this dying
Is a royal house too? and he a prince forever there.

Does it matter that Latona could smile at last?
It is hard to believe that a sunbeam, even then, so long
Before us, could kill, could maim, could strike them low—
Leaving their horses to stand quietly on the green plain.

Dear lady, how pleasant to be a name in a story:
How lovely do your seven daughters look, so many
Sharp letters on a harmless page, their bright hair
Falling like timid birds through fable's pretty sky.
Does it count very much that their warm little breasts
Opened under the cruel spears?—how swiftly, soundlessly,
They lost what we can never lose; until that moment,
That awful moment, the moment when their seven throats
Became lakes of crimson, when words would not come,
When their hands grew still—until that moment, Niobe,
They had not known that there was nothing to say,
And everyone everywhere saying it.

Palms for a Catholic Child

The first flower,
Fields' document
Unto God,
The giver,
I give thee.

Not as church,
Or chapel,
(Jerusalem has not died.
Our lands are still green.)
But as a house
Of high wonder,
Wilder than their God,
And less heathen.

Inasmuch as War Is Not for Women

If she be loving, if all that matters leaving her
Is said: if she were cold and sad and lonely for me

The tiger rends the rabbit! O God she kills
Unkindly slow.
I guess her bloody hands will go warm
Around the name which soldiers' screams have chilled.

THE OLD LEAN OVER THE TOMBSTONES, the
young try to read them, and the youngest play upon
them. O God! Hear me! "I shall don my best clothes
and doff them too o'nights, honey, all one for my be-
ing married and going away with you," said the tender
girl. Ah, it's merry, merry, the Lord quickening in the
sea and the sun, moon, stars, rooks, swallows, vines,
mushrooms, roses, nettles, melons, pinks, rams,
calves, mermaids, wolves, horses, eagles, urchins, ele-
phants, pigs, hares, lions and the thing you want to
say and the thing I want to say, the wrecks and the
wreckers, the sleek and the starved, Tom and Madge
and Mr. Kek, merry, merry with pain and cold and
being so damned alone, stirring around here for a
little while and going away to live with whatever god
they can scare up

My horsemen wheel in a great circle shutting out the sun.
They take my lightest word as their unbreakable law.

The days of my murder are at an end. They guard me from
disaster.
Our camp faces the war. No leader gets over us. No trench
conceals.
Recruiting goes on everywhere. There are no emblems,
and no awards.
We have our music and that is enough to conquer this world.
We are on the move always. Records are kept. Files made.
Our scouts are in your city now. No stone has escaped our maps.
We know where you are and what you will do when the time
comes.

It would interest me to make a partial report.
The names used are authentic. No mythical place is intended.
All of the crimes are your own.

MIGA (*a shoe salesman whose small salary supports wife, three
children, father, mother*): H'lo.
SHERNSH (*a bottle baby*): Up your brown!
MIGA (*laughing*): Heh. Heh. Hoh.
NOLLY (*a nice-looking whore*): Anything today, boys?
SHERNSH (*taking her up*): I've only got a buck.
NOLLY: Well, half a loaf . . .
MIGA (*moving off*): This is whoreable.
STREETLAMP: Now the bride and groom . . .
CURBSTONE: Enter this hallowed room.
TAXICAB: Zlug. Zlug. Erh! Ehr!
POCKLE (*a decent gunman*):
He was remembering his fathers and there was no woman
around.
What better than a fish you may well ask.
Being near the sea, lived in a shack, he did.

A conch shell can be heard for miles but no tart
Showed up, blow as he might and he was a big man.
Bearded like a goat. So he finally made a swordfish

87

Which he called Roberta and they did all right until
The little one came. The rub was that Junior took
To following his old man about the beach and though
The Beard went in heavy on philosophy with the kid
He could never break him of doing what was in front of him
To do. Then one day Roberta's Big Sword came back home
And after polishing off the old boy he fell to figuring
What could he do with the queer little tike who knew
All about Plato but never got off home plate with
Any of the cute little swordfish lassies. Poor Junior
Had a lot on the ball but nowhere at all to throw it.

CLAUD KOWL (*reading from the almanac for 1853*): People come
and make a hole in you. When it's animals, it's not their
fault, but human beings needn't. They make a hole and they
go away and leave it.

(*Now the scene shifts to a cheap boardinghouse such as can be
found in any small town.*)

DAISY (*girl of twelve summers, long hair of golden color, pretty
in a pretty way*): Mother!
MRS. REEK (*herself ugly as hell*): Yes, dear.
DAISY: Mother, kin I wear my new dress to the funeral?
MRS. REEK: What funeral, child?
DAISY (*stabbing her*): Why yours, you old witch.

(*Office of* LITERATURE, INC.)

ELIOT (*on the telephone*): H'lo.
BEARDED VOICE: Hi, T.S.
ELIOT: What's new, Mr. G.?
BEARDED VOICE: Guy here thinks you all stink.
ELIOT: What guy, Mr. G.?
BEARDED VOICE: Name of Dante.
ELIOT (*reaching for his* Inferno): Ah, to ell with im.
EZRA P. (*entering breathlessly*): How about a canto thru. the Pk.,
Possum?

ELIOT (*glowering*): I've just been called out on a maternity case. The Mother Church is pupping.

EZRA P.: It wd. But what does that make her?

(*Phone rings.*)

SECRETARY: Yes?

R. JEFFERS: America calling.

SECRETARY: Mr. Eliot. It's America . . .

SPENDER, LEWIS & AUDEN (*who has been in the wastebasket the whole time*): Give me that telephone.

SECRETARY: Yessir, Mr. Triumvirate.

S.L.A.: Helll-o.

R. JEFFERS: Is this Mr. Eliot?

S.L.A. (*chuckling*): No, but you're getting warm.

R. JEFFERS: I wish to speak to Mr. Eliot.

S.L.A.: Mr. Eliot has spoken.

R. JEFFERS: What's that?

S.L.A.: I say—Mr. Eliot has said all he has to say.

R. JEFFERS: Well, so have I. Put him on anyway.

EZRA P. (*grabbing*): Give me that phone. HEL. O.

GREGORY MACLEISH MILLAY (*who has taken the phone from poor JEFFERS*): H'lo, England? I want to be remembered when I die and even after I am dead because what lips I kissed last make me feel very very empty inside.

EZRA P.: Horsefruit, sailor.

ELIOT (*stirring moodily as scene changes*): Knitting I loved and, next to knitting, nothin.

(*Ward in a private asylum; nurses in blue uniforms move along the rows of patients, looking an awful lot like policemen.*)

CRITIC (*reading paper in a sleepy voice*): "He would accumulate formidable apparatus, logical swim-bladders, transcendental life-preservers and other precautionary and vehiculatory gear for setting out; perhaps did at last get underway, but was swiftly solicited, turned aside by the glance of some radiant new game on this hand or that into new courses; and ever into newer; and before long into all the universe, where it was uncertain what game you would catch or whether any at all."

MR. KEK (*a mild little man who has just kicked the hell out of a particularly burly truck driver*): Balls.

(*Note For Staging: The machine-gun nest should be in full view of the audience; gun transports may be utilized much after the fashion of a Greek Chorus, a raucous laugh here and there, etc. Shock troops may be kept in the wings, depending on the conditions, domestic and foreign, that pertain at the time of the performance—usually real bayonets should be used for all passages of controversial action. Suggested title: "Much Adon't About Everything."*)

MR. KEK: There comes a time in the life of a man or of a nation when he or it (or he she it) must decide a vera import prob— is a woman the less a lady iff er slip shews?

Now then: so we know that the girl could not have been keeled by A cause he were sleeping wit the cook at the toime; likewise D wass reading Bunyan to er faderinlawr; while, and dis'l slay yer, the Marster wass puling hisself erf in ther cellah. They can sail into rages, all on em, even Cooc-the-Kissy, and that is why I am frying th' leaves so they'll all turn brown, so the wind kin blow them away.

GARBAGE SCOW (*pensively*): Hym that is of a contrary opinion they counte not in the numbre of men, as one that hath avaled the heighe nature of hys soule to the vielnes of brute beastes bodyes.

For you maye be suer that he will studie either with craft prively to mocke, or els violently to breake the common laws (*Here the actor should belch delicately.*) of his countrey; in whom remaineth no further hope than of the bodye.

For deceit and falshod and all maners of lys, as nexte unto fraud, they do marvelouslie admir and aplaud.

MAE WEST'S TOENAIL: O eloquent and slaphappy dream! whom none could devise, thou has persuaded; what none hath had the nerve at, thou hast kicked through; whom all the world hath flattered, thou only hast cast out of the world; thou hast drawn into one sack all the cruelty of man and thrown it on thy magnificent back.

SUBWAY TURNSTILE: We shall this day light such a conflagration, by God's Grace, as I trust shall never be put out.

FIRST LAY OF THE LAST MINSTREL: He was good.

SECOND LAY OF THE LAST MINSTREL: He was good when he had it.

LAST LAY OF THE LAST MINSTREL: He was all gone when I got there.

THE NATION ITSELF: T's the uttermost thou hast in thee: out with it then. Up. Up. Whatsoever thy mustard gas findeth to do, do thou likecase with thy whole might.

OUR OWN SCARS AND STRIKES: The *great* idea began in words and ended in warts yet.

MR. KEK (*as though to himself*): Balls.

STAGEHAND (*unable to contain himself*):
Put it in a crock, hide it in the hunter, howl it
    in the forest,
Seek for it in this womb, in this fist, in this sickness.

OSTAS (*mystic and soured seer*): Night's black penis probing the heaving cowl of the sea . . .

PAVING BRICK: Mother of lunacies and the suggestress of suicides.

MR. KEK: And God brushing his beard aside went good on Mrs. God.

CHORUS OF NUNS ALL IN WHITE: You will write to me from heaven, won't you, Puszwortle?

MR. KEK (*ad libbing*):
And indaid that I sal, because of because shite
Ye marble bathtubs alive with lidies in heat
Mamie, Mamie, gie us a quator fer a w' nip
But the King of Sweden isn't needin no meat tahdie.

OSTAS (*dreamily*): The keel of dusk noses the rooftops.

MR. KEK (*with deep conviction*): Balls.

SHERNSH: Two dollars to put my man on your pretty girl.

NOLLY (*angrily*): Cheese and rabbits! blast you pink, Mr. Picka-nose.

MIGA (*rushing in*): The Nazis are coming!

MR. KEK: Where in hell you expect them to come from, stupid? Just take the cover off that little pot marked Americanism.

LIBERAL-INTELLECTUAL (*bristling*): Do you mean to say that you won't fight to save democracy from the fascists?

MR. KEK: Balls, Jack. You said the same damn thing in 1914. Whose democracy did you fight for then?

LIBERAL-INTELLECTUAL: But it's *different* now . . .

MR. KEK: Horsefruit, sailor. Let the capitalists of democracy fight it out with the capitalists of fascism. France, Italy, England, Germany, the U.S.—what the hell have the working classes of those countries got against each other? Don't come yapping to me with murders dripping out of your pockets.

THE CONSCIENCE OF THE PEOPLE: Just give me time enough.

STINKY DOONUT: To form a judgment in this interesting case, the progress, rise and genius of Morris Piddle must be explained. The circumstances in his tragicall fictions and manners, which are proper to the end of poetry . . .

MR. KEK: At least one end.

STINKY DOONUT: . . . must be pointed out. Reasons for the decline and rejection of this quaint . . .

MR. KEK: Wack.

STINKY DOONUT: . . . man must be given.

OSTAS: Hear! Hear! The life and opinions of an asslicker.

NOLLY: I feel very burnt out.

MIGA: Pood dear Nolly.

SHERNSH: Poor Nolly and Miga.

STINKY DOONUT: Poor Shernsh too.

OSTAS (*looking after a schoolgirl pantingly*): There is no cathedral or battle-machine that the least sparrow cannot fly over.

MR. KEK: Blue balls.

OSTAS: Must you have the address of Death tonight?

BROWN BIRD SINGING: The Lord tries all things and we are tried.

HANGMAN'S TREE: The Lord gives and the Law takes away.

JUNIOR'S ROADSTER WITH THE SIREN: And we are tried as the lame are tried by all things.

SWEET ALICE BEN BOLT: Well, I repeat—we have seen each other *somewhere*. Could it have been at—but no, no . . .

THE OLD OAKEN BUCKET: This dog leaps at my throat. Get the hell outa his way. How would you like it if some dog jumped yuh and I put my gawdum two cents in?

MR. KEK: I saw you put that general in your pocket.

NOLLY AND MIGA (*smiling tenderly at each other*): Oh, we fit the battle of Jellyroll . . . Jellyroll . . .

OSTAS: Into Thy hand I commend my spirit.

MR. KEK: Up, and into the saddle of my pea-green pony to set down first me then my journal of the last thoity days, and then back to bed, then up, and atum. Three statesmen to lunch, brainy chaps but unhonest as all hell; and then with my little bow and arrow to the opree where Ah bagged a rather cherce tenor; put my bum down. Thence to a beer jernt where met Ike and Mul and a wise guy with twa' burlesque queens waiting for him out front. Said to him Mack it's my inning and fanned him. Home with the skoits. Had it out with them. So back to my little nest, shaved, et, read the sporting page, put my bum down, and tottled erf to bed. Dreamed of my babyhood. And were sad.

NOLLY (*dreamily*):
"This ae nighte, this ae nighte,
Every nighte and alle,
Fire and sleet and candle-lighte,
And Christe receive thy soule."

MIGA (*with good grace*):
"Mother and maiden
Was never none but she;
Well may such a lady
Goddes mother be."

SHERNSH (*lifting a flower to his swollen lips*):
   "Now with his love, now in his colde grave
   Allone, with-outen any companye . . ."
MR. KEK (*putting himself outside a pint of Scotch*):
   "Get up, the caller calls, get up!
   And in the dead of night
   To win the bairns their bite and sup,
   I rise, a weary wight.
   My flannel dudden donned, thrice o'er
   My burds are kissed, and then
   I, with a whistle, shut the door
   I may not ope again."

      (*smiling hungrily at all of them*)

   "Thus Lullabye my youth, myne eyes,
   My will, my ware, and all that was,
   I can no more delayes devise,
   But welcome payne, let pleasure passe:
   With Lullabye now take your leave,
   With Lullabye your dreams deceive,
   And when you rise with waking eye,
   Remember then this Lullabye."

      (*passing bottle to* NOLLY)

   "The house is swept
   Which sin so long foul kept:
   The peny's found for which the loser wept.
   And purg'd with tears,
   God's Image re-appears.
   The peny truly shews whose stamp it bears."

      (*aside to* NOLLY) Feel it yet, Nolly?

      (*with careful eye on her, continuing*)

   "Here lies a piece of Christ, a Star in Dust . . ."

94

NOLLY: Fill er up, Short, Stark and Hideous.

MR. KEK (*with a warm glow in his voice*):
"Great, or Good, or Kind, or Faire
I will ne're the more despaire:
If she love me (this beleeve)
I will Die ere she shall grieve.
If she slighte me when I woe,
I can scorne and let her goe,
For if she be not for me,
What care I for whom she be?"

(*sternly to* NOLLY) How about it, Baby?

MIGA: Lay off that stuff.

SHERNSH: You licentious old man, you!

NOLLY (*to* MR. KEK): I know why you want me—but that won't
help you either.

(*There is a long silence: all of the principals are crying, without
shame, almost without interest.*)

MR. KEK: The world is getting dark. There is nothing to say
now. There is nowhere to go. There is . . .

NOLLY (*quietly*): Let us go home.

MR. KEK: Where, Nolly?

NOLLY: To our old dwelling.

MIGA: In the temple.

SHERNSH: Of our own sacrilegious hearts.

MR. KEK (*reverently*): Baa—alls.

The days of your murder are at hand.
This is your city and it is time to die.
All of the deaths are at your door.
My horesmen wheel in a great circle shutting out the guns.
I sing for the flame and against the ever-grinning darkness.

Heine, Too, Lived in Germany

The pavements are quiet under press of their feet;
Their voices bud into the dark like flowers sick
From too much care. They are the herders, beautiful
In uniform
Why does this blood scream Liar Liar
Somewhere a door bangs, somewhere a window flies up.
The hunted are awake. Fear is heavy as butter over
Their houses
Why does this blood scream Liar Liar
It was well-timed; they took the ones wanted;
Tortured the others. They did it cleanly, without fuss.
　　　Their calm faces,
Posed in rapid-glare of slick machine guns, are cinches
To make the very first edition of that EXTRA—
Which is our duty to give the hurt and sick of earth.

Do the Dead Know What Time It Is?

The old guy put down his beer.
Son, he said,
　　　(and a girl came over to the table where we were:
　　　asked us by Jack Christ to buy her a drink.)
Son, I am going to tell you something
The like of which nobody ever was told.
　　　(and the girl said, I've got nothing on tonight;
　　　how about you and me going to your place?)
I am going to tell you the story of my mother's
Meeting with God.
　　　(and I whispered to the girl: I don't have a room,
　　　but, maybe . . .)
She walked up to where the top of the world is

And He came right up to her and said
So at last you've come home.
    (but maybe what?
    I thought I'd like to stay here and talk to you.)
My mother started to cry and God
Put His arms around her.
    (about what?
    Oh, just talk . . . we'll find something.)
She said it was like a fog coming over her face
And light was everywhere and a soft voice saying
You can stop crying now.
    (what can we talk about that will take all night?
    and I said that I didn't know.)
You can stop crying now.

Nice Day for a Lynching

The bloodhounds look like sad old judges
In a strange court. They point their noses
At the Negro jerking in their noose;
His feet spread crowlike above these
Honorable men who laugh as he chokes.

I don't know this black man.
I don't know these white men.

But I know that one of my hands
Is black, and one white. I know that
One part of me is being strangled,
While another part horribly laughs.

Until it changes,
I shall be forever killing; and be killed.

MAN IS TO MAN A BEAST: a fawning dog, a roaring lion, a thieving fox, a robbing wolf, a treacherous jackal and a rapacious vulture. The civilest, I think, of nations, are those whom we account the most barbarous; there is some moderation and good nature in the Toupinambaltians, who eat no men but their enemies, while we civilized people prey upon everything that we can swallow. It is the great boast of culture and philosophy that they united men into societies and built up the houses and the high walls of cities. I wish they could undo all that they have done; that we might have our woods and our innocence again, instead of our empty buildings and our blood-fed politics. They have assembled many thousands of scattered people into one body: it is true, they have so done; they have brought them into hovels to rot and starve, and into armies to murder one another: they found them hunters and fishers of wild creatures and they have made them hunters and fishers of each other.

The nobility of living like men on this dark earth is certainly not to be counterfeited into this pig-fouled coin

The strange thing I said to Sam is the way they die.
All day our guns centered fire on the town, pounding
The very hell out of them, but do you think they'd give up . . .
Sam, I said why don't they quit? why in the name of God!
He grinned through his broken teeth. Boss, they don't like you.

So what? They're out of ammunition, food and water petered out,
They're up to their necks in their own dead—they haven't got
        a chance.
No but they don't want you to get her. But I need her I need
        her, Sam.
All right then blow their guts out. Jesus Christ look, Boss,
Your men are throwing their rifles over the wall and they've swung
The machine guns on us . . . This is it, Sam, we're in for it
        now boy.
Lead slugs get him in the belly. He tries to crawl but it's no go.
Take it easy, kid. Boss . . . Yes, Sam. Would you mind, Boss,
        it hurts
Like the devil. So long, fellah. I put him away with my revolver.
Now you bastards. Men, I yell. Blah, I get back. So that's it eh?
I see her standing at the city's gate. Her face makes me crazy
She's my woman and when you know that they can't keep you off.
I am walking at them now brother I'm goddamned if I'll go down.

Sweet Christus they're just standing there shooting me to ribbons
I can't see anymore I'm down on my knees clawing to get along
Brother, if you've got a little private army send it on I need it
More than you do you sonofabitch letting me take them all alone.

What did I tell you here comes Sam riding in at the head of
        a bunch of nice
Cleancut cutthroats there's Larry England and German Jackie
And Italio the Boot and Spinker Spain and good old
        Rotchop Russia
Well here is Little Free-Ass France and America the Shootemful
But *where* is Louie dat Crap and Jest A Sweet Pee
        In The Moonlight
Once while riding in Our Great West
Sleeping openmouthed awakened by a dripdrip from the
        rack above
Madam, your dill pickles are leaking
O that says she laughing them's not pickles them's puppies

Greatest sight our country has to offer
When the groundhog crawls out of his hole . . .
Have you got her I ask and Sam says, Boss, she's right in here.
What shall we do with the prisoners he wants to know.
What have you done I say and he says come over to the window.
All right, Sam, but I wish you had put the stakes farther away
I never liked the smell of frying meat. But you want to hear them
He says and I say yes but I don't like that stink. Well here she is.
I remember her as being younger but then I haven't seen her
    in twenty years.
Molly dear, I breathe softly O God how lovely she is and so pure.
What's that on her cheek I ask Sam. That's mold, Boss, he says,
She don't hardly ever get time to wash with so many guys at her.
How many's she get a day I ask. Some days maybe two hundred
    or three.
We'll incorporate I say. I always wanted a nice little business
    of my own.
Well, babe, I say brightly taking off my coat. I walk over
    and pat her bust.
She can't speak English, Boss. That's all right, Sam, she can
    speak whore.

Elegy for the Silent Voices
and the Joiners of Everything

The featureless ghost under the wall cannot jerk out at us,
    like a pig would, or shriek, like the guns will,
    or be our own fallen human face, as madness is
(Therefore) And he cannot have tense, wakeful girls and fall
    vaguely into heaven, like Shelley did, the sexual balloon
    coming down to spend its gas in his baby-blue eyes

These are the survivors: a drunkard, two shepherds
With tan beards, an office force consisting of bookkeeper,

Typist and errandboy, several scrubwomen, a rapist,
Four Germans, a whores' union, a signpainter, no boxers,
Wrestlers or policemen, one gunman and one half of a Japanese
How soon can we expect Murphy, the Snag-Tooth
    they asked eagerly

Therefore: (They took a quick gander at the steam readings:
                DANGER   ZERO,
    and saw that some twenty or more sailors with big skins
    and endless ribs had brought the ship, *Lonedeath,* up fast
    to a shivering dock: hove to: and it all going God-high,
    town, engine room, skipper, cripples, spotted dogs,
        with a diamond
    of thunderous sound, splitting the sky up like a fat
        fish's belly)

(People hurry along like pictures taken through milk)
A pretty girl gave birth to a child in a muddy field
And the ragged wonder of it was featured on the radio,
A pleasing description being given of what the mother wanted
    her son to be
"Castrated," she said simply—and somebody is very likely to

With dignity, continuously pure and fortunate,
Something lives and taunts that disappearing ghost,
As Melville did, intangible as an idiot's dream

Behind shouting trees the figure glides like blood in a mouse's side
Within our faces the poor move their awful hands
    in desolate proverbs
Jesus Joseph and Mary it is not thus, it is not thus, it is not thus
That the whole round world is broken

There is nothing to be afraid of
Our houses need holes for new air and we will get them
    through our heads.

*HE IS GUARDED BY CROWDS AND SHACKLED
WITH FORMALITIES: the whole hat, the half hat,
the whole smile, the half smile, the ditto ass, the nod,
the embrace, the positive parting with a little bow,
the comparative at the middle of the room, the su-
perlative at the door: as if there were such rules set
to these leviathans as are to the sea "Hitherto shalt
thou come, but no further." (Job XXXVIII:11)*

The half-starved goat followed the man
Everywhere: folks wondered about them;
The gent, in his old coat, hatless in the cold,
Rubbing blue nose on sleeve, watery-eyed,
Stroking the billy like a Memphis Man
After the fourth bottle, shoved people round
Like he didn't like anything except maybe
That mangy old goat—"Lie down, lie down,
Fair Elaine," he softly sang—and the pair
Of them crushed along like sodden blisters
On the big dirty foot of the city. Singing
"Lie down, lie down, fair Elaine."

Death Will Amuse Them

A little girl was given a new toy
That needed no winding and would never run down
As even the best of everything will

And all day she played with it
Following happily over the floor of heaven
Until finally it rolled to the feet of God Himself

Who said: "You must give it back now."
Then He pointed down at two soldiers who were staring up
Hopefully

"You see, it is a very popular toy."
And He tossed it down to them
Whose eyes would stare up in earnest when they touched it.

I GOT THE FAT POET INTO A CORNER and told
him he was writing s———t and couldn't get away
with it

Now, it is night and time
for sleep. Everyone is
tired

from garbage-glutting
lifting their snouts
from the trough
long enough
to ease their gut—
I won't urge the point.

Gold-plated poems
to stuff up
their mind's ass

or politics
watered down so as
not to scare the blue bloods
Boo! you well-fed bastards

The Quantity of Mercy

The quail flutters like a forlorn castle falling
I do not mean her harm
She thinks I wish to hurt her young;
The little things are somewhere hidden.
They move their tiny mouths but do not cry.

I cannot ever hurt thee, little bird
I cannot ever hurt thee

I have but a bullet left
And there are so many things to kill.

Eve of St. Agony, or the Middle Class
Was Sitting on Its Fat

Man-dirt and stomachs that the sea unloads; rockets
Of quick lice crawling inland, planting their damn flags,
Putting their malethings in any hole that will stand still,
Yapping bloody murder while they slice off each other's heads,
Spewing themselves around, priesting, whoring, lording
It over little guys, messing their pants, writing gush-notes
To their grandmas, wanting somebody to do something pronto,
Wanting the good thing right now and the bad stuff
        for the other boy.
Gullet, praise God for the gut with the patented zipper;
Sing loud for the lads who sell iceboxes on the burning deck.
Dear reader, gentle reader, dainty little reader, this is
The way we go round the milktrucks and seamusic, Sike's trap
        and Meg's rib,
The wobbly sparrow with two strikes on the bible, behave
Alfred, your pokus is out; I used to collect old ladies,
Pickling them in brine and painting mustaches on their bellies,

Later I went in for stripteasing before Save Democracy Clubs;
When the joint was raided we were all caught with our
    pants down.
But I will say this: I like butter on both sides of my bread
And my sister can rape a Hun any time she's a mind to,
Or the Yellow Peril for that matter; Hector, your papa's
    in the lobby.
The old days were different; the ball scores meant something then,
Two ball in the side pocket and two bits says so; he got up
    slow see,
Shook the water out of his hair, wham, tell me that ain't a sweet
    left hand;
I told her what to do and we did it, Jesus I said, is your name
    McCoy?
Maybe it was the beer or because she was only sixteen
    but I got hoarse
Just thinking about her; married a john who travels in cotton
    underwear.
Now you take today; I don't want it. Wessex, who was that with
    I saw you lady?
Tony gave all his dough to the church; Lizzie believed in feeding
    her own face;
And that's why you'll never meet a worm who isn't an
    antichrist, my friend,
I mean when you get down to a brass tack you'll find some sucker
    sitting on it.
Whereas. Muckle's whip and Jessie's rod, boyo, it sure looks black
In the gut of this particular whale. Hilda, is that a .38
    in your handbag?

    Ghosts in packs like dogs grinning at ghosts
    Pocketless thieves in a city that never sleeps
    Chains clank, warders curse, this go is wenting fast!

Take it from me, neighbor, there's one hell of
A cowardly new world a-sneaking up on you.

Fog

Rain's lovely gray daughter has lost her tall lover.
He whose mouth she knew; who was good to her.

I've heard her talk of him when the river lights
Scream "Christ! it's lonely; Christ! it's cold."

Heard the slug cry of her loneliness calling him
When the ship's mast points to no star in the North.

Many men have thought they were he;
Feeling her cold arms as they held death in theirs—

The woman-face in the frame of nothingness;
As the machinery of sleep turned its first wheel;

And they slept, while angels fell in colored sound
Upon the closing waters. Child and singing cradle one.

O sorrowful lady whose lover is that harbor
In a heaven where all we of longing lie, clinging together
as it gets dark.

If We Are to Know Where We Live

I came to the house. It was dark.
It was hell standing there.
No one answered my knock.

WHAT ARE THEY DOING IN MY HOUSE

I tapped on the window. I banged on the door.
They pulled the shades. They threw the heavy bolt.

But I knew what they wanted
And I saw what I was not to see
And I heard what I was not to hear.

They wanted to murder the thing within the house.
I saw my own face with the knives above it.
I heard my own screams as they tortured me.

And I was everyone. We all stood there.

Autumn Is the Crows' Time

They come in low, wings like dark bandages
Slung on their backs: air-minded monks
With bright devil eyes: these thieves
Would never hang beside our Christ!

The corn does a yellow dance in the wind.
Hills bleed grays and browns and the sky
Is dull blue. Nature's drabbest season
Sprawls like a clown in church, not
Knowing whether to laugh or pray

      but the crows
Do both, coming in low, not concerned
With the farmer's anger, quite equipped
To handle the shot that lifts at them.

Leave it so: suspended:
The farmer's ragged angry face;
The earth, upon which all things are quick or slow,
Dependent on the gun of the farmer and the wisdom
      of the crow.

AND HE HAD WILDER MOMENTS, when he would hurry to and fro by the margin of the demented December sea, when its black waves, white-topped, towered mountain-high, threatening to bury the lonely wild-haired being, with extended hands, standing just within its last line of water-wrack. There he would stride, drenched with spray, roaring forth rage even to blasphemy, as if he would outroar that ocean, against that inscrutable decree of fate which had hidden the whole race of his fellows from him; and scowling up dumb curses to that scowling heaven, as if he would dare, in his reckless misery to frown back the very frown of God, which had withered him, heart and hope, life and love

My heart says, puzzled, "Why do men kill each other?"
Ask the smug-faced stars.
Is it ever Easter on the cross?

My hand wanders to the control-stick.
I kick out the first bomb.
It is pretty good.
Most all the town, messed plenty.
Two weeks without sleep;
Months without a woman.
Suppose it's still the same.

Rats gnaw at the dead.
Filmed over, eyes, world, music.
Mozart flaking open to the flies.
What voluptuous graves they have here.
Backfire of the sodden ages.
Why are they moving that gun up?

Maggots skate into the castle through silt of kings.
Oh no, not the Queen lying in her dirt!
Notice the lovely rings on her plump fingers.
My eyes watch all the other eyes, warily.

The Overworld

On alternating levels the world pounds in
And there is not such another one anywhere

The city awakens to the whisper of bells
And sleep melts like a snowstorm in the sun

We are awake, Lord, Lord God, we are awake

Tumble swallows out of warm caves
Watch their naked hands as they haunt the foaming air
O push tigers through the flaming bushes and let brides
Quit the booming arms where they have lain through the night
Their licensed heat like a dumb-craft lamp
Haunting the place where the dead lie
Hoppity hippity pretty little piece of clay
Buy us sell us pay us want us praise us, harlot banker priest
Put us in the way of something
We'll bed with you; we'll bleed for you, hoppity hippity hop
Trust us love us touch us take us leave us alone

We are awake, Lord, Lord God, we are awake

Do not tell the horse that his rider can't hold the reins anymore
Do not talk of murder to the man who has a knife in his back
Do not gossip with the killer but push tigers through
      the flaming bushes
And place the baskets exactly for our heads
For we are kneeling here for we are kneeling here

Plow Horses

They stand contentedly, chewing
What does it mean to live now?

They are solid and the muscles move
Easily in the oil of their blood
What does it mean to live now?

They put their faces together like children
And their great gentle eyes look at me
What does it mean to live now?

I run my hand along their necks, lovingly.

Career for a Child of Five

At night, when I can't sleep,
When the faces won't back,
When horror touches my chest
And I start up screaming . . .

It was long ago in a strange land,
Child, that I shall kill you

My mother got the palms from the hands
Of the priest himself; and being doubly blessed
As they were, she would put them on the bureau
Near candles, where their shadows reeled
A devil's walk through my childhood.
But I never cried, being too near terror.

You may repeat your nice prayers,
Child, that I shall kill you

Then one night, after hours of torment,
I started to say all the foul words
That boys had taught me; beginning
Softly . . . then louder, louder,
Until mother came and put soap
In my mouth to rub them away.

Was ever son so willed in love,
Child, that I shall kill you

And now, when I can't sleep,
When shadows bring the boy back,
It's always he who is able to cry;
The foul words remain to me.

· Hymn to a Trench Gun

Is it that you feel not our dying?
We would not lightly go this way.
Trees look dark as ghosts; the streets
Are dimly lighted behind us—they seem
Ruts of slow fire pouring across the valley.
This place is not home: it's rough and wild.
We crawl upon our knees; we bend our heads.
Something calls from somewhere . . . something cries . . .
We look down on you. We cup our hands and scream.
Something dies . . . something calls from nowhere . . . dies . . .
We are already dead. We are already dead.

"Let us go down and walk into their houses;
Let us show them the place where the bullets will enter;
Let us ask them to bury us now . . ."

Nobody can kill the dead. We look at you.

23rd Street Runs into Heaven

You stand near the window as lights wink
On along the street. Somewhere a trolley, taking
Shop girls and clerks home, clatters through
This before-supper Sabbath. An alley cat cries
To find the garbage cans sealed; newsboys
Begin their murder-into-pennies round.

We are shut in, secure for a little, safe until
Tomorrow. You slip your dress off, roll down
Your stockings, careful against runs. Naked now,
With soft light on soft flesh, you pause
For a moment; turn and face me—
Smile in a way that only women know
Who have lain long with their lover
And are made more virginal.

Our supper is plain but we are very wonderful.

Eight Early Poems

I

This room has mystery like trance
Of wine; forget-me-nots of you
Are chair and couch, the books your
Fingers touched. And now that you

Are absent here the silence scrapes
A secret rust from everything;
While sudden wreaths of sorrow's
Dust uncover emptiness like halls
To stumble through, and terror falls.

Your name includes the shadow flight of birds
That curve a longing cry near home;
In garden loveliness of cottage smoke
The flowering wings arrest the traffic
Of a sadder prophecy . . . for you

Are bird and summer sky and all
I know of home. Your face awakes a fog
Like blossoms to drape my eyes
In streets where noise and duty are.
And
     if words I knew to speak your body, then
Flesh of me would have no way to you.

III

THE SEA HAS CAVES AND URNS

The sea unlocks a child's castle and an angel's
Eye: my father's blood runs through the whale . . .
     here where an infinity of hands
     pursues a stumbling, shoreless world . . .

The footless worm remarks of hill and sound
Where waves convince the pilgrim's feet
     that there awaits
     the final, monstrous sleep.
     My father's bones are continents made . . .

IV

I know the hair, tissue, skin,
eyes: the lilies, locking and singing
in the bone, growing into your face

113

and through your face—I know
the pressure of the spirit's skeleton
and point the gentle word "love"
    at it;
but beneath the play of tags
on everything, I know my words,
like whisky in a corpse, to be
    of little use
to one lost in the golden pasturage
of this "you" which is the journey's
drive into the land of a human heaven.

v

It is a lonely walk into the mind's retreat
    finding
That air is green against the couch of grass;
That water is wooden beneath a ship's hull;
That the spinning petals of a flower,
    held between the fingers,
Are a perfect talking of color;
                and yet, this
Is not more strange or less obscure
Than that each time my eyes
Explore the spreading world in yours,
I do not see, sharp face, the floating
Timbers of Eden washed high
    on the hanging question in mine;
                    or that
Each time I touch your body,
Like a mirror held to music,
I do not plant a splitting beauty
Upon the lives of all the things I am.

FRAGMENT FROM "A SCHOOLBOY'S ODYSSEY"

Come wind an Easter lily peace in your hair . . .
Let boy be true to girl . . . river smells and your hand
    warm within mine . . . a pedlar saying "Good morning
    children" . . . and I had the world to give you . . .
Oh God how I hated the mills and our dirty lives
And the sunshine creeping an Africa of sleep over our faces.

VII

GEOGRAPHY OF MUSIC

Let me be prodigal as sun in praising you.
I take the peeping angel, frolicking
    in the branches of Time;
The dreamless churchyard on the wings
Of this gypsy moth; the face
Within the river's mist; the footsteps
Of this throbbing flower; water's rapture, leaf's
Melody in delirium of sunrise—
I take these things as factions
    in the spirit's lens
Through which I look at you. And yet,
    how can
I trust to word's furniture in moving now
Within the swarm of mountain worlds
Your lightest touch has built for me?
It is the ocean's sound of sorrowing,
It is the wonder of a thousand singing,
It is the world with all loveliness
Lost within the moons and suns of it,
Beloved, that you are.

AT THE NEW YEAR

In the shape of this night, in the still fall
  of snow, Father
In all that is cold and tiny, these little birds
  and children
In everything that moves tonight, the trolleys
  and the lovers, Father
In the great hush of country, in the ugly noise
  of our cities
In this deep throw of stars, in those trenches
  where the dead are, Father
In all the wide land waiting, and in the liners
  out on the black water
In all that has been said bravely, in all that is
  mean anywhere in the world, Father
In all that is good and lovely, in every house
  where sham and hatred are
In the name of those who wait, in the sound
  of angry voices, Father
Before the bells ring, before this little point in time
  has rushed us on
Before this clean moment has gone, before this night
  turns to face tomorrow, Father
There is this high singing in the air
Forever this sorrowful human face in eternity's window
And there are other bells that we would ring, Father
Other bells that we would ring.

*AND IN ANOTHER PLACE USES THE SAME
PHRASE "Secretum iter & fallentis semita vitae."
(The secret tracks of the deceiving life.) Which is*

very elegant in Latin, but English will hardly bear up the sense; and therefore Mr. Piddle translates it very well: "Or from a life, led, as it were, by stealth." Yet we say in our language: "A thing deceives our sight when it passes before us unperceived!" And we may well enough say out of the same author: "Sometimes with sleep, sometimes with wine, we strive the cares of life and troubles to deceive." But that is not to deceive the world, but to deceive ourselves, as Quintilian says: "vitam fallere," to draw on still, and amuse, and deceive our life, till it be advanced insensibly to the fatal period, and fall into that pit which nature hath prepared for it. The meaning of all this (and I am speaking now for critics alone) is no more than that most vulgar saying: "Bene qui latuit, bene vixit" He has lived well who has lain well hidden

Mr. Kek is seen dusting a wall-motto that hangs over the fireplace directly facing the door. He hums a little tune as he works: They were all gathered at the wedding but the bride was too fagged to walk. Backing off he squints fiercely at the motto, the ornate characters of which proclaim:

> "I closed my lids, and kept them closed,
> And the balls like pulses beat;
> For the sky and the sea, and the sea and the sky
> Lay like a load on my weary eye,
> And the dead were at my feet."

A soft snow dulls the sound of city traffic and the occasional meek truck noises may be imagined as the punctuation of slightly boiled

*angels chatting together in the sky. Rare cheer dominates the room
with its roaring fire. It is Christmas Eve and* MR. KEK *anticipates
a goodly crew of clients. The girls in their beautiful shimmering
gowns sit sedately in a row near the paneled stairs which lead to
the upper rooms.*

MR. KEK *crosses the brothel with jaunty step as the door opens
to admit the first celebrants of the gala night.*

THOMAS DEKKER (*stamping against the snow*): Did you bring the
    bottle, Mr. J.?

BEN JONSON (*holding it out*): Want one now?

JOHN DONNE (*taking a slug in turn*): Ah, it's good to be alive.

BEN JONSON (*anxiously*): Where's Stevie?

WALTER SNOWBEARD WHITMAN: He'll be along. Stopped off at
    Tony's.

MR. KEK (*heartily*): Greetings, gates!
    (*Greetings are got out of the way.*)

MR. KEK (*continuing*): You will find some nice girls here. (*He
    points.*)

MATTHEW ARNOLD (*walking over*): Good evening, dear ladies.

O HOW THAT GLITTERING TAKETH ME (*a neat trick in a low-cut
    dress who seems more eager than the others*): I've waited all
    my life for you.

BEN JONSON (*taking her arm*): You'll like me better. (*They go
    off.*)

MATTHEW ARNOLD: Damn!

THE GRAVE'S A FINE AND PRIVATE PLACE (*lovliest wench of all*):
    You may have me, sir.

MATTHEW ARNOLD (*doubtfully*): You're not exactly my type.

ANDREW MARVELL: I'll have you, my bonnie lass. (*They go off.*)

GO AND CATCH A FALLING STAR (*rudely taking* ARNOLD'*s arm*):
    Come on, stupid, you'll lose out altogether. (*They go off.*)

ROBERT BURNS: Ha! Here's Stevie now.

STEPHEN CRANE: There's trouble brewing in the town. They've
    closed all the roads and some say that troops can be heard
    marching in from the West.

JOHN DONNE: What sort of troops?

JAMES THOMSON: Troops of the Enemy.

RICHARD CRASHAW: But we have no enemies.

BARUCH SPINOZA: Father, when does the hurting cease?

DANTE ALIGHIERI: When do your horses lift their sharp hoofs from our torn flesh?

ARTHUR RIMBAUD: When is the thing said made still on your white throne?

BEN JONSON (*descending like a sleepwalker*):

> We are the hunted whom all things harry.
> We are the wretched whom every sound wakes.

(*turning to the girls*) And they must die too.

SOFTLY, NOW SOFTLY LIES SLEEPING (*a buxom blonde with a hard face, brilliantly painted*):

> We are like the gull-capped water
> That never lies under sleep as men do.

BEN JONSON (*sadly*): They are too fragile to be wanted by death. (*He goes out into the night.*)

FRANÇOIS VILLON (*coming in with a voicey rush*): Well, which is it to be? (*All of the girls smile tenderly at him.*)

POOR SOUL, THE CENTER OF MY SINFUL EARTH: Please, take me.

FRANÇOIS VILLON: That's one. I'm in fine fettle tonight.

BLOW, BLOW THOU WINTER WIND: And me.

FRANÇOIS VILLON: Two. But wait! Who's this! I haven't seen your face . . .

THE GRAVE'S A FINE AND PRIVATE PLACE (*who has deserted MARVELL*): I have waited all my life for you. (*They go off arm in arm.*)

SAM'L T. COLERIDGE (*coming in from the night*): They've taken Ben! They're dragging him through the streets to the gallows outside the town.

JOHN DONNE: Then the Enemy has taken the city!

HEINRICH HEINE: The Enemy has been here always.

RICHARD CRASHAW: But the marching troops . . .

HEINRICH HEINE: Enemy to fight Enemy. The people die at the bottom like flies under an idiot's boot—but they never fight in their own war.

John Donne: Poor Ben!

François Villon (*clattering down the stairs*): Pluck your swords from their softness, mates; we've enough here to fight God Himself!

(*As they rush out a heavy rumbling not unlike the sound of artillery is heard: woog! waan! waa-wooog!*)

Mr. Kek (*listening gravely*): A fine birth He's getting this night.

Matthew Arnold (*coming down with a black eye*): Where is everybody?

Mr. Kek: They've gone courting a prettier girl than I've to offer...

(Arnold *leaves, muttering to himself.*)

(*Now the room is quiet again. The fire crackles merrily and the girls whisper together.*)

Mr. Kek (*looking them over critically*): Guess it'll be you tonight.

Cherry-Ripe, Ripe, Ripe, I Cry (*youngest and frailest*): I don't like you—you and your frog's face leering at everybody and everything.

Mr. Kek (*grabbing her arm*): My face is what it sees and you don't have to do with it anyway.

(*It is some hours later. The room has been transformed into a banquet hall. An enormous table bridges the walls. Mr. Kek, napkin on arm, administers to the needs of his hungry guests; a singularly beautiful smile wreathes his battered features. Barmaids move about filling glasses and making themselves generally useful.*)

Bix Beiderbecke (*lowering his trumpet, still hot with "Jass Me Blues"*): I may get that note before the night is over.

Phantom Mike Gibbons (*helping himself to more turkey*): You'll never hit that note—and you know it.

Bat Nelson: Just like my left hand never quite did what I wanted.

Carl Hubbell: If a guy had some little thing more nobody could hit him.

Peter Jackson: Seems funny to think that we won't be getting in there anymore.

JOE GANS (*lifting his glass in mock toast*): Yeah, it's up to the kids now.

PRETTY AMBERG: None of them can touch you guys.

BOB FITZSIMMONS: But they're getting in there . . .

BIX BEIDERBECKE (*crossing to piano*): Mind if I try it this way, boys? (*The room is hushed as he plays "In a Mist."*)

STEVE FOSTER (*as the last note dies*): I never belonged in your league.

BIX BEIDERBECKE: How about "Beautiful Dreamer"?

STEVE FOSTER: I liked that one.

EDGAR POE: The three of us should go on the town sometime.

OWNEY MADDEN (*suspiciously*): What can you do?

VINCENT COLL (*putting his hand inside his coat*): Leave the little guy alone.

HERMAN MELVILLE: Eddie can take care of himself.

HART CRANE: Better than any of us.

   (*There is a sudden commotion in the hall and the door is flung open to admit half a dozen green-shirted men armed with heavy automatics.*)

FIRST GREEN SHIRT: Any you seen two guys and a girl come in here last ten minutes?

MR. KEK (*stepping up to them*): Sure. Sure. Lots of people come to my house. What about it?

SECOND GREEN SHIRT: Wise boy, huh. These two mugs and the jane won't be hard to spot. (*He looks over the room*). They're dressed up in nothin—nekked as plucked monkeys.

MR. KEK: It's cold as the grave out tonight . . .

FIRST GREEN SHIRT: Yeah, well you figure it. Come on, boys. (*They go off soldier-style.*)

GYP THE BLOOD (*testily*): We could pick them off from the windows.

STRIPTEASE SARA: Let them go. Why spoil our fun with the likes of them.

JACK "LEGS" DIAMOND: Guess you're right. We should mix with bums like that . . .

GLORIA DAWN: Let's ride em, Bix. Point that ole horn at Mr. God.

(BIX *puts his trumpet through "Wabash Blues," "Tin Roof,"*
and good old "Basin Street;" one by one, Red Allen, Teddy
Wilson, Coleman Hawkins, Earl Hines, Jack Teagarden,
Cozy Cole, Ziggy Elman, and Louis The One And Only put
that big train on through the night.)

NATHANIEL HAWTHORNE: I don't see much in that.

HERMAN MELVILLE (*easily*): You wouldn't.

NICKY ARNSTEIN (*taking a barmaid's arm*): How's about it, kiddo?

MR. KEK: Lay off that stuff.
(*The door is thrown open violently and two men and a wom-*
an stumble in: their naked bodies are blue with cold.)

NOLLY: Stop them! Oh for God's sake . . . stop them! (*She sinks*
to the floor.)

MR. KEK (*putting his coat around her and motioning* MIGA *and*
SHERNSH *to the fire*): What do they want with you?

MIGA (*warming himself frantically*): We were in a hotel room
playing cards and they come banging on the door . . .

SHERNSH: They stripped us and clamped us all in one cell. Nolly
was nice to a guard and he let us out.

MR. KEK: What do they want with you?

NOLLY (*shivering*): That's what's horrible—they didn't say any-
thing and they kicked us quiet.

MR. KEK: They'll be back. You three go upstairs and I'll have
food sent up. We'll see that they don't get beyond this room.

AL FABICCIO: We'd better get ready.

ABE ATTEL: All you guys with gats stand near the stairs—us
boys'll use our fists up front.

VINCENT COLL (*extracting a tommy gun from a bag at his feet*):
This oughta be easy.

GYP THE BLOOD: You never know what them rats are liable to
pull.

WOODROW JENNINGS TAFT: Why should we risk our lives for that
whore and her two nogood lovers?

MR. KEK (*without bitterness*): You wouldn't understand.

(*A tense, watchful silence pervades the banquet hall. Somewhere a clock booms out over the City—hushed somewhat by the falling snow and the voice of human murder . . . one, two three and* TWELVE.)

GYPSY BUD MURPHY (*as the last echo dies*): Christ is born.

MR. KEK (*cheerfully*): They may not be back for hours. Anybody know any stories?

J. WILKES BOOTH: Let's go around the table.

MR. KEK: You start, Hanner.

HOTBUTT HANNER (*looking thoughtful*): During all the time I was with him, never once did his motor stop running.

MR. KEK: That's not exactly a story.

HOTBUTT HANNER (*taking* SAMMY KATZ' *hand off her leg*): It's mine.

MR. KEK: All right then, anything at all.

TUCKER NELSON: It was a wet day. We were camped out in a little wood. Their guns chewed up the country all around us. Larry took his rifle and shot two of our officers. Then he yelled across the lines, "Hey! you guys, throw down your damn guns!" Timkins, in charge of Company S, coming up on the dead run, put a bullet through Larry's head. The men stood there, tense, not knowing what to do.

CHUEY THE CHIMP: The hotbum woulda come off oak but the match went out . . .
(*A sudden noise at the door and the noses of their revolvers sniff expectantly.*)

MR. KEK (*rifle crooked on his arm*): Let them make the first move.
(*The door opens slowly and . . .*)

BEN JONSON: I didn't think I'd ever get here. (*His face is a bloody bag: his clothes are in shreds: one arm is shot away at the shoulder*) I wanted to tell you that his real name is . . . (*He dies.*)

MR. KEK: Real schmeel . . . (*bending over him*) But it sure as hell wasn't Shakespeare.

NOLLY (*calling down*): We can't stand it much longer. Wouldn't it be better to kill ourselves . . . (*Her voice breaks off hysterically.*)

123

MR. KEK: We'll see you through, Nolly. *(to the group)* Well, let's get on with it. Who's next?

CAPT. JOHN SMIFF: I knew a charming trolley once name of Terrance.

PRETTY RED WING: A stromberry pie can be a cute character.

MAJOR ED MARTIN: Nine out of ten of the fellahs had doses, but they figured a soldier wouldn't be using it much anyhow.

AUNT POLLY: He used to come to my gate every evening just as the sun was setting back of the red barn. I never really liked the man but all my sixteen children were his spitting image. My husband never suspected anything but the neighbors talked so one day me and him went quietlike into the orchard and made our plan for doing away with my legal mate but I got cold feet at the last moment and shot my lover through the head and they hanged some hobo for it.

SCHIZOPHRENIA AND THE SEVEN SHTOONKS: Mister Mose could chin himself in its nightshoit. All his erl were changed come dark by divers damsels as he would mount the platform saying my velly friends foo feathor'd at the post ten berries on yer docement mademosel O bride of Teccadema late of Rhodes with yore image weping Oook oott par la course

Evlilthin is swek notor ekes paw wont lik le lok ma bele beeg justa minut sir, wel th yelo besterd will rite a bes seler erbot a younge man who maid a made an thes peep liv lik peegs ev'r sense, h'lo wifey, gotta dinnar hot, never ment me wooman ter slav oer stov all diy; pert ye bonnert on bitchling we gerin ter paint ther towne blue.

CASEY JONES *(reading from the back of an old calendar)*: "Many methods of making steel were in use prior to 1855 but none of them produced the metal in large enough quantities or at a low enough price to satisfy the demand. Pig iron or cast iron were easy to make from the ore but to get the extra carbon out of pig iron was a laborious and expensive process. The first step in making steel is to get the oxygen out of the ore . . ."

(A rifle is heard outside the window and one of the barmaids

clutches her breast; a red stream gushes out over her fingers as she sags to the floor.)

MR. KEK *(as the men make a rush for the window)*: It's just a trick to draw us out . . .

HENRY ADAMS: But we can't sit on here—to be picked off like clay pigeons.

(Another shot and JOHN BROWN *slides from his chair, the top of his head gone.)*

MR. KEK: There's no help for it. We must wait our chance. You can't fight a thing you can't see.

FRANÇOIS VILLON *(staggering in with a prisoner)*: God's rod! Here's one of them at last.

THE PRISONER: I swear to you! I have nothing to do with them! I am a citizen just like yourselves.

MR. KEK *(to VILLON)*: Where did you find him?

FRANÇOIS VILLON: He was skulking in the shadow near your door.

MR. KEK: What are we to do with him?

(A bullet sings in and THE PRISONER *slumps in his tracks, his eyes accusing them.)*

FRANÇOIS VILLON *(rushing back into the night with drawn sword)*: I'm match for any coward!

(All are silent expecting the fusillade which does not come.)

MR. KEK: My God! Like a cat with a mouse . . . *(Several others follow* VILLON *in a frenzied rush; immediately a storm of shots breaks out.)*

DOLLY VARDEN *(hysterically)*: There's no escape now.

(The sound of airplane motors can be heard: a bomb explodes somewhere nearby.)

MR. KEK *(putting out the lights)*: Everybody quiet. *(A shot rings out—from inside the room—someone groans.* MR. KEK *throws the light-switch, revealing* VILLON *standing near the door, blood streaming from a wound in his head.)*

MR. KEK: You damn fool! Why did you rush off like that?

FRANÇOIS VILLON: I was shot by someone *in this room.* Funny . . . *(He chuckles as he falls in a bloody heap.)*

MR. KEK: Who fired that shot?

> (*All are silent. The bombers are almost overhead now.* MR. KEK *again fills the room with darkness. The faint glow from the fire reveals terror on every face.*)

A VOICE IN THE DARKNESS: Are we all to die like this? Trapped like rats in a well . . .

NOLLY (*screaming*): Someone is climbing across the roof . . . A-a-a-h!

> (*There is the sound of a whispered conversation, then silence.*)

MIGA (*yelling down*): It's all right. Nolly's taking care of him.

MR. KEK (*breathing heavily*): There's no hope now.

> (*A powerful searchlight floods the room.*)

VOICE FROM THE NIGHT: Come out one by one—you will not be harmed.

MR. KEK (*as several move to comply*): Stay where you are.

VOICE FROM THE NIGHT: We are your friends. We have rounded up all the killers.

MR. KEK: Then why don't you show yourselves to us?

VOICE FROM THE NIGHT: We are not ready for that.

(*The night grows silent again: the planes have flown over and armored trucks no longer move through the streets.*)

PADRAIC PIERCE: I don't trust this quiet.

ANDREAS NIN: The murder is not to end so easily.

MR. KEK (*putting the light on*): I have a terror of dying in the dark.

NIKOLAI LENIN: There is no darkness when men know what they are fighting for.

MR. KEK: Well let's get on with our little Canterbury.

HUGO THEIL: I remember little of my childhood. There were never shoes enough to go round. Mother did a bit of hustling when dad couldn't get work and she caught it, one of my brothers being born a drooling idiot which stopped her and us kids worked up from little rackets to the big money and The Chair for Tom and ten years for me. It's better in jail than out.

LESTER GROOSE: I found her in a quick-lunch joint in Dallas. We set up house and I got a job in a garage. We named our son Gene Debs but it didn't help him none when he fell under a freight somewhere in Montana.

SHERIFF HANCOCK: We had some kicks, sure, people don't understand the workings of the Law. For every nigger my boys nicked I gave them a buck raise. It don't hurt a nigger when he burns anymore than a mule when you put a cigarette under his tail. Once on a bet we made a supper of black meat and it didn't taste half bad.

HENRY M. SUNSET: Gabble from too much cake, gabble from too little clover, munch then, mertch then, as the gray crocidile goes bloop, girth of a bible lesson, but we are going, going, goon, why, or when, they are all drawbridges and I am a turkeygobbler in Mrs. Beef's mothermachin. A litle nolege gues a loong loong wah. Some folks is screws.

AUGIE OAT: In front of a front of a what is so rare as a stake fumbling in front of a filly named Nan I mean when drink doops me doon. When a hitch to horse a post to. Ride cooboy! I have been thinking boot oh the duck deeves doone bul ther are no fly on M. Fletch, but would I care so much for parsnips enyhoo. Take the moth in grandpa's attic or month Devembar, tidy, touchy, extraordinary tail on that snail. If you want a quail just add some feathers of cos. Suggest you get a shootgun. Now a word or two about swallows. They are stained boxes of filth. Adequate jewels for Matilda God. A green is rooster rot. He were the dater of a Rear-Admiral.

MR. KEK (calling upstairs): Are you all right, Nolly?

NOLLY: Yes, he's gone now.

MR. KEK: Who was he? Did he say anything about the others?

NOLLY (without bitterness): All I know is that I gave him what he wanted and he went away.

SHERMAN MITCHELL: I think I'll go home. (He moves off.)

MR. KEK: Wait! (MITCHELL is shot as he opens the door.)

ALFRED WHITSTEED (in mounting hysteria): Thas be tha poora-thee going down thi seagoes leving lutes in Hagen, in Mozalbach to mirth-throat. O dayey . . . (*There is a thunderous knock on the door.* WHITSTEED *is almost sobbing as he continues.*) O Divay, herd trumhorns in grass lik mi lov; this es yor younge halcyon mithglos in purple balboo weed-voice, on these dead. When are hompeec (*The pounding is resumed.*) ganging for glee through that fevermiste! (*His voice rises in stuttering terror.*) Grate anteloop danc there: welcom mi wegflesh down thi ocean-rool from wave who slaeps beside crossthief. An gullen fli mi dear aroon ont gosen ta glide foe en goloved delgad greepec. Woken sing blue hes mergrav ild skigon deth.

(*The door growls-to and soldiers clothed in metallic blue march into the room brandishing a new type of rifle used here for the first time by any nation—plans on request.*)

THE LEADER (*to* MR. KEK): We want you and the three who escaped us earlier tonight. The others may go.

MR. KEK (*as his friends make ready to defend the stairway*): No, all that is useless now . . . (*His face goes slack in bewilderment:* except for himself the room is empty.)

MR. KEK (*swaying on his feet*): Then I . . . (*A shout from the doorway and he unlocks the door of his wretched little room.*) Nolly!

NOLLY: What's all the excitement about?

MR. KEK (*slowly*): Excitement . . . ?

NOLLY: Sure, you were bawling your lungs out. I thought you were being torn limb from limb.

MR. KEK: Has anything happened tonight?

NOLLY: The usual.

MR. KEK: Where are Shernsh and Miga?

NOLLY: They're pulling a job on the West Side. (*putting her arms around him*) Do you really love me?

MR. KEK: Nolly, you haven't lied to me? There wasn't trouble out there?

NOLLY: Murder. Rape. Burning and butchering. The usual.

MR. KEK: Are you afraid to die, Nolly?

NOLLY: I don't know, I never tried it.

MR. KEK: Isn't it strange that people have to die?

NOLLY: Being strange doesn't alter anything.

MR. KEK: All the rest of it is nonsense—yowling at the moon.

NOLLY: You're not really afraid.

MR. KEK: The world seems sick, almost as though man had grown tired of being shut up in himself and was trying to get out— and Nolly . . .

NOLLY: Yes?

MR. KEK: There isn't a Goddamned place for him to go.

NOLLY: There never was.

MR. KEK: But only a few knew it.

NOLLY: And they were the good guys.

MR. KEK (*slowly*): Yes, they were the good guys. Kicked and splattered around by fools—spit on, hounded—and for what?

NOLLY: For the thing that happens when we put our arms around each other and know that there is no ugliness or madness in all the world.

MR. KEK (*listening*): Do you hear something moving up the stairs?

NOLLY: I have been listening to it ever since I came here.
    (*The sound as of something heavy being dragged up the stairs is plainly audible now.*)

MR. KEK (*moving to the door*): Shall I open?

NOLLY (*after a moment*): Wait. It's going away now. (*They stand close together, waiting.*)

MR. KEK: I . . .(*As he opens the door a heavy wooden cross falls into the room.*)

NOLLY: Look! There is blood on its arms.

MR. KEK: And flesh still warm caught in its nails.
    (*Somewhere in the distance an auto horn toots three times, echoing with the clarity of a cock crow.*)

NOLLY: We can't keep it here.

MR. KEK: Where can we take it?

NOLLY: Back to Him.

MR. KEK (*stubbornly*): But where?

NOLLY: Out into the sickness that is this world.

129

HE WAS ALONE (AS IN REALITY) UPON HIS HUMBLE BED, when imagination brought to his ears the sound of many voices again singing the slow and monotonous psalm which was interrupted by the outcries of some unseen things who attempted to enter his chamber, and, amid yells of fear and execrations of anger, bade him, "Arise and come forth and aid;" then the coffined form, which slept so quietly below, stood by his side and in beseeching accents bade him, "Arise and save what is beautiful"

Come back when fog drifts out over the city
And sleep puts her kind hands on all these poor devils

Come back when the policeman is in another street
And Beatrice will let you see her thin soul under the paint

Come back to the corner and tell them what brand
    of poison you want
Ask them why your very own dear lady is always on the lay

Somebody will pick up the pieces, somebody will put you to bed
You're a great guy, and she's the finest broad in all the world

Take it easy, partner, death is not such a bad chaser
And you didn't mix this one anyway

They were all right, the lot of them, it wasn't up to them
And they knew it; if somebody had come along and said,
I've got a spot for a two-legged animal in the world
    I'm working on,
They wouldn't have made anything like they had been made.

They were wise that this man-business was just a matter
Of putting it in and taking it out, and that went all the way
From throwing up cathedrals to getting hot pants over Kathy.
Maybe there was something to get steamed about, maybe it was
Baseball to grow a beard and end up on a cross so that a lot
Of hysteria cases could have something to slap around;
Maybe the old Greek boy knew what he was doing when
      he hemlocked
It out, loving the heels who hobbled him; maybe little
      French Joan
Got a kick out of the English hot-foot; the boys at the corner bar
Were willing to believe it. No skin off their noses. But what
      was hard
Was when you get a snoot full and all you can think to say
      starts with s
And you know damn well you're a good guy and you'll never
      meet a dame
Who really has your address, who can really dot your t's or cross
      your i's

Come back when it's old home week in this particular hell
And you can bum enough nickels to take the fallen angels out

I sat down and said beer thinking Scotch and there by God
Was my woman just as I had always known she would be
And I went over to her and she said come home with me
Like that, raining a bit, will you get wet? no, let's hurry,
Climbing the stairs behind her, watching; what's your name?
Lorraine, don't make so much noise, the landlady; buzz her, I said,
Wondering how God could have gotten it all into this little tail;
Key in the lock, light; hello, you're lovely did you know that?
She was all right, all of her, it was up to me and I knew it; let's
Talk first, do you mind? I said no and she said some female stuff
Husband on the lam and I've never done this before tonight; me, I
Put all my cards on the table and dealt myself five aces, great God

I was wanting it then but she said some more things and started
To cry and I slammed on my coat and said you lousy bitch
   which shut
Her up and I put my key in the lock

And when it's open, when you've got it, when it's all yours,
When nobody else in all the world is where you are,
When your arms have really gone around something,
When your thighs know all the answers to all the questions,
Why is there always one bead of sweat that doesn't come from
      either of your faces?

Come back when sleep drifts out over the city
And the good God puts His hands on all these poor devils.

*ALL THAT NIGHT LIGHTS WERE SEEN MOV-
ING IN EVERY DIRECTION, and voices heard call-
ing her name, re-echoed by the hills, and only an-
swered by the sad owls, or some fishers lying off
the land's edge, who thought themselves called to
from the shore; some thought that she had perished
at the hands of a roaming gang of robbers, others
that she had never been alive on this earth at all*

O beauteous daughter, the bright pitcher of death
Is on its last way to the well, said the Crippled Wren;
Sway and bellow, let earth put up its dukes,
Go down swinging, girlie, said the Ocean Wild;
The sea wants you, trust not his wet love . . . sleep
Here, sleep here, the Elm Tree said; it is late and cold,

Brother, she sobbed, and I have no mate under this sky.
    God be kind to her, wind move softly
    For she has no grave, she has no grave

Somewhere an idiot set fire to a city, fought in a war;
Houses rotted and people made love at quick-lunch counters.
Put out the light
The clock has stopped
The third cock sounds
Humor the thing called human
Tell them not to name us
The city is not here now
Black horses stamp dust
The tiny child cries
The tiny child cries in its dream
I say these words and they are you
The new moon saddles night's purple colt
And its poor mouth drips white blood to stars
Sleep here, sleep here, the Jesus-Wing said.
    God be kind to her, wind move softly
    For she has no grave, she has no grave

The heart is not here now
In the sky Christ's people trim the wicks of night
I think His hand is at the door
Why do I watch the child's sleep?
Thou art as pure as my love, I said
Why do I linger in this awful dark?
I hear the death bells keening through her heart
Black horses shake their clammy harnesses
I see their brilliant feet on the floor of morning

Why does this minstrel weep?
Why did the child dream at all?
I shall ask my love when death is done with her

Tomorrow

We to your story, game and smugness, do add
This death, our death. We to the clown commit
The glory given us; we to the further, after-breath
Of fame declare our dividend of fire, our mite
Of trampled ash. We to that cavernous place
You call "our time," commend an anger charged
To rip the face of worlds so simply snuggling in
Above our rotted heads; we to the wily saviors
Send warning, sound a war's depth
That shall be a stop to their stuttering guns,
That shall be a sound which no battle's strut can scare.

We were your only decent war; we were answer, aim.
We were that rooted story, Man's game. We to your bare lands
Lend prestige, dead. We to others' sons spell glory.

The Executions in Moscow

*"I am convinced—and this is the conviction that I have tried to express in
all my writings—that to arm ourselves against Fascism we do not need
material means above all. To oppose Fascism, we need neither heavy arma-
ments nor bureaucratic apparatuses. What we need above all is a different
way of looking at life and at human beings. My dear friends, without this
different way of looking at life and at human beings, we shall ourselves
become Fascists. And I refuse to be a Fascist—even a Red Fascist."*

IGNAZIO SILONE

I

Then if this clay thing calls
So blindly; its stern game spent
In the torn navy of killing
Where flaps that Magdalen, pity sent:
How like to Power is our nature slain,

The peace of evil which we now endure,
With death to dignify this honor's slum;
Since nothing living has a wound pure.

Why die for the dead? that soft trip
Through freedom which only they know.
I'm taking myself inside. There troops
Move like sun over wholesome snow;
And wind can cry in spirit effect
While ink-orators bay and despise—
But I shall endorse no bloody erect
Murder and go on looking with my own eyes.

II

Like a woman in a warm room
Will make a church of her hands

When she touches her lover:
I put my heart to the revolution.

But what do they know of the soldier
Whose gun is calibered on that star?

Men fight best when there is no blood.
And I put my heart to the revolution.

III

The poor thing crying at night
Putting blunt head to our door

How the sky over these houses pushes itself
Against God's great agile hand

Hush . . . be still

In the village are lights and the voice
of a woman who knows your name

Hush . . . and sleep

"Who'd blame us for their dying?"
"Cheap candles for the dead?"

And the heart puts a fence around heaven
As snow a privacy over the least sparrow fallen . . .

"Who'd bind the wound?"
"Cloth to cover terror!"

On this last hill strides that stranger and the voice
which is not to be stilled

The door opens and it stands there, horribly,
As the hungry of heaven have always stood

IV

To do now what war will do later
To be the warrior who destroys our weapons
To be the traitor who has nothing to turn to
To be the killer who kills his own kind

The beauty of a girl hangs in the sky
like an innocent wheel writhing in heaven

This bleary day moves over us
Like a bird ready to empty its belly.
We see a face whose demented features

Hang over our work like a fancy whore.
Better that our books be burned
Than leg be lifted to our lives.

And never still is that strange voice saying
I am the shadow of that which has never been

It is not a question of choosing an enemy;
But rather the nature of the war.

October 1937

The Body Beside the Ties

Can't seem to wake you, kid, guess it
put you to sleep getting cut in two
    I wonder what my mother will say
To hell with your old lady, kid, it's you dead
like you read about being dead
in the schoolbooks with medals all over
your chest and all the girls saying
Boy is he ever something on that big white horse
hell's fire a hero dying for his ahem country
    What is my country?
And all the fine buildings with flags fluttering
thataboy some class a first-rate bloke
with bubbles of blood in his hair
There are a lot of jails in America . . . a lot of poor boys
trying to get somewhere.

Hello, kid
still dead?

    I had a lot to do a lot to see

Portrait on an American Theme

I have your coat. Your gloves are on the chair.
"Where are we going?"

This room is cold. We can't stay here.
"It's snowing out and your shoes are through."

We must leave here.
"But why? You said last night . . ."

How can I tell her that she is dead?
She wanted never to leave me.

I am glad that she can't hear the hearse
Crunching through the powdery new snow.

Peter's Diary in Goodentown

PETER RECORDS THE SPARROW'S FALLING FEATHER

The boy steadies the air rifle on his arm.
I hear the gentle *poof-th*: my eyes on the bird.
Its gray-pegged feathers fidget; one slight leg
Is off the ground. (The sky is too small, I keep thinking.
Where will it fly?) The sparrow's hit! bends over
    slightly,
Then springs. All is panic a moment:
    this is not June; this is death—
Settling in a little fluff
    if I could see the battered castles
    this bird quits
    if I could hear the wee-thingish calling
    this throat leaks
Then I could lift it in my hand and take it
To my little daughter, telling her that this
Had been to Dying
And all the flags of the place lapping summer air.

THE DAY-MISTS ARE STREWN WITH US

Then it is plain ah plain that I love you,
Bya Deena
Like in the book, the one about the white hart whose doe
Was proud to think that his horns forked heaven
And we could never believe that a hunter took him from her
Or that their fawn isn't living wonderfully somewhere
With innocent eyes looking at us forever

I lift you in my arms and your breasts are warm
Against my face, like slim white swans on lake water

What did the book mean when it said that the two deer stood
Upon a distant hill under a strange congress of stars
And that someone said "It can't be terribly far to Heaven"?

SPRING IN GOODENTOWN

Suddenly, with surprising quiet, in my slippers,
Threw open the door. You won't believe it—
Nobody could. Only, just to the left of the barren lawn,
About twenty feet from the fire hydrant,
A group of little people crept along. I suppose this green clan
Had fine reasons for crossing the pavement, but
The curb was high and they were tired (for the woods
    are far away)
So I've—and you won't believe it—been busy all morning
Lifting the gay little creatures into the soon-green lawn.

FOREST NEAR GOODENTOWN

Where day sits calmly, perched on a monstrous box:
Look alive, fantastic lord; these silent hours labor
Through the cracks like flattened mice. They gnaw
Your scattered gown; its shine is ripping wide:
Trees and lovers, roofs and bridges lie
Along the tears, and I, Peter, guess creation's
There, numb and blind, under the hook of night,

Like this horrible hour
Upsetting the secret box of our generation—
At dusk even minutes have an eternity's power.

PETER READS EMERSON:

"Things are in the saddle and ride mankind."

And it was by the great calm stars that they came riding . . .
A company of flaming men.
 Oh I guessed by the names they gave me
 And the roll of their blood in the street
 That the people they came for were killers
"Then have you any famous hidden round these bricks?"
I told them: Look to their conquest; the desert is a watered city.
"Then have you any good men buried in this painted junk?"
I told them: Look to their trying; they've turned it in and out.
They did not question further; they did not ride away.
 Oh I knew from the beating they gave me
 And the clash of their dreams in the street
 That the killers of killing were ever the Christ
They did not ride away. They'd been there always.

BYA DEENA

Above us, Bya Deena, all unboughten glory is.
The tiny spires lean up their darling pencils,
But that dark paper is clear. Man's speech
Is not the sky's: It's frightfully quiet there,
And satisfied. We'd need more, my gentle dear,
Than all the pale will of our civilized wishing to learn
That a straight line is a circle in that other compass
Of God's, where to be is to be without being, and glad.

Already, under our kisses, we find that,
Quite like any other,

Our lungs love the barbarous air; and,
As we hear the little star call to its brother,
We know that more than geometry is there.

PETER GAINS A SON

The doctor fusses through the rooms with their lives
In his pocket: the pale crazy light chokes the cherry tree
At the window. Distant and calling, steel of church bell
Melts into sound.
She is screaming! I, Peter, father, murderer,
Sit in superficial doom and hear the changing fate
Of property. That cry holds her within the course
Of my fatherhood: me it shakes in mother's hell,
Extending sex.

They are slapping something in that other room.
My son cries. They hit the breath into him . . .
Lungs are new, unused: air hurts. It may be that those makers
Of new worlds can learn from these ways of natural birth.

PETER REPORTS ON HIMSELF

Much of all I know, I can't understand.

These are my hands, my eyes, and these
Are the things I believe, love, trust;

And yet I alone can lift these fingers,
Open these eyes or believe in this way.

There is nothing in you that I can be,
        or give a mouth to clay—
There is no one where you are unless I am there.

There is so little to say

but the birds take the sod in their claws
beautifully
and carry it into the sky where the sun is.

What uniform shall I wear when I tell them what I think
about war?

PETER'S LITTLE DAUGHTER DIES

That she must change so soon her curving city;
Leave this travel scarcely started; never see
Stars again reposeful in that dear room
Where death strays not and little birds
Are never split by shot—is it like this,
Dying? Just the moment going over
The edge of body, nothing left there
That grass cannot solve?

I'd wish to settle nothing here with chisel;
No cold angel with well-fed eyes shall rest above her . . .
She once said "The Snow Queen must be very beautiful."

She was so tiny . . . She won't know what the dead are
supposed to do.

THE SHELLING OF GOODENTOWN

Fog reigns; its plural features soft in the ointment of space.
O God this absolute and floating peace above the town.
The candyshops are filled; buying children place
Their pennies down and lessen trade with laughter.
The knobbed nose of the meeting house clock sniffles in the fog.
Time strays without a hat, his bald head smeared by little birds
Who fly above the steeple. Half the sleep I ever had is loose
Over the hills of this quiet land. Fog is a woolly blur . . . fog . . .

O God

The dark lips part
If the world has a brain, where is it? The bombs shriek down.
Earth and sky retch in their thudding glow . . .
My people have hurt no one my people have done no harm at all
Who will pray for us who were not skilled in hate or fear
But who believed that killing is murder even though
    they call it War.

Summer 1936

THE FIGURE MOTIONED WITH ITS MANGLED HAND TOWARD THE WALL BEHIND IT, *and uttered a melancholy cry*

It was rumored on the block
Ethel is going to let go tonight.
I made big about it, strutting
Down 5th eyeing the babies over,
Thinking they look like mudhens
Next to my little piece of tail.
She was hard to get. Her old lady
Was saving her for dough, but hell
I had class, want the moon, kid?
And I'd give it to her. Funny thing
Though, this is all a lie, I never
So much as touched her hand, she
Thinks I'm dirt, nobody else ever
Always got the wrong end of the stick.
I'd carry the mail for you, Ethel,
Stop running around with that pup,
He's got a car, sure, and jack to throw
Like water but what does he want?
What do they all want? something easy,
Something that somebody else worked for.
Ethel, lay off rich kids, you'll end dirty.

Join the world and see the army
The slime is quiet tonight, along the Jersey coast
The chippies discuss Democracy in awed tones
Breathes there a heel with man so dead . . .
Shoot the liquid fire to Johnnie, boy
With every rendezvous-with-death we are giving away . . .
An autographed photo of J. P. Morgan taken in the frontline
     trenches

They took him down stone steps
To a cellar thick with rats.
The guard gave him a cigarette
And slapped it out of his mouth.
Moral. Don't ever knock off a cop.
Ethel, looking like a movie queen,
Descended on his cell in a mink coat.
When they fitted the black cap over his head
He knew that he'd never have another chance to be president.

Can the Harp Shoot Through Its Propellers?

And I had it neatly written
                    this is the secret
   of your earth: this is its one greener tree;
   its only deep sky
                    nicely settled—holding it
The way a lover is held; stubborn of its lack
Of shame—but, a blind man, passing
In great haste, bumped my arm and gave
My words upon the dusty wind

And I stand here silent now while all the breath
Of the damn beasts snuffs about my empty hands,
Not knowing that the fashion of my art
Could not design a submarine or bomb a city.

ON THE SOUTH-WEST COAST OF EREHWEMOS STANDS A ROMANTIC LITTLE VILLAGE, *inhabited chiefly by the poorer kind of people, consisting of small farmers and oysterdredgers, whose estates are the small craft in which they glide over its interminable deep fields in search of the creatures which they wring from its bosom. It is built on the very top of a hill, commanding on the one side a view of an immense bay, and on the other of the peaceful green meadows and valleys, cultivated by the greater number of its quiet folk. The approach to it from the nearest town was by a road which branched away into lanes and wooded walks, and from the sea by a beautiful little blue lady of water, running far up into the land, both sides of which, and indeed all the rest of that coast, were guarded by craggy and gigantic rocks, some of them hollowed into caverns, into which none of the inhabitants, from motives of superstition, reverence, and fear, had ever dared to penetrate. The farmer who followed his own plow in the spring, singing the wild sweet chant of the season, and bound up with his own hands the sheaves in the autumn, was not richer, greater, nor finer than he who, barelegged on the strand, gathered in the hoar weed for the farmer in the spring, or dared the bitter winds of fall and the wrath of the winter in his tiny boat, to earn with his dredging net a yet harder subsistence for his family. Distinctions were unknown in that village; every man was the equal of his peaceful neighbor*

The mouse was startled by its own unimpearled shadow.

Why can't Hogan come to your house like other people?
You can't lay eggs like a hen, can you, with shells?
You can't have puppies, can you, with little spots, Madam?
Then why won't you let Hogan come to your house?
Oak trees don't invite you to visit them, even the tiny ones.
God hasn't put any different gut in you, has He, Lady?
I'm afraid I don't get it, what has Hogan done to you?
I'm afraid I must tell the police, I know one with a blind mother.

The truth is that we were going to make a night of it, just
    the four of us,
in the Cave-Bear Tavern, Flossie, Al, Jordan Tim, and
    faithfully yours,
walking in there like you see us now, a wagon-maker, a hawk-boy
    out of work,
and not exactly a whore but not stingy either, and myself of
    course, as usual,
finding our table in the corner and ordering a wee un, a tall un,
    and a whopper.

Where Hogan was I can't say, never having seen the guy except
from hearsay. He'd come in at about 190 when he was just right,
but Newark Ned was too many for him, Lord how that guy
    could hit,
I'm just coming out of my corner there's his glove and it's
    two hours later.
Jordan Tim hasn't got a look-in to live the year out, TB'd
to hell and gone but he's company in his cups; Al here, well
I wouldn't trust him in bed with the Pope's grandmother, already
making his play for Flossie but Christ she won't honey his horn,
she's Hogan's girl. I'm no quitter though. Where there's a wench
there's always a way. I am a pretty decent lad I tell her, my room
fronts the ocean, marble bathtubs and all. I'm not dirty says she.
I've got two maids and a cook. Then what do you want with me?

Just at that time Jordon Tim starts to cough and spoils
    the tablecloth.
Let's get out of here Al says getting to his feet and looking around.
He sees the barkeep's daughter and goes over his pants
    starting to smoke.
We get to her in a dead heat but Jordan Tim's already there,
    saying
Babe you've got the cutest damn fanny in the business,
    Sugar it's you
and me for us, huh? All right Al I say let's toss for this lass Flossie.
He says tail and it comes down heads and I marches off with
    my love.

When she turned her head I went into her
and this is what it's like in a woman I thought,
looking around; and the funniest thing it was,
her wanting me and me inside there, watching
myself just standing like a fool afraid to make
the first move
and I felt her think Why doesn't he take me?
but she said I'm glad it's you and not that Al
and It said Yes Flossie I'm plenty glad it's not that louse
and It put Its arms around us and I left her
and went back into me.

All my ghostborn dreams are stilled now
    is this white flesh all, Father?
are my prayers to end between these pawed-over legs?
    is this all that your noble clay can do?

It came to pass that Hogan became the favorite of the mouse
and now and then it would let him look through its eye,
but that woman would never stand to have him in her house.

How do *you* feel, you smug lug . . .

Meditation of My Lady of Sorrows

Upon my throat your kisses blur their man
to be mine
as a child I lead to my breast.

There is madness in this city.
Are they arranged, the days of treachery
and murder? Are they made blind,
the nights when we are not together?

There is sorrow in our world.
Now my will, against your frantic wooing,
urges no dead soldier on me
for nights when we are not together

My hand smooths your hair that will grow out to my fingers
when you have been taught to love in the way your country wants.

Stayed No Longer in the Place Than
to Hire a Guide for the Next Stage

The little silver rain-children were laughing in the street
When the good man tied his horse and went into the tavern

I have come to tell you not to sorrow
The copper kettle spat into the fire
"Did you say something, buddy?" it asked

I shall be late to my father's house
The barwench put the soup down with a sloppy bang
"That'll be twenty cents," she said

In this large body, towns and the shabby wail of sheep
The poem is not enough without us, darling
Above your head and my head, the quiet heavens
Within what we are together, thy face and this star
Between us as we stand here, no blackness, no death
Upon this green altar that is earth, your body and my body
And all the world would dwell therein and I sing of thy beauty
Until the cock-boat and the whale, the bison calf
    and David's sling
Were put within a pattern, yea, the whole dear tit of everything,
Not to break, not to wear thin, not to end like tracks in the snow,
Not to hurt anyone, never to lie to anyone nor to kill anyone

It is not enough to say that the heart mutilates sleep
I have been sent to explain your sorrow
There is Judy's cough, the cry of the sick and the hurt
And I am to talk quietly
Keep my voice down
Breathe warm stuff at you
Cut my lines out of bread dough

But I shall sing of thy beauty, of the caged goat
    and the infant Christ
Of the bull's hot glee and of the naked girl in the briary bush
I shall celebrate the blood on the floor of the runaway boxcar
And in this town, and with this gun, and for this scab's child
I shall explore the tempest in the frog's groin
I shall put my fingers on the forehead of this star

It is enough that we have listened against the third cock
In my father's heart are many mansions
Night's sword riding harmless as a bird over us
It is that thou art the answer to what I would say
The wreath, the grace and the good robe
As of now and forever

In Judgment of the Leaf

And we were speaking easily and all the light stayed low
Within your eyes; I think no equal glass has since been ground:
My love was looking through the throng that gave you mind.

We were quiet as the stars began to ride the billows;
And watching them we took an only mortal stair.
We wandered up the stable rays, were startled, lost
In a child's land whose stars are glory of jangling buoys,
Gunned by the froth of eternity and space.

    Something snapped a twig at a distance from us:
    it seemed real: a bird called its little bonfire of sound:
    thickets flamed with the trial of a leaf in the night

Gentle hands were warm, scared within my hands; the moment's
Church wavered through Time's dripping tapers . . . was torn away.

    Suddenly
We knew that we could not belong again to simple love.
I saw your opening eyes reject the trade of tiny things
And I reasoned that the whole world might lie naked
In the earth of your eyes, in easy wonder building God.

Biography of Southern Rain

Rain's all right. The boys who physic
through town on freights won't kick
if it comes; they often laugh then, talking
about the girl who lived down the block,
and how her hair was corn-yellow gold
that God could use for money. But rain,
like memory, can come in filthy clothes too.

The whole upstairs of space caved in that night;
as though a drunken giant had stumbled over the sky—
and all the tears in the world came through.
It was that. Like everyone hurt crying at once.
Trees bent to it, their arms a gallows for all
who had ever died in pain, or were hungry, since
the first thief turned to Christ, cursing . . .

Then, out of the rain, a girl's voice—her hand
on my arm. "Buddy, help me get this train."
Her voice was soft . . . a cigarette after coffee.
I could hear the clickdamnitclick of the wheels;
saw the headlight writing something on the rain.
Then I saw her face—its bleeding sores—I didn't
ask her if she had ever been in love
or had ever heard of Magdalen and Mary
or why she wanted to leave that town.

Do you see what I mean about the rain?

The Black Panther and the Little Boy

Such was the power of sleep over him, his unfolded heart sway-
ing gently as a frond; padding by on remote feet, the antelope of
dream that could not be eaten—such was the peace of the animal
heritage that the cage could not shut out. The child's full-open
eyes looked long on the great beast's peaceful face. He turned
then to an attendant and put this sly question:

"You won't let him out, will you?"

The man, whose daughter had just brought him lunch in the
usual worker's pail, did not think it important enough to answer;
instead he selected an item of food and ate.

"Please let him out. He must get very lonesome shut up in this way."

The attendant thought it best to answer at last:

"I can't do that. He'd make a meal of us."

The panther moved slightly as something went through his sleep; perhaps a bird, a snake, a deer.

"Then he should if he wants to!" the boy said rebelliously. "He is very beautiful."

That child will live to be eaten by something. May he be blind to the atrocious beast that does make a meal of him and his kind.

I Suddenly Became Conscious That This Thing Was Looking at Me Intently

With the help of three dwarfs from a nearby world
I contrived to detach my head and placed it on a rock near the sea

Ships butted the shore down
Horses trampled my hapless face
But the eyes continued to stare at me

"Do you understand now?" asked the little men
"What are they trying to see?" I asked

The morning star made her cold puddle on the hill
Shepherds cried their terror but the eyes did not stir

"Shall we return them to you?" asked the little men
"Not until I know what they see," I said

Like a merciless black paw a great wave thundered inland
And with a little gulp of pleasure scooped up my two eyes

"You have waited too long," muttered the little men
"But they are still watching me!" I said

"These Have Gone with Silent Hands, Seeking"

These have gone with silent hands, seeking, in shadow,
folding palms down over the cities, offering secret praise.
Was it this they wanted? Was it for this they followed the voice,
the dark sea, the strange continent, the names, lights crying
on the water, faces grinning from the sky, the startled child,
and over all the shadow, the murders, crime, disease,
the awful voice calling, crying "Come to me! Come to me!"
Yes, they have tried, have grown tired in combat, tired
      unto death;
and we had meant to speak of them, of the voice, the fire, night,
candles, the pitiful whore, the scab, the crippled wren, the nun,
the dancer, the Jesus-wing over the watchers in the village . . .
but there was pain, hunger, fighting, hatred, no peace,
and wings folded, dread, and no singing, God,
there was no singing, there was darkness and ignorance,
dissolution, poverty, the wound unhealed, and the sound
of a great breaking, a complete death . . . no one said
anything very important, people went on dying
and the dead stayed where they were.

> *What bodies do together in the dark is beautiful*
>   *and lips*
> *may move in wonder as a man does love with a woman*
> *that which is of her essence, uniting with his*
>   *and it will be all fire and roads leading somewhere*
> *not darkness, not rain on the tortured faces, nor shadows*
> *falling, falling*

shadows that mean nothing, and no one to care
They won't be afraid
There will be birds flying through their upturned faces

This is the forest inn, the sleepbound city
Bells cough soundlessly, swinging in the warm dark

We walk silently on sleep's moss
We have come a long way

The dog at the gate is too drowsy to bark
Lights go out in the village
There is wonder in us

Stars that shift and ebb like fog on the tranquil seaface;
Lights returning, blurred, swinging away; snatches of old songs;
The rough hand of my father; cities of my people sinking
through vast space.
Troubled stars are staked out in the pastures of sleep . . .
Turn to me, my darling . . . face blurring . . . the human fog . . .
diving lights . . .
The solstitial hand over storm and bitterness, over death's
awful oblivion,
High, high, holding the dark folly of clay to the mute
drench of eternity.
Look! children are laughing at their games . . . there is
no sadness, no death,
There is no question, no answer, no decay, no pain . . . there is
the quiet of earth
When the lights go out and we walk together or lie alone
as our fathers do,
There are eyes looking at us and we should be beautiful
in battle, devout in sleep.

1933

I DON'T WANT TO STARTLE YOU but they are going to kill most of us

I knew the General only by name of course.
I said Wartface what have you done with her?
I said you dirty louse tell me where she is now?
His duck-eyes shifted to the Guard. All right, Sam.
I saw a photograph of the old prick's wife on the desk;
Face smiling like a bag of money on a beggar's grave.
Who is that fat turd I said—he hit me with his jewelled fist.
While his man held me he put a lighted cigarette on my eyelid.
I smelt the burning flesh through his excellent perfume.
On the wall it said *Democracy must be saved at all costs.*
The floor was littered with letters of endorsement from liberals
And intellectuals: "your high ideals," "liberty," "human justice."
Stalin's picture spotted between Hoover's and a group-shot
    of the DAR.
I brought my knee up suddenly and caught him in the nuts.
A little foam trickled from his flabby puss. All right, Sam.
They led me into a yard and through a city of iron cells.
I saw all the boys: Lenin, Trotsky, Nin, Pierce,
    Rosa Luxemburg . . .
Their eyes were confident, beautiful, unafraid . . .
We came finally to an immense hall protected by barbed wire
And machine guns: Hitler, Benny Mussolini, Roosevelt, and all
The big and little wigs were at table, F.D.'s arm around Adolf,
Chiang Kai-shek's around the Pope, all laughing fit to kill.
As soon as a treaty was signed, out the window it went;
But how they fumbled at each other under the table!
I snatched up a menu:
        Grilled Japanese Soldier on Toast
        Fried Revolutionaries à la Dirty Joe
        Roast Worker Free Style
        Hamstrung Colonial Stew, British Special
        Gassed Child's Breast, International Favorite

Wine list—Blood 1914, '15, '17, '23, '34, '36, '40, etc.
So much fresh meat I thought! A butchers' holiday . . .
The General paused to enjoy the floorshow: ˙
On a raised platform little groups of people stood.
Flags told their nationality; orators told them what to do.
As the bands blared they rushed at each other with bayonets.
The dead and dying were dragged off and others brought on.
Sweat streamed from the orators; the musicians wobbled crazily.
The Big Shots were mad with joy, juggling in their seats like
    monkeys.
And they never get wise the General said as we moved on.
Out in the air again . . .
A line of petty officials and war-pimps waited before the door.
As we approached they drew aside respectfully to let the
    General in.
I heard a woman moaning and I knew what they wanted there.
Now do you know what we've done with her the General said.
To go mad or to die . . .
They forced me to watch as the General went up to her and
Her eyes were looking at me.

*HARROWED BY THESE APPREHENSIONS HE
RESOLVED TO COMMIT HIMSELF TO THE
MERCY OF THE STORM, as of the two evils the
least, and penetrate straight forward through some
devious opening, until he should be delivered from
the forest. For this purpose he turned into the road
watched over by madness and terror, knowing that
his pursuers would never follow him there. After he
had continued in this way through a succession of
groves, and bogs, and thorns, and brakes, by which*

not only his clothes but also his living skin suffered in grievous manner, while every nerve quivered with eagerness and dismay, he at last reached an open plain, and following his course, in full hope of arriving at some village where his life would be safe, he saw a devil-light in the distance, which he looked upon as the star of his good fortune, and, running toward it at full speed, arrived at the door of a lone cottage, into which he was admitted by a beautiful young woman, who, understanding he was a lost man in a lost world, gently led him to the great bed where they went at each other without any delay whatever

I

She is lying on my outstretched arm.
And where are we to go? what are we to do, God,
When the dream falls to the ground?
For the dream is falling to the ground.
For the dream is falling with a dull dead sound.
She says the dream is falling to the ground.
She is lying near me through the night.
But holy holy hell the drums begin.
The drums are spreading their hideous sound.
I say the drums are going like mad!
The drums are going, the drums, the drums,
The drums begin the music of the blood.
Run, run, run, I say run, poor devils, run!
I say we are running before the hounds.
The hounds are at our heels.

You say she is lying here beside me. No!
I will not believe it,
I will not believe that she is in my arms now.
She is not in my arms, she is not anywhere near.
To hell with the dream and the girl and all.
You heard me say to hell with all of it.
You had better die and be done, better die and be done.
The Hangman says you had best leave your boots on.
Take your boots off and lie down and be quite done.
Do you hear the ass braying in the swamp?
O the ass is braying in the swamp.
Oh! Oh! in the swamp, the ass, braying.
Put my war-boots on.
Put my helmet of steel on my head.
Good night my sweet baby, my pretty piece . . .
They are not far off now!
Where to?
They are not far off now!
Where to?
I say good night my nice little lay . . .

II

Because above your loved body I have lain,
O my pretty, my pretty dear,
You know what I want to say (my darling, O my darling,
Of course I'm a sonofabitch, a lousy skirt-mad bastard,
O my sweet, my sweet, we'll both be dead after while,
Because we'll both be dead after while) when I say
Take off your dress
Across the hall somebody coughs
A toilet is flushed, a baby cries
Cats put their sordid love over us
 A truck is always running over some poor guy
 And the bastards are always starting some war or other

You know exactly what I mean and you take your dress off
    letting me
Run my hands over your breasts and your soft thighs O my pretty
    my pretty
Lying under my eager body the two of us breathing hard
    and I enter easily
Like a star pressing into a child's hand
. . . and the warm-vowelled singing of your hair

Now I lie content beside you,
My arm cradling your head,
O my dearest, my sweet, my pretty,
Go to sleep, go to sleep . . . to sleep . . . go to sleep . . .
I'll always be beside you when you wake.

III

I am turning the lights out now.
A red wind crawls in over the water.
Before I come again, in my own honor,
Men will have gone down like pricked guts;
Murder will walk the world.
All the nice young kids will be puked clean.
Who will listen? who will care?

Don't fight their war!
Tell them to go to hell!

This isn't a poem. This is a sob and a death rattle.
Who will listen? who will care?
A black wind blows in over the graves.

I will not believe it—
But it is true.
It is true.

EARLY IN THE MORNING, then, of the eventful day, a man with an arch importance in his sun-bronzed face, was seen marching from house to house, in deep dingle or on windy hillbrow, and followed by half the idle and the young of the great parish; in either hand he bore a wand of peeled willow, tied with ribands and wild flowers, and his whole person was fantastically decorated with a veritable madness of humility

I am the world-crier, and this is my dangerous career

Since she has put the dirt between us
Since she has hurried on before me
Since she has left the little hut of men

Seven black cities are buried where the Virgin sleeps
The waves of the water hurl her clean-throated lover home

"Darling" and I address the rot of her pure body, her purity
That neither beast nor man can despoil, that no one knows

Since her heart is silent
Since her eyes are closed
Since her arms are empty of me

"Darling" and I speak against the slain as well as the slayers,
Against you and against myself, against the creak of our bellies,
Against the smug Tower, against all our treachery and
     human sloth

Since the room is cold and the light is growing feeble
Since she has gone to join the things of God
Since she is dead, since she is dead now

Since men are dying for things that have no meaning
Since nobody seems to care anymore

I know what you do when the crowds have gone
I followed you when you went to sell us out
I understand what they want and how they will get it

"Darling" and I have lain on her white breast as she lies now,
As alone as she is, as lost walking earth as she is beneath it

I have seen you undress before them
I could smell your terror when they took you
I could feel their bodies as they stripped your flesh-star

"Darling" and I have knelt by her side as Joseph Mary's, praying
Against the black world and the rain falling on our two faces,
And the rain falling on the two faces that look up
     through the grass

Since the guns are aimed at us
Since the trenches have been dug
Since it remains only to die
Since she lies quiet in her grave
Since she has gone to live with her God

I am the one to call your bluff, and this is my climate

Rage and harry, O wind; roll thunder, be a maddened storm;
Buckle, gouge and shatter; roar, howl, foam, splinter;
Level the cities, send their hideous buildings down;
Plow them to their knees; fling up the blinding sand;
Let your lightning go; lean against their flimsy bridges;
Scream, curse, sing! O wind of a peoples' wrath!
Soar in a million tongues. Flay all hate from the earth.
Rise up, rise up in strict beauty, be lullaby for all these slain.

The Hunted City

How at the midnight of his age the Poet hurls himself on the green lance of his country.

What do I know that is unknown to the bright weasel in the cornfield? How along the shore fish roll in grooves of bluegreen laughter! The great shaggy bulls in rut write their poems in living flesh.

I shall not respect your insular customs.

This is not a family report. How our heroes swept in over the smoking rumps of young whores . . . and the great blue skirt of eternity billowing out over the little shops where lard and tobacco could be bought. Poor Stevie Crane! river fog coughing in over the kerosene lamps and the battlefields adrip with printer's ink. O sheriff, hold those quaint guns steady: new names for bad men; site of forgotten campfires: authority to make the Poem.

There are no roses on the approaches whence my people come.

Twenty-six years have gone through my body . . . whirlpools of beggars and maddened angels. How I have wanted the Good in my hand.

There shall be no ship out of this harbor until the workmen have been paid for their work; and I like the smell of morning to be around the ancient faces where history went.

How the jail in Macon stank of Negro miseries
the open gut of the South growling with flies.

I shall remember the savage dogs that sat like furred-guns before the farmer's barn. Rotten belly of rain on my cold face.

God! God! do not let me go alone with no adequate word in my mouth.

My man is eaten by the gonorrhea of war.
My Poem will be building in the blood of young men
and I shall remember what they will have been forced to forget.
There is a desperate task here.
. . . I have no right to expect you to listen now.

II

Gatherers of wild seed and froststained fruit; mixers of fantasy and the steel dung of bombing planes; bringers of fair women to terrible grief in the night; cheats, devils, saviors, assassins; inventors of the water wheel and legal systems, of machines and religion, of the sailing ship and the cavalcades of locomotive and cart; makers of new ways of doing and being's renegade; self-shacklers, creatures of shadow and madness; signers of magical speeches and spenders of human blood; keepers of sheep and cattle, of horses, dogs and swine; planters of barley, wheat and the eleven kinds of corn; builders in stone, bronze, steel.

I have watched the four skies and have seen no sign
    to kill there
Do you understand that I am building a city
    for your children!
I have been standing here in the dusk and it is
    getting darker
Fire floods the three-breasted church but it is
    getting darker
O horrible eyes float in this dusk that settles like

a body into its grave
      and it is night over all the faces of mankind
and it does not cease to get darker on those doomed faces.

      O cringer in the animal dark
      tracing your image on the steaming wall of a cave—
What did you want from your pottery, your weaving, your
      implements of building and of war?
Where are the museums of the Soul!
Awesome whirlwind's raven whose stalk legs shatter
nocturnal flesh of cities. Great sleeping girls joining
      stone hands round this human parade . . .

For the sake of my own beliefs pausing to be with you
To ask you what you will do when the hurricane hits, knowing
that it is getting darker and all the Jesuslights are going out.
      (Clock's tick. Plow's warm flower. Letters on
            the idiot's desk.)
Awful whirlpool's rook and the drowned feathers
on the war helmet of a young Roman lost in a Christian war.
      (Fire flings its hot salt into the wounds
            of the sacked town.
      . . . A little girl placing a red flower on the grave
            of an old man
      and two merchants haggling over the price
            of godmanure.
      Lark's chapel. Gun's deadly gut. Prayer on
            the virgin's lips.)
In my own voice pausing to be understood.

Make me a Law that will do for all time and for all men.

Remember the hot fretting of this human kind; the gods set up
and washed away in the blood of children; the towering huts
of steel and the stinking rot of flesh that lived nowhere;
the cripples; the hideous shadows

495,000 years pouring into the museums of science
  histories of men who stood outside history
Remember the pitiful handful of broken pots and scattered bones
Horror howling across eternity!

Luckily we can record what our machine guns will do.

III

I compel you to question me about my motives. Who raises the
breasts of water? the mutilated shroud where dawn's serpent
sleeps? Have you seen how the black ant stands on his destiny in
a stupor of trained festivities; more sober than the Orient;
  between chemical talks, an avalanche of eager bodies
coupling on shelves marked with the teeth of learned surveys . . .
  the sheathing as of vegetable steel that men begin in
  and would end in, crying *Mother Mother* while
  its gets darker and ever away from the womb that is
  mortal and ever nearer the cold one which is death.
Firm-limbed sleep, O gentle sleep, sleep of men and of beasts
  Plunge the magnificent writ of thy organ along
  the singular staircase of Eternity.

  I stumble like a duck on a pontoon of greased dollars.
  If you are going to sell your soul to the devil, make sure
  that he doesn't give you religion as part of your change.

What a glorypot of pleasure men and women have had
  of each other.
God has written all His poems on the hilarious skin of lovers.

  The shining tongues of the sea
  fondle the night's roaring ass
And the cloud-god lowers his white hand straight down
through the drowsy stars . . .
(The weight of a great pain falls on my heart!)

That blue hole, Heaven, carry its tide over the wounded within
my heart. My special men and clean-breasted women, how they
went down at daybreak and found a dead child in the road—
    making him their only cathedral, and lighted
    green candles in the field with his willing body.

The trapper was held in his own trap until a leopard had aroused
the village with her wild screams.
That death was made for me, she said:
I will allow no other to die it.
    The horrible reaches in the sparrow's eye!

To explain the murders. Yet there will be peace in certain parts
of the city; sonnets dripping like moss from the walls; women
holding their gifts out, arms, thighs, their quick song; singing of
the male too, not refined entirely, but pure enough to push the
chores along; dancing set on human sex; and the liquor going
the rounds, a domestic product, quite shabby it is true.

Call the prettiest girls . . . summon their less pretty sisters too
    I shall rely on no single map or hearsay.

Of the City itself we know little; the few songs of good melody
say nothing. There should be a church there for the creatures of
the field and sea; bells of fine quality; choirboys without rifles.
There should be a few old men weaving heraldic designs in rugs
new from the looms; they would have no interest whatever in
local jealousies. Windmills might well be down if the City boast
of any age.

    All this is said that you may be watchful for the first
    sign of trouble at the gates
Ah! at the boulevards ankle deep in surprised blood.
The dream surpasses our vigil.
Americans have learned neither to live nor to die, but they have
made an art of being loudly between the two.

. . . It is raining in Alabama and the drummers in their
little honkytonk souls have forgotten all about the
helenface that could launch ten hundred ships
Steam makes hairy puddings of the tired horses and the sullen sky
eats them greedily
. . . It is winter in Vermont. Snow has a long talk with
the suicides and wretched cows do their odd singing in
cold choirs; chickens stare wickedly at the back of God's
hoar head, wanting to be the world and the world a miserable
chicken in a filthy coop. Beauty counts her cancerous toes.

I shall forget every evil face as the male fox the hound
which hunts him unto death.

v

The little hill climbs up to the village and puts its green hands
tenderly round it; women have their days in the cider-sharp sun
and men their work riding over the infested land of the fog-
widowed sea and lowering nets that convulse like stomachs.

The earth has its milk to give.
Beautiful horsemen bathe the immortal slopes with the rich
yellow blood of wheat and men say as I continue to say
This is a battle worthy of our weapons.
But a different sort of soldier is seen prowling about
like a pod holding death's fat grub . . .
Purer than a man's first girl the sky floats in virginal peace
above the pallid snouts that jut from the stone of the war statues.
I have seen the crippled lark rise like a dream
to the fugitive kiss of the wind's delirious mouth . . .
and there is no report whatever that fish have ceased
to have their admirable babies down deep in the sea.
I have heard the noiseless talking of our graves
and the worms have evolved a very effective way of writing
history.
Man is all around the things that men do

but there is little enough to be happy about . . .
I do not accuse you, little fellows, I only declare
that instead of drums to beat you consider your miserable
breasts, and I caution you to know now that this world is
fashioned of pain and of murder. You will not recognize the
hangman until your own poor human head is in his noose.
The poet should wear comfortable shoes and see a lot of children.

Listen! is that the third throat of the cock?
Has the mariner built his last desolate fire on this coast?
The moon rubs his great clean face against the roofs of the city
and harlots display their green sores which are the slum flowers . . .
O pity the backward ape who has no flute, who has no Christ,
who has no civilization and no poison gas to protect it with;
pity those in asylums whose fists cannot reach faces to smash;
pity the dead for their weight is not measured in military pounds.

Evidently those are deathbells keening through the night
and there are no horses saddled in the inn yard
there is no light at any window, no warmth, no hope . . .
This is indeed a battle worthy of our weapons.

VI

I saw three hundred fat cattle putting their forlornly comic faces
down to feed in the white grass where the skeletons of mutilated
soldiers were; great white gulls dipped into the sea which hacked
wetly at the stone toes of that coast;
        sad white girls lay under monsters and the ground
        shook as though charged with unborn armies.
    Then the white eyes of God looked upon me and His voice
    said
You must help me. My only son, begotten of Mary, dead once
on the cross, hallowed in name by the generations of men,
the hair of whose head is like the whips that scourge evil,
my son, my only son, born of woman, conceived in pain.
    His voice ceased. His white eyes lifted in terror
    and my throat His great hands found

My son, my son Jesus, He cried, *why hast thou forsaken me!*
    and His tears spattered my hot cheek.
One death was given thee, one betrayal, one agony,
but thou hast willed to die as men do, finding death
at every inn, in every lost city, among all peoples,
endlessly, and without the very gates of thy enemy.
    And God lowered His hands from my throat,
        asking forgiveness.

    But another voice spoke, a voice which I had heard
    in all my wanderings, and it said
"While you were speaking these cattle have moved out of sight
and a storm has arisen on the sea, the earth wakes from its
white sleep and the true church approaches over the water . . ."
    God's death! it was good to see the red blood
    on the ground again: thirty men could watch all at once
    and not see more than I saw.
    How the wind tore at the skirts of priests!
    God's death! I have never seen more efficient-looking guns,
    or in better repair.

I have seen the cold white eyes of night watching us, brothers.
Come, soldier, break your sleep; how beautiful are the wings
    of your chrysalis as it throws down its guns, killing war.
I have heard the calm wise voice of Christ calling us, brothers.
Thus I have learned to laugh and to grow roses in the black
    stone of the meeting halls.
A desire for truth is treason only for liars and dunces.

VII

I despise these poets with their puerile little chalk-talks of the soul,
these fat ducks waddling through the stink of the publishing
houses . . .
To shut the door and draw the shades! I am come upon an exile
that means this world is held off for a short moment. Arrange
living skin over the war drums.

The body of an age lies here (And I refuse to jump
upon it with my two feet, though it should be made
to wake—sprawling there like a stabbed whore, and
the eyes wide as spiked wine) Beneath what haunted
sky do we press against the bodies of our women!
. . . incorruptible boroughs through which have snaked
the vines of our unsleeping sex.

How all the halls were scented with the woman-smell and lined
by ancestral portraits of great louts who'd seen the night out
on the exposed banks of the Mississippi, who'd muled the farthest
reaches of the Rockies, their boots grinding out an empire for
the flabby bellies in swivel chairs—and their wives: little
bone buckets into which the desert had poured a puritan flesh—
and we, their grandchildren, looking all ways at once
      and seeing nothing

I have consulted the tribal books, the unpublished journals and
the diaries of certain mental cases; it is remarkable that I can
proclaim a growing literature of intensity and consummate pure-
ness. It is clear to me that when the reader has digested "The
dog ate the cheese and the small boy in the yellow coat coughed"
he has embarked on no mean adventure. Our more advanced
critics have interpreted American Letters from several highly ex-
citing angles; I read only yesterday a magnificient statement con-
cerning the mean diameter of the fourth vowel sound in the
eleventh line of Greer's "Annihilated Café"—this, of course, even
with one reading alone, can cause the most profound skeptic con-
siderable pride in the creative spirit applied sensitively, and sacri-
ficially, like a lamb with nosebleed. The young writer may well
thank his steadfast star today. I have thought betweentimes of
starting a school modeled somewhat along the lines of a well-
managed nursery: certainly there is no lack of incentive.

      Humanity is a good thing. Perhaps we can arrange the
            murder
      of a sizable number of people to save it.

from *The Teeth of the Lion* (1942)

For Miriam

Do I not deal with angels
When her lips I touch

So gentle, so warm and sweet—falsity
Has no sight of her
O the world is a place of veils and roses
When she is there

I am come to her wonder
Like a boy finding a star in a haymow
And there is nothing cruel or mad or evil
Anywhere

Kibali-Ituri

I told her that my mother would make
A bed and supper for us; but it was
Already dark and I had lost the way.
"Mother will give us food and coffee,
And we shall sleep in my old room.
The moon will stand at the window,
And we shall be as children again,"
I said; but I had lost the way and it was
Already dark in the forest. "Mother will cry
"A bit, because she is old and . . ."
"Does your mother speak English?" she said.
"As well as a book," I told her, rubbing my sleeve
Over my nose which had started to bleed.

"And your father wears shoes?"
"Of course he does. My brother can drive
A car and my sister is noted for her beauty."
We had by now reached the bank
Of a swollen river and I told her to undress
And we started across; but the water
Was full of tiny horses that snapped
At our ankles with long, pointed teeth.
So we swam back and we stretched out
Under a giant tree. "Does your mother dye
Her hair?" she asked, slipping into her panties.
"How should I know?" I said, beginning to shiver.
I took her coat and slipped it over my shoulders.
"Where did you say your mother was born?"
"She was born into a gentle house
That sat high on a hill overlooking a valley."
I put out my hand to her and touched
Something that felt like thick water.
Striking a match I saw a fat man
With a little round black hole in his head.
He had been grinning happily when he died.
A large dog sat at his feet. He held a box
In his left hand, from which spilled
A number of picture postcards. Big drops
Of water were hitting down through the leaves.
"It's raining," I said, opening our lunchbox
And taking out a bacon-tomato sandwich.
"How long has your mother had these dizzy spells?"
"She will put the supper all out on the table,
And after we've eaten we'll climb the stairs
Up to my old room and it will be like . . ."
"Say! it's beginning to rain," she said, pushing
Over near and trying to snuggle under
Her coat. I shoved her off and she got up
And went crashing away through the trees.
I called after her once softly but

She did not answer; so I caught up
And ran along at her side until we
Came to a little town. Lights were on
In all the houses and people were singing
And there was the sound of children laughing
At games. I knocked at a door and my mother
Opened it. She smiled when she saw me
And I stretched out my arms to her but
She turned quickly and the house grew dark.
Then, one by one, the lights in all that village
Went out, and we stood in the cold rain
While somewhere a little way off
The rumble of heavy guns shook the ground.

The Grand Palace of Versailles

An elephant made of cotton . . .
Towers of lace under which satin-heeled
Gentlemen sit, playing with the bustles
Of slightly desiccated Grandes Damns.
Good morning, Louis; it's a fine day
In the mirror.

A chaise longue carved
Out of the living body of a white leopard . . .
Spools of silk placed in buckets
Of gilt milk . . . A three-headed dancer
Prancing to the music of a little bell
Languidly swung by a Negro with a hairlip.
Two visiting kings having their canes reheaded,
While a painter to the court tints their eyebrows
With the juice of mildly sickening berries.
What does Salvador Ernst Matta, Louis?
It's a fine day in the mirror.

The Reason for Skylarks

It was nearly morning when the giant
Reached the tree of children.
Their faces shone like white apples
On the cold dark branches
And their dresses and little coats
Made sodden gestures in the wind.

He did not laugh or weep or stamp
His heavy feet. He set to work at once
Lifting them tenderly down
Into a straw basket which was fixed
By a golden strap to his shoulder.
Only one did he drop—a soft pretty child
Whose hair was the color of watered milk.
She fell into the long grass
And he could not find her
Though he searched until his fingers
Bled and the full light came.

He shook his fist at the sky and called
God a bitter name.

But no answer was made and the giant
Got down on his knees before the tree
And putting his hands about the trunk
Shook
Until all the children had fallen
Into the grass. Then he pranced and stamped
Them to jelly. And still he felt no peace.
He took his half-full basket and set it afire,
Holding it by the handle until
Everything had been burned. He saw now
Two men on steaming horses approaching
From the direction of the world

And taking a little silver flute
Out of his pocket he played tune
After tune until they came up to him.

Turner

They rocked on iron benches on the sand
That aproned the sea. From time to time
One of them would look around at me
And all would bob and jounce—pinching
Their ears and shaking their breasts—
Shouting: "Who has seen the furious man?
O who has seen the man of murder made?"
But I noticed that their eyes were sad
And their lips had been bitten through.
Thinking, then, to give them fun,
I started to spin, first on one foot, then
On the other, until the seas and the sky and
The black houses and the pain and the hurt
And everyone I loved and everything that
Was evil or clean or to be afraid of or
Killed or made love to was as one thing
And I neither awake nor asleep but like
A wheel turning in a bucket of colored fish—
And staggering I fell among them
—Their rough tongues salting my face
As their hands sought under my coat.
I admired the children which slept
In huge shells at their feet, and the custom
Of the oldest women to drop dead
At spaced intervals and be borne away
By the more savage waves. But I did not like
The way the maidens sat, their knees drawn up
And skirts pulled down unto their very toes;

Especially since their language was inviting
Of pleasures less confined, and their upper parts
Were completely unclothed. "When I have rested
A little," I told them, "I am going to stretch a rope
From that steeple there over to this gray crag;
Then I am going to balance myself
Back and forth above the water until
One of you consents to walk away with me
Into the hills where we can beat
Great dishpans with knobbed clubs
And after three days have the courage
To count the sorrows of the shy red squirrel."

"The Lions of Fire Shall Have Their Hunting"

The lions of fire
Shall have their hunting in this black land

Their teeth shall tear at your soft throats
Their claws kill

O the lions of fire shall awake
And the valleys steam with their fury

Because you are sick with the dirt of your money
Because you are pigs rooting in the swill of your war
Because you are mean and sly and full of the pus of your
    pious murder
Because you have turned your faces from God
Because you have spread your filth everywhere

O the lions of fire
Wait in the crawling shadows of your world
And their terrible eyes are watching you

Midnight Special

There were no antelope on the balcony
And Thomas had not yet appeared
At the barred window above the precipice

A little snow had fallen since the afternoon
But it was warm in the thought
Of distant forests and I said: "God
Will not suffer if I run my hands
Out over these deeps and shy groves
Until I touch my own undertaking"

But Thomas was busy at his gruel
And when the antelope did come
The management had rigged up a loudspeaker
On the balcony and I was asked to say
A few words to the present George 6th
So I said: "Let the Midnight Special shine a light on me.
O let the Midnight Special shine its everlovin' light on me."

"I Have Lighted the Candles, Mary"

I have lighted the candles, Mary . . .
How softly breathes your little Son

My wife has spread the table
With our best cloth. There are apples,
Bright as red clocks, upon the mantel.
The snow is a weary face at the window.
How sweetly does He sleep

"Into this bitter world, O Terrible Huntsman!"
I say, and she takes my hand—"Hush,
You will wake Him."

The taste of tears is on her mouth
When I kiss her. I take an apple
And hold it tightly in my fist;
The cold, swollen face of war leans in the window.

They are blowing out the candles, Mary . . .
The world is a thing gone mad tonight.
O hold Him tenderly, dear Mother,
For His is a kingdom in the hearts of men.

The Origin of Baseball

Someone had been walking in and out
Of the world without coming
To much decision about anything.
The sun seemed too hot most of the time.
There weren't enough birds around
And the hills had a silly look
When he got on top of one.
The girls in heaven, however, thought
Nothing of asking to see his watch
Like you would want someone to tell
A joke—"Time," they'd say, "what's
That mean—time?", laughing with the edges
Of their white mouths, like a flutter of paper
In a madhouse. And he'd stumble over
General Sherman or Elizabeth B.
Browning, muttering, "Can't you keep
Your big wings out of the aisle?" But down
Again, there'd be millions of people without
Enough to eat and men with guns just
Standing there shooting each other.

So he wanted to throw something
And he picked up a baseball.

A Theory of Nato-geography as Advanced by the Tiaphidian Man, With a Comment on the Character of His Penal System

Rivers were made by the commingling
Efforts of the milkweed and the bullsnake
To rid the world of too-arch bishops. Snow
Came about through an error done
By the Evil One in thinking that
Summer would last just as long
With cold weather. The rain falls
Because what it has to hold on with
Is weaker at the bottom than at the top.
Flowers come to bloom because they get
Lonely sitting off by themselves. Same
With starlings, they fly better when
In motion. Then It built the first man,
And, after a bit of pleasant ribbing, proceeded
To make the first woman. This was more fun
Indeed. Hence the rabbit.

They have bars on all the windows.

Cleveland, Oh?

There were only two things anyone would want
        at that particular moment in a place
        such as that one was:
The bed where God lay.
The sound the boats made at seven each night.

But the rest of it was uncertain.
Nothing was as good as being dead.
The old men were never tired of saying it:
Nothing was quite as good as being dead.

A few trees and a dismantled 1932 Buick.
The rope which held the red stag to his
      miserable circle. A china closet
      with a little porcelain bride and groom
      on the middle shelf. Her tiny pink ear
      chipped off.
Not much to grow wings over.
God was far away and the boats never came by
      anymore.
Nothing was very good or even
At all evil in any ultimate sense.

"O My Love the Pretty Towns"

O my love
The pretty towns
All the blue tents of our nights together
And the lilies and the birds glad in our joy
The road through the forest
Where the surly wolf lived
And the snow at the top of the mountain
And the little
Rain falling on the roofs of the village
O my love my dear lady
The world is not very big
There is only room for our wonder
And the light leaning winds of heaven
Are not more sweet or pure
Than your mouth on my throat
O my love there are larks in our morning
And the finding flame of your hands
And the moss on the bank of the river
And the butterflies
And the whirling-mad
Butterflies!

rain wind light cold cold dark late stem gate bar flame knife garden blue

noise morning son loud art alive net tiger storm lily job tear maker shove

Moon

SUN

mirror
coast
deer
frog
tunnel
grave
noose
supper
beauty
fear
heights
garden
taste
climb
will
look
wing
valley
rule
name
knock
angel
shadow
terror
quest

work
star
good
soul
book
lift
world
body
stone
town
weave
center
break
afraid
skill
thing
laugh
grow
three
keep
force
other
charm
soar
fence

I am the music you make

the blue wings of the ocean

the crying of the black swan

I am the friend
of your childhood

SLEEP

Birds

It is in my heart to wish you

no sorrow

no pain

no betrayal

for I am the will of your last being

the shudder of the breaking open

of terrible gates

O thou art good

and wise

and kindling

a new fire

I am the cave and the light

the watch God keeps

when His children go mad

LIVE

I am the death you seek

the life you are afraid

to know

behold this eye of blood!

power rise tree knowledge innocence fall hand thorn get father chain spool

law peace turtle grass snow prayer life black deep first tie hit see eye

Polly—An Almost-True Story

Polly had a kind of electric beauty—it flashed out of her eye and ran up and down over her face like little mice coated with jewels.

Polly was in love with a teamster who used to ride around in front of her house on Sunday in a red buckboard pulled by two blooded mares. He never looked in but he would whistle "Painted lips, painted eyes, she's just a bird of paradise" and then whip the mares into a fireman's waggle.

For some reason this made Polly very angry. She would walk back into the parlor and grab her little brother away from the funny papers and clamp him into a tub of cold water. This always surprised her mother, so Polly got into the habit of having two tubs ready. Sometimes the old man would be home, and that'd make three tubs. Anyone happen in—they'd get a tub. It went on like that until one Sunday the red buckboard didn't show up. Polly's folks were much relieved, of course; and Polly was just as pretty as ever. Three weeks later they found the teamster in a little clump of elderberry bushes near the road. Someone had taken a knife and damn near sliced off his head. What happened to the buckboard and the two mares is just another one of those things that nobody ever seems able to get to the bottom of.

"Under the Green Ledge"

Under the green ledge
Sits a curious thing (I am walking
        through the snow. Two men
        with rifles follow at the distance
        of a long yell. Their eyes are sleepy
        and they don't seem to hate me.)

It has a tin cross
On its head. One ear
Is shaped like a dog's
And hangs down into the water. An old woman
Pours cocoa into a china mug and feeds
Her infant son. He gurgles like a tiny engine
Designed to amuse angels. But this happens
In another country where only people live.
For under the green ledge
Sits an awesome thing (I turn around
     and the men begin at once to build
     a great cart. They have no horse; fools,
     I think—O a fine strong cart—but
     what will pull and what will race
     them round this ancient world! Then
     I feel the shafts against my ribs
     and I set off at a nervy clip—as
     they sing and O they sing: "Blow away
     the morning dew, the dew, and the dew,
     blow away the morning dew; how sweet
     the winds do blow!") Under the green ledge
Squats a curious thing (All the greenery and
All that's of the sea and of the land and of snow
That falls on my cold face; *and this heart*
Thus the taste of blood
The whip!
And I am running upon the world O
Sing blow away. The two men shine their rifles
On the velvet rag of my fear. Where running?
Whence the chase and the prized award?)
Men kill. Under the green ledge
I huddle with what life I can steal.

Legend for a Little Child

In the shadow of the second world
An old woman sat on a lacquered milkstool
Carding wool for the beautiful coat
Of the Prince of Light

At her thorny feet He played
Filling His hands with birds
And making copper kettles from the thistledown
That blew in across the sweet groves of childhood

Huge blue dogs romped upon the hills
And their tongues lanced the air like butterflies
That had flown out of a toy circus

Now tenderly she beckoned Him near
And taking His head in her wrinkled fists
She told Him the story of mankind

"Then I must go to them!" He cried, and tears fell hot
    on her ancient hands.
"Yes, You must go to them . . ."
"But they are blind—they will not know me!"
"Be happy then, my Little Prince, there will be
    no danger for Thee."

from *The Dark Kingdom* (1942)

For Miriam

The sea is awash with roses O they blow
Upon the land

The still hills fill with their scent
O the hills flow on their sweetness
As on God's hand

O love, it is so little we know of pleasure
Pleasure that lasts as the snow

But the sea is awash with roses O they blow
Upon the land

A Temple

To leave the earth was my wish, and no will stayed my rising.
Early, before sun had filled the roads with carts
Conveying folk to weddings and to murders;
Before men left their selves of sleep, to wander
In the dark of the world like whipped beasts.

I took no pack. I had no horse, no staff, no gun.
I got up a little way and something called me,
Saying,
"Put your hand in mine. We will seek God together."
And I answered,
"It is your father who is lost, not mine."
Then the sky filled with tears of blood, and snakes sang.

The Forms of Knowledge

We moved down the valley
Past the stalls where the sun horses
Champed their bits of gold; and whence
Night's murmuring rivers flow
Onto the world.

Her two legs were beautiful
When we paused on the green bed
And I lifted her down. She sobbed
Once, then her mouth bruised mine;
Her hands turned to fire. She made
Red flowers on my neck when
I took her.
    At cloud level we ate,
The crumbs falling unheeded from our puffed lips. Below us
Stretched the unknown lands of sorrow.
Men had little wisdom there. They sat
In their filth like sick dogs, vomiting up
Their food. And they fought that nothing
Might be changed. In the image of God.

Now that we really see them, the other beings,
Our eyes are not strange.
Alive! standing just out of reach
Beyond where the dead cry.
So the challenge! So this destiny
Builds pleasure. My wish
Is gathered unto the silent breast. My gain
Is for all men. My eyes gleam steadily
Above this night.
    The other creatures
Come to taste my will. I separate the seeing
From the thing seen: my eyes

Think the new islands. I have heard
The sound of immense wings
Beating over their unshadowed hills.
Not to be separated from my world . . . O walk
At my side on these endless heights.
Who will? O who will harry the dark
At the side of the damned . . .

Calling to each other across the graves,
The beautiful and strong whom
Horror eats, whose bones are already
Bleached in city deserts, whose stars
And moons bestride another world—
These, these few, these *holy*—
They are not drowned by the great white rains
Of this winter; they are not trampled
By the horses of murder and death;
Instead, they try to live above life,
As the birds above their flying,
As the dead beyond their dying.

Leviathan's scales sparkle in the heavens
And the whole fish of the universe
Turns on the enraptured spit of God.
Through the flames I can see the lowered faces
Of creatures that watch us in amused love.
We live on only one side of the world.

As we moved down the valley
The petals of the snowflower
Dropped gently on all that had been ugly
Anywhere on this principal star.

The Rites of Darkness

The sleds of the children
Move down the right slope.
To the left, hazed in the tumbling air,
A thousand lights smudge
Within the branches of the old forest,
Like colored moons in a well of milk.

The sleds of the children
Make no sound on the hard-packed snow.
Their bright cries are not heard
On that strange hill.
The youngest are wrapped
In cloth of gold, and their scarves
Have been dipped in blood.
All the others, from the son
Of Tegos, who is the Bishop
Of Black Church—near Tarn,
On to the daughter of the last slut,
Are garbed in love's shining dress;
Naked little eels, they flash
Across the amazed ice.
And behind each sled
There trots a man with his sex
Held like a whip in his snaking hand.

But no one sees the giant horse
That climbs the steps which stretch forth
Between the calling lights and that hill
Straight up to the throne of God.
He is taller than the highest tree
And his flanks steam under the cold moon.
The beat of his heart shakes the sky
And his reaching muzzle snuffles
At the most ancient star.

The innocent alone approach evil
Without fear; in their appointed flame
They acknowledge all living things.
The only evil is doubt; the only good
Is not death, but life. To be is to love.
This I thought as I stood while the snow
Fell in that bitter place, and the riders
Rode their motionless sleds into a nowhere
Of sleep. Ah, God, we can walk so easily,
Bed with women, do every business
That houses and roads are for, scratch
Our shanks and lug candles through
These caves; but, God, we can't believe,
We can't believe in anything.
Because nothing is pure enough.
Because nothing will ever happen
To make us good in our own sight.
Because nothing is evil enough.

☆

I squat on my heels, raise my head
To the moon, and howl.
I dig my nails into my sides,
And laugh when the snow turns red.
As I bend to drink,
I laugh at everything that anyone loves.

All your damn horses climbing to heaven.

The Watcher

Someone is present.

On the earth are laid the crowns
Of his pride.
These unreturning cobramen
Have not fouled his home.
They matter not to him.

Why are you crying?
What have you killed?

☆

The shorelights of heaven flicker palely
Above these whining hosts.
Men lift their hoofs in useless walking
Over the dead lands; and the bending
Brain grows sour on its mash of dread.
But he does not falter.
Before him plume his faultless deeds.

Why are you calling?
What would you kindle?

You matter not to him.

These Unreturning Destinies

The columns glow faintly white
Under this comfortable moon.
In their wisdom pass
The cathedral airs of heaven.

Here night's immortal toad sings,
Its black throat puffed with mockery
Of all narrow determinations.
        Old dancers sleep
In feathery cribs, their green rhythm stilled
By the swaying of stone bells
In churches of water.
The figure of a man appears
For a moment on the steps of the temple,
Then sorrowfully withdraws to his place
In the attended shadow.
Before and around him stand
The brick and steel forests of the dead city,
And perched in the cold branches
The birds of madness clamor.
Now is the hour of silence come.
The magnificent heads shine faintly
Upon the roads of the fish,
And are gone, O they are gathered
Unto the thoughtful breast of victory.
Destiny and youth sleep in the lands
Of the walking sword.
Each one is larger than his other.
In their alternate life men hold
Untarnishing peaks.
On what man is write
Other landscapes, other fairer caverns,
Other more welcome-radiant islands
That peacefully float on his luminous waters.

The columns of death glow faintly white
Within the forests of this destroying planet.
Here gleeful beasts track each other
Through lanes of winter and rotting heroes.

The Second People

We are warned by slow footsteps
Resounding above the daily towers
Of the forest.
These branches arch over clearings
Where lizards reduce their prodigious love.
Snouts of the white bat furrow
Through dark battlements, pursuing
What has not dared life.
There are dwellings
But our position is empty to meet
Even the commonest of this second people.
Almost mournful light seizes
Upon the creeping aisles, surprising
Leopards and herds of tangled snakes.
The waters of the river are covered
With hair that the wind blows
Into monotonous curls.
Nothing has changed on the landroads
But we do not promise to return.
We do not expect this love to perish.

Among us there is a man accused
Of devotion.
His wound seems to ask no revelation
But enables the panther to sleep.
What it is to assist in absolutes,
If only to match the hyena's love.
Who will not allow us conduct
That this second life decides?
Look at the sickness!—we are only foolish
To prolong the unclean splendor of children
Who have no bodies to take their crying to.

These then connect with tubular suns
That grow out of lakes
Tranquil as black light, and their weight
Lowers the earth by the size of journeys.
Lament for the natives of these brighter worlds!
I hold this terrible storm-lantern
Above the empty waters.
Why does no one return to greet me?
What have I done that the wound rejoices?

☆

Among us there is a man accused
Of defiance.
His way seems to answer all running.

"Into Another Mission"

Into another mission
Circling my exposed continent . . .
Intimate with God . . .
Follow me, explorers of humanity. O gentle

Fullness, sweet as a girl

So darkly watching the hours ride their horses of air . . .
O all that withering! My skeleton boy picks roses
In the infinite river of my walking.
Light grows in the camps of death.

Even now a solemn Presence chills the beast,
And darkness speaks kindly to his bride.

The Cloth of the Tempest

These of living emanate a formidable light,
Which is equal to death, and when used
Gives increase eternally.
What fortifies in separate thought
Is not drawn by wind or by man defiled.
So whispers the parable of doubleness.
As it is necessary not to submit
To power which weakens the hidden forms;
It is extraordinarily more essential
Not to deny welcome to these originating forces
When they gather within our heat
To give us habitation.
The one life must be attempted with the other,
That we may embark upon the fiery work
For which we were certainly made.

What has been separated from the mother,
Must again be joined; for we were born of spirit,
And to spirit all mortal things return,
As it is necessary in the method of earth.
So sings the parable of singleness.
My comforter does not conceal his face;
I have seen appearances that were not marshalled
By sleep.
              Perhaps I am to be stationed
At the nets which move through this completing sea.
Or I have hunting on my sign.

Yet the ground is visible,
The center of our seeing. (The houses rest
Like sentinels on this hawking star.
Two women are bathing near a trestle;
Their bodies dress the world in golden birds;
The skin of their throats is a dancing flute . . .

How alter or change? How properly
Find an exact equation? What is flying
Anywhere that is more essential to our quest?
Even the lake . . . boat walking on its blue streets;
Organ of thunder muttering in the sky . . . A tiger
Standing on the edge of a plowed field . . .
What is necessary? What is inseparable to know?
The children seek silvery-pretty caves . . .
What are we to teach?)
The distance is not great
To worlds of magnificent joy or nowhere.

"In the Footsteps of the Walking Air"

In the footsteps of the walking air
Sky's prophetic chickens weave their cloth of awe
And hillsides lift green wings in somber journeying.

Night in his soft haste bumps on the shoulders of the abyss
And a single drop of dark blood covers the earth.

Now is the China of the spirit at walking
In my reaches.
A sable organ sounds in my gathered will
And love's inscrutable skeleton sings.

My seeing moves under a vegetable shroud
And dead forests stand where once Mary stood.

Sullen stone dogs wait in the groves of water . . .
—Though the wanderer drown, his welfare is as a fire
That burns at the bottom of the sea, warming
Unknown roads for sleep to walk upon.

The Village Tudda

Not all of them were human.
They laughed at me, hunting through
My coat for knives or contraceptives;
Running their hands up the front
And gently touching my hair.

Their house stood in a forest
Near the famous river.
Here all day the weather was cold,
Or warm; the sun or the unchanging stars
Put in their work.
Schoolboys piloted yachts on the same bay
Where dragons had been seen
Not twenty years before.
Plumbers sat on the meetinghouse roof
And fixed the pipes of heaven
So that it never rained on Tuesday,
Which was held to be in bad taste.
Plowgirls wandered in the verdant fields
Seeking the answer to the universe.
They were a gentle lot;
Their legends, too.

It is said that
Once, before the coming of man,
A hill caught fire, and the goddess Anna
Died, screaming in the flames, her womb
Burning like a sack of oil.
Next day the world split into four parts:
The place of water,
The place of heaven,
The place of mind,
And the place of air—

It is told that land did not exist at all,
Though many people knew nothing else.

On that hill strange things embraced
And their children hated the earth kind.

☆

I believe that to deliver myself
Is to deliver you.
I seek only to have less.
It is not enough that my things strive;
Myself I lead.

☆

The old women sat upon the couch
And made obscene gestures of love.
I did not fail my trust.

Three naked girls hung by their hair
From the pole of the roof.
When they cried, brightly-clad fools
Did hi-jinks at the door.

Dirty, torn, and weary,
The day squatted on the town
Like a blind watchman, picking
His sun-pocked nose.

☆

They brought the fairest then.
I had no rest.
She unbound her hair
And we lay down near the world.
I was drunk with her scent.
Coming back from that place of mystery,
She made me weep.

Irkalla's White Caves

I believe that a young woman
Is standing in a circle of lions
On the other side of the sky.

In a little while I must carry her the flowers
Which only fade here; and she will not cry
If my hands are not very full.

Fiery antlers toss within the forests of heaven
And ocean's plaintive towns
Echo the tread of celestial feet.
O the beautiful eyes stare down . . .
What have we done that we are blessèd?
What have we died that we hasten to God?

And all the animals are asleep again
In their separate caves.
Hairy bellies distended with their kill.
Culture blubbering in and out
Like the breath of a stranded fish.
Crucifixion in wax. The test-tube messiahs.
Immaculate fornication under the smoking walls
Of a dead world.
                    I dig for my death
        in this thousand-watt dungheap.
        There isn't even enough clean air
To die in.
        O blood-bearded destroyer!
        In other times . . .
        (soundless barges float
        down the rivers of death)
        In another heart

These crimes may not flower . . .
What have we done that we are blessèd?
What have we damned that we are blinded?

Now, with my seven-holed head open
On the air whence comes a fabulous mariner
To take his place among the spheres—
The air which is God
And the mariner who is sleep—I fold
Upon myself like a bird over flames. Then
All my nightbound juices sing. Snails
Pop out of unexpected places and the long
     light lances of waterbulls plunge
       into the green crotch of my native land.
Eyes peer out of the seaweed that gently sways
Above the towers and salt gates of a lost world.

On the other side of the sky
A young woman is standing
In a circle of lions—
The young woman who is dream
And the lions which are death.

"Where My Stag-Antlered Love Moves"

Where my stag-antlered love moves
Across your warm springing hills
In lengthening music to enter your cave
Is my world.

Where my wet coinage carries the price
Of an architecture as incredible
As ever His in Whose image it is.

The Lasting Seasons

I had not much thought of mercy.
All the solemn events
Be damned. Who are the happy
But the dead? That they had come to me
With good intent, that the cool sides
Of their faces shone in gentle joy, even
That they were ordained to show me peace;
These things . . . but why only this! Why do I
Stand here in this place with the whole sound
Of horror on my heart? What have I done
That I am separated from my kind?
Does no one remember . . . O Jesus *is no one
Alive now* (What I felt, wrenched out
With my bleeding hands—wanting
To touch something living
O how I wept in the dark)
(Wake) O God all Your surging little beasts
Are dead God
There is only the sound of crashing
In the thickets where sick death walks
All Your crying little white-eyed fish . . .
       It is fun
To play a flute or clean out a well. Let
The yellow bull want a better pasture,
And he will get it. I like running
After anonymous seers: "You dropped
Something, Jack."—handing them an orange
Or a bottlecap. What has anybody
To complain about? We either mix
With the best people or we cut our throats. Each
Rose is pink or white or a Red Red
Or some other color. Trains run on tracks
Or they now and then get tired of it. Almost
Every sort of thing has been done or said

Or lied about or killed by somebody. You
Can't beat the game with a cold deck anymore
Than a cow can sit in a teacup.
            So I hadn't much thought
Of mercy when they hunted me up that morning.
It had been raining. The hollows in the valley
Were filling with things that seemed to call
To something in the sky. A great white body
Moved slowly shoreward over the water.
I was obliged to watch several figures
Float down from that gigantic craft.
                        They gathered
Me up about twenty miles, when, being made free,
I realized that I could walk alone.
There were roads and gardens, floating cities
That had harbors in the air . . .
I moved without effort
Through that peaceful sea . . .
Lights shining in the dark crust which hangs
Above the sun . . . stars . . .
Moon not an ocean's width away from the earth . . .
Green beings swimming beside me;
Smooth-limbed, the insides of their mouths
Covered with a fine, golden hair . . .
Live! live! *only to live!*
Plunging down at last, unsheltered
In the cold rain . . .
But why only this! To end always
On this stricken land . . . What have I done?
What did I love that I expected mercy? What
Have I killed that I can endure their murder?
      O
What unfouled constellations above there!
O quiet, hidden forms . . . awake!
Man does nothing. And a black rain
Falls from my unreturning heights.

The Expectant Shelters

These, we are told (in an hour of legends),
Shall not be expected to drink of these waters.
They do not delight in our laws.
The cages of terror impress no weariness
Upon their spirit. They have not fallen;
But they have with flame stood
Where He who has care cries.

A breast they flower on . . . it calls them
Home. O Thou Beautiful
How shadowy all things are!
               O bend
Nearer Thy breathing eyes and make us
One with Thy will!
(It is not life that builds these vigilant walls.)
Silently guarding the entrances,
The watchers do not lament.
It is we who are vanishing;
They have delight in their laws.

That we have in death no remarkable dwelling
Does not confine our path.
We have not been taken from home
When we count the firesheds of heaven
As our surety in towers.
We shall not have fallen
If we entertain our flames.

Something has called . . .
(*The proud unopening entrances sway*)
O Someone who is kind cries to us . . .
This pure breast they flower on . . .
O still do the unclean cry out to Thee!

Meben

Below the wall in the lake-garden
Some creatures waited round
The arena for the old lion
To be brought out.

Chained to a tree stump, her white little
Breasts on a level with the water,
Sat a young lady. She lifted her voice
To God and cried.

Around the wall stalked a yellow luthe
And seven eyes squirmed in its face.
The first eye had seen the flood;
The second eye had watched Christ die.

Now the lion leaves the worn chute,
And wades to her side.
He puts his teeth into that white arm.
She is stained.

Above the wall there is a track
That runs along the air.
God sits at the wheel of that spinning car,
And He watches all the little seasons
Of the poet and the lion.

I am sure that He does not laugh
When I stand on this wall and raise
My guns against the creatures who stand
In the arenas of murder
Howling for the blood of everything I love.

A Devotion

For the scaffold spreads its gray flower
Over my world.

All creatures lie in its doom.

Master, we are the divided hearers of death; all
Turning to an inward hell; all murdering
In the name of our terror.

Ever more cunning! We know each other by our look
Of cannibal supplication.

O jibe, prance! commune with fire . . .
O incredible toss and curve of dying planets
O whose hallowing . . . circling hordes!

Will that one of hunting hound my clay slave?

The Crowded Net

The flute of water . . . green deep and hearing
Monsters walk my island sleep

Fables tap along the sunken corridors—
                    O thou radiance
Of my sorrow,
Why do all the wrecks and murders lodge in me?

Neither a reaching eye nor a branching name . . .
Stone, drum, carriage (rising, weep; gazing, moan)

I am heavy with the funeral of things that do not die.

The Naked Land

A beast stands at my eye.

I cook my senses in a dark fire.
The old wombs rot and the new mother
Approaches with the footsteps of a world.

Who are the people of this unscaled heaven?
What beckons?
Whose blood hallows this grim land?
What slithers along the watershed of my human sleep?

The other side of knowing . . .
Caress of unwaking delight . . . O start
A sufficient love! O gently silent forms
Of the last spaces.

"As We Are So Wonderfully Done with Each Other"

As we are so wonderfully done with each other
We can walk into our separate sleep
On floors of music where the milkwhite cloak of childhood lies

O my lady, my fairest dear, my sweetest, loveliest one
Your lips have splashed my dull house with the speech of flowers
My hands are hallowed where they touched over your
      soft curving.

It is good to be weary from that brilliant work
It is being God to feel your breathing under me

A waterglass on the bureau fills with morning . . .
Don't let anyone in to wake us.

The Manifold Fusions

The skinned corpse of a lion
Completes that magnificent part of the landscape
Which extends from Rega to the golden corridors
Of Solomon Trismosin. The country there
    (with its black deer, red and silver
    river birds, yellow milk, and baby
    monsters eating out of dishes shaped
    like arrows which humble mutes
    have decorated with fur) is not
Surpassed by anything seen in the old times.

A pack of defiant men hunt naked
In the Caducean hills. To the left of the cathedral,
Where Tonlin saw the weeping lovesayer,
And heard the concert of destinations, a totally
Different amusement rises on the sight; for here,
Shooting butterflies from her green mouth, the mother
Of our hopping climates fingers the prosperous heart
    of the sun.   (*Yet people do not waken*
    who only walk in the remote distance.
    Meaning one thing, and achieving another,
    they drop no shadow on that golden ground.)

The inside of this land is represented by the practice
Of christs to have three heads. A similar watching
Causes the serpent to stand to his swords when
Man threatens him with resurrection.

Beneath the fourteen nude ladies
Who stretch upon the sky like glass flowers
In a pot of blue snow, Tonlin gathers her hunting
    into the radiant caves of sleep. (*Holding*
    them lightly she turns the three faces together,

their single neck at ease, lips touching,
until the selfsame blood fills every mouth
and they flip like idiot fish in their terror.)

But an ornament has been attained.
The circular figures of men and women
Blow carelessly about in the singular foliage
Of this island. Finny wings beat over
The strange crucibles that hold my childhood.
I, too, seem to walk in the remote distance;
Mastering one thing but failing all others,
I fire no villages on this black land.

The Blind Maidens of Our Homelessness

And their murder towns me sick O it red-streets
Through the smoking island where I stand.
Where are you, mask-shadowed assassin?
O gunman of my appointed surrender . . .
I am lost in this valley of wounds and talking voids.

So I cry out against these living gates (*at me, Lord!*
Look at me! why must Thou assume
That this wild wrong face despairs of Thee?

—I hear a tiger-hum foaming in all I hold . . .)
Let the gates close on the blood! I cast myself
Into the fire of Dream's high cold—seascape of sparkling beasts
That fester under this dying star—

O could they have seen him—
What mask of flesh weeping
Between the worlds!
The Unnamed Name where the soul is.

Heaven and Earth

The scales of the monster
Glitter as he bends above her,
Forking a red power into her moving sex.
And she thinks
(Her face is small and white.
Her eyes are innocent, her mouth pure.):
They will have reached the Cumber Road,
—Where the Geggan sings by the rock,
Their rifles unslung and their ears alert
For the sound of my voice, but
It will be too late—all things are lost
To them and to me, for I am the daughter
Of Death, his slave and his maiden bride.
Then thought the monster
(His tail was a spool of snakes.
His hearts were ten, and his eyes seven.):
The taste of her is as a side of kid
Left in the sun for a thousand days;
Her breasts pop in my shining paws
Like saplings in the fire of sleep;
But she does not turn her woman to me.

I am as a fire raging in an empty world.
Next thought the horsemen
(Their saddles shone as brown suns.
Ten cubits were they tall, their horses seven.):
She will have need of us
And we cannot wait on the Cumber Road
—Where the Geggan sings by the fiery rock,
For we are her sons and Mega is her mother.
Then at last thought Death
(His hands were fat with ice
And his beard was as black as his heart.):

No one will need her when I have done
O no one will know where we have gone
But there will be such wonder in her eyes
When she has seen what life does not show.

And he took her tenderly into his living house.

"There Is Nothing False in Thee"

There is nothing false in thee.
In thy heat the youngest body
Has warmth and light.
In thee the quills of the sun
Find adornment.

What does not die
Is with thee.

Thou art clothed in robes of music.
Thy voice awakens wings.

And still more with thee
Are the flowers of earth made bright.

Upon thy deeps the fiery sails
Of heaven glide.

Thou art the radiance and the joy.
Thy heart shall only fail
When all else has fallen.

What does not perish
Lives in thee.

Continuation of the Landscape

Definite motion is accomplished
Where all seems fixed in the orderly molds
Of sight (through the mastery and knowledge
    of natural signs we can renew
    ourselves with an ancient innocence):
These forests have the sanctity of the quiet tides
Rolling over their green reaching, yet
They do not improve upon their real station,
Which is to grow as it was first decreed.
The white bird and the snail vary the world
By the exact condition of their being; only man
Would change his distance from that beautiful center;
Only man, undirected and naked, would run
From the creature which inhabits his kind.

That to this dark village, unsummoned, unattended
By guide or acclaim, with more joy than sorrow,
I come; is not without its moment on the clock
Of my endeavor. Only through losing our place
    in this overlapping circle of wombs,
    can we attain to that ultimate pattern
Where childhood selects its running wing and grave.

☆

A queen with transparent breasts is found
On the slope of the black hill.
She has a flowing and a meaning
Which the distance dims.
Shape of head distorted by three long swinging poles
That seem to batter through her skull—
Though this may be no more than the lances
Of her companions, who are obscured
By the way the air is torn across in that place.

In fact, this whole scene is frayed and indistinct,
Almost as if it had been too long in the world,
And seen by no one really to make it luminous.

A man made of water and a shoulder-high heart
Are proceeding at a slow pace before.
Just behind come two pretty scintillating claws
Dressed as tavern maids, one of them
Riding on the horns of a small yellow wolf.
They are all intent on an object or ideal
Which seems to be harbored just above me.
The heart moves its head from side to side,
And in each of its eyes there is a tiny slit
Through which a cross looks.

"From My High Love
I Look at That Poor World There"

From my high love I look at that poor world there;
I know that murder is the first prince in that tribe!

The towering sucking terror . . .
Schoolboys over whom the retching crows sing.
There is no lack of hell in that mad nest.
Gray horns hoot dismally in skeleton paws . . .

☆

There is a little inn in the valley.
I wet my finger and put it to the wind:
Death whistles at his pitiless fun.

On the innwall I tack our two hearts;
Let not the bullets go through one before the other.

"For Losing Her Love All Would I Profane"

For losing her love all would I profane
As a man who washes his heart in filth.
She wakes so whitely at my side,
Her two breasts like bowls of snow
Upon which I put my hands like players
In a child's story of heaven.

For gaining her love all would I protest
As a man who threatens God with murder.
Her lips part sleep's jewelled rain
Like little red boats on a Sunday lake.
I know nothing about men who die
Like beasts in a war-fouled ditch—
My sweet . . .

O God what shall become of us!

"We Go Out Together into the Staring Town"

We go out together into the staring town
And buy cheese and bread and little jugs with flowered labels

Everywhere is a tent for us to put on our whirling show

A great deal has been said of the handless serpents
Which war has set loose in the gay milk of our heads

But because you braid your hair and taste like honey of heaven
We go together into town and buy wine and yellow candles

O this is celebration enough for twenty worlds!

We Are Not Worthy, Lord

The dwarfs shuffle up the white steps
To take their peace
On the velvet bellies of young whores.
Menda and Cuu, children
Of sick play; black-eyed
And dirty-tongued—cold little whelps.

Did the king speak?
What does the poet here?

(I spent last night feeding the green swans
At the pool of Our Lady Marie.
Yesterday there were no lilies
In the swamps, but only
A toothless hag mumbling her beads
By the Nesbar's wall.)

After their rude movement has stilled,
The dwarfs mince away
With flowers on their sweating flanks;
Then do Menda and Cuu adorn
Themselves in silken robes
And play at house with golden shrieks.

What do the people love?
Whence comes the traveler here?

(I followed the sea to his cold hall
And there was silence round me
Like the thinking
Of a mad man in a woolen cell.)

Yet murder waited at the Nesbar's wall.

Virtue

Writhing vines were her only apparel.
Her body rippled like a serpent's
As she crossed the lamenting ground
And entered the throne-place of monsters
Which stood in a loathsome glade.

It is said that a hundred years passed
While she lay in their hair-wreathed love—
Then, on a day of storm and mystery,
She walked back into the world
As young and quick as a new watch.

The Meaning of Life

Heart, heart, heart . . . yes, I know thee!
Spirit. Sheltering hurt. The soul breathes
Its alien conquest, like a mother her baby's milk.

It is enough to be innocent.

O burning snake! So far to God. Place
Of water, the dawn of land, the separated
Wing. So near to winter. In my own tongue,
Without fear or prayer, speaking to you,
Who will die, who will go down in pain, sobbing,
    "My God! O my God!"—
Let it suffice that I have found my grail.

The heart sees
What is repellent
And what benevolent
But judges all within itself.

Paxdominisit Sem Pervobiscum Etcumspiri Tutuo

Not to be shattered

Smooth opening ears of the monster
Lower me down, God
Stumbling, weak, *disappearing*

Torn coughing, twisted in blood (now
Flinging my constellations back at God O
Almost daring a multitudinous horizon
No hearing bird dismembers paradise) none

Tastes my faring. Scream christs on embracing shores.

"The Wolf of Winter"

The wolf of winter
Devours roads and towns
In his white hunger.

The wolf of winter
Sticks his paw into the city's rancid pot,
Wanly stirring its soup of whores and suicides.

O the wolf of winter
Crunches on the bones of the poor
In his chill white cave.

The wolf of winter . . .
The grim, the cold, the white
Beautiful winter wolf
That feeds on our world.

Like a Mourningless Child

The rescuing gate is wide
On villages that drift through the sun.
I do not listen to sleep anymore.
Cows pasture on stalks of green hours
And a haze of joyous deer drinks eternity.
Bells make blue robes for the wind to wear.
Summer whistles for her dogs of tree and flower.
The old faith plays jacks with idiots on church lawns.
I am so close to good. I have no need to see God.

The Known Soldier

The balancing spaces are not disturbed
By the yes or no of these cantering brutes.
Frequently another hate-stained robe is placed
On the unriddling skeleton of man's labor
To destroy his life-enchanted animal;
Then do the hordes of murder howl
On the solemn islands of death.
But these unsorrowing angels
Still hover above my city,
And they pick golden fruit
On the orchard slopes of our destiny.

We cannot wish to—it seems—hear confessions
That teach innocence; we are not possessed
Of mercy enough to pardon those whom evil
Has not fattened, whose use has not kissed guns.
What is this crazy croon of nobleness,
Of ancient human wisdom and honor?
What majesty itches on the grinning tongues
Of these who have died
That men might not live?

How God Was Made

On the first day
A weed led her young to drink at Eternity
But there was only one hanging eye
That withered them with its look

On the second day
A wondrous hand fashioned a bubble
And the stars sang
His branching head awake

On the third day
His heart began to beat
And the heavens foamed along their gathering roads
Where the mad and the dead would walk

On the fourth day
His ribs bent around the air
And the pillars of nothingness toppled down
To become roosts for the birds that foul dreams

On the fifth day
His body stirred upon the sun
And the fiery kingdoms raised their flags
That would be lifting over us forever

On the sixth day
His mouth breathed the first word
And all the things of wonder and pain and beauty
Were made ready for the poor flesh of man

On the seventh day
His sweeping eye saw what had been done
And moved into the great, gentle face
Where not even God could see its terror

An Examination into Life and Death

Someone has fallen to the earth
Beneath the white tree.
As often as I say life I am confronted
By that falling O I am determined now
To grow within my saying until I see God
      until my branches grow again
      on the Tree O until my branches
      bloom again on that rootless Tree . . .
I am determined to turn my pattern
Into the costly rooms of the tempest:
To write my storm-name across the world.
Do you see him lying there? On his head
The surpassing climates lean; his mouth
Has the countenance of my saying O warm
And clothed in strength his body was
That is cold now. Written to the end that I may
Bury what is no longer of his element
      (was he of houses and sand towers
      of fruit on broken stems, dry dead flowers
      on a blood-sticky table O did he grow
      upon his rightful Tree, upon his Tree
      that alone covers him now) . . .
I make my peace with the mystery.
But where have the fallen gone?
O what hardens when all is so still and kind
In the manifold rooms of the dead? The first cry
Will be mine, God, O the first cry will be mine!
I am the man all men would be.
I have opened.
These are my forms; this is my soil:
In the beginning there was light
And I held my hands to cover it out
But they came—my quest found bodies
In the hills whence the earth formed;
Bodies which no one has seen

O some are flaming now
they lift up the sun to new grounds
Where the eye of God walks serene and allknowing.
O meaning is a fool's disguise!
Deprived of his clay position
Man fondles the shells of darkness
Where his real life waits.
I think that the fallen of earth
Are alive in the original world.

No one has really fallen
Whose house was prepared by fire.
Beneath the Life-Tree
The still figures rise to their sun,
And they are enveloped in skins of joy O they fall not
As we fall who are not yet arrived to taste journeys.
Do you see me lying here? On my heart
The uncaring heavens lean . . .
What can I believe!
I am the voice all men hear.
I have been cleaned.
These are my people; this is my haven:
At the end there shall be light
And you will welcome the perfections
Of an endless world in which nothing is stained
    where you will dwell in wonder
    beneath the freed suns of your eight senses
    O where you will die not as they of living
    die who are not yet prepared to receive God.
I make my place in the mystery.
I am the branch surely fallen from that rootless Tree.

When the one thing is completed,
The other may grow.
Each acts on his own nature,

And it is not necessary to die
If death be not present in you.
No one has really departed
Who was himself a beginning.
What collects in the human cave
Harbors the waters of birth.
Those who do understand this
Are wiser than any evil or good.
God is wiser than nature
Because it is unnatural to be God.

.   .   .   .   .   .

All sounds
All cryings
All events
All colors
Are His. He belongs nowhere.
He is the Being all men are kind to O He kills
For death is the eye which alone sees His Kingdom
For death is His eye.

Lenada

Great glimmering wagons rumble across this sky.
Phantom whips flash above unseen horses,
And the cursing of enraptured drivers is heard.

The spit of the dove holds the world together
And down in the water bells sound to ears
That grow on the luminous heads of sea beings.

On their webbed feet the Anthian women
Stand above the earth

And they are taller than the gray towers
Of Westerfell. Upon their heads stars frolic;
They hold red lions in their white hands.

But I cannot stay here. Today something
Followed me across the sand to the edge
Of the cool forest where I have my home.
(It made a soft purring sound in its throat . . .)
I was afraid. As I wrenched my door shut,
Its teeth closed on my hand.
Though I felt pain, no wound showed.
Its breath had been cold
And it smelled of the sea.

The countries which are closest to Lenada
Are at their loveliest now. The slow rivers
Move like pretty serpents down their serene paths.
The wishes of children ride handsome yellow horses
Around the tents of the sun. Beautiful women comb
Their hair in the churchyard of Anthia's Penitents.

The ancient islands
Drift upon the rivers which flow through the air . . .
As for the rain, it is green
From the trampled grass where soldiers fall
In other worlds.

As for the satisfying precipice, the skylarks
Of our love roost there.
As for the American death
And the wet teeth of our legends,
O the spit of the wind will hold them together

On an earth where no one can stay
Until first he coldly leaves.

What Happened in the Camps

We had come from being kind
To want murder.
It was quiet at first;
They had left the victims chained
In filth-green cellars, where their cries
Only traveled twenty feet.
A man's time is not sacred
In the camps.
Religion, or the desire to enjoy
A personal public-God, is, like everything else,
Only a habit.
We soon forgot the promised sacrifice,
And spent our days gazing at each other
For the first sign of disease.

One night, however, when the snow hung
On the branches of the sky like cotton birds,
And the sleighs of the wind belled down
Unseen roads, a messenger came with news
Of joyous danger.
The prisoners must be destroyed at once,
Because . . .
Because they had built cities in themselves.
       It was bitterly cold.
       In the field the purest lambs
       Perished; water froze
       In the ancient wells of Lleba.
They had built cities in their sorrow,
And it was beautiful there.
But in the world the snow fell on the lances
Of an aroused army; and their innocent blood
Caked the boots of the soldiers
With the ugly juice of death.

They had built cities in their sad kindness,
And the shadows were filled with light.
But on the earth the animals perfected
Their unlimited ways, and every tooth
Found a throat to warm.

☆

Clear cold heaven!
What are the wounded
That they be wounded again!

It is quiet here in the ground.

"I Suggest That This Day Be Made Holy"

I suggest that this day be made holy
In the records of my kinsmen.

O there was wonder abroad . . . such waves
Of beauty that the very earth wept.

Yet I can tell little. O love
When can I turn my star on
That you may see what was only Light!
The vast and secret core of radiance!

Two women swimming in a river
Which flows through an orchard—
Ripe warm fruit glistening in the sun
And the beautiful bodies of the women
Playing idly in the water . . .

Oh there is not room on earth for such glory.

Saturday Night in the Parthenon

Tiny green birds skate over the surface of the room.
A naked girl prepares a basin with steaming water,
And in the corner away from the hearth, the red wheels
Of an up-ended chariot slowly turn.
After a long moment, the door to the other world opens
And the golden figure of a man appears. He stands
Ruddy as a salmon beside the niche where are kept
The keepsakes of the Prince of Earth; then sadly, drawing
A hammer out of his side, he advances to an oaken desk,
And being careful to strike in exact fury, pounds it to bits.
Another woman has by now taken her station
Beside the bubbling tub.
Her legs are covered with a silken blue fur,
Which in places above the knees
Grows to the thickness of a lion's mane.
The upper sphere of her chest
Is gathered into huge creases by two jeweled pins.
Transparent little boots reveal toes
Which an angel could want.
Beneath her on the floor a beautiful cinnamon cat
Plays with a bunch of yellow grapes, running
Its paws in and out like a boy being a silly king.
Her voice is round and white as she says:
"Your bath is ready, darling. Don't wait too long."
But he has already drawn away to the window
And through its circular opening looks,
As a man into the pages of his death.
"Terrible horsemen are setting fire to the earth.
Houses are burning . . . the people fly before
The red spears of a speckled madness . . ."
"Please, dear," interrupts the original woman,
"We cannot help them . . . Under the cancerous foot
Of their hatred, they were born to perish—
Like beasts in a well of spiders . . .

Come now, sweet; the water will get cold."
A little wagon pulled by foxes lowers from the ceiling.
Three men are seated on its cushions which breathe
Like purple breasts. The head of one is tipped
To the right, where, on a bed of snails, a radiant child
Is crowing sleepily; the heads of the other two are turned
Upward, as though in contemplation
Of an authority which is not easily apprehended.
Yet they act as one, lifting the baby from its rosy perch,
And depositing it gently in the tub.
The water hisses over its scream . . . a faint smell
Of horror floats up. Then the three withdraw
With their hapless burden, and the tinny bark
Of the foxes dies on the air.
"It hasn't grown cold yet," the golden figure says,
And he strokes the belly of the second woman,
Running his hands over her fur like someone asleep.
They lie together under the shadow of a giant crab
Which polishes its thousand vises beside the fire.
Farther back, nearly obscured by kettles and chairs,
A second landscape can be seen; then a third, fourth,
Fifth . . . until the whole, fluted like a rose,
And webbed in a miraculous workmanship,
Ascends unto the seven thrones
Where Tomorrow sits.
Slowly advancing down these shifting levels,
The white Queen of Heaven approaches.
Stars glitter in her hair. A tree grows
Out of her side, and gazing through the foliage
The eyes of the Beautiful gleam—"Hurry, darling,"
The first woman calls. "The water is getting cold."
But he does not hear.
The hilt of the knife is carved like a scepter
And like a scepter gently sways
Above his mutilated throat . . .
Smiling like a fashionable hat, the furry girl

Walks quickly to the tub, and throwing off
Her stained gown, eels into the water.
The other watches her sorrowfully; then,
Without haste, as one would strangle an owl,
She flicks the wheel of the chariot—around
Which the black world bends . . .

    without thrones or gates, without faith,
    warmth or light for any of its creatures;
    where even the children go mad—and,
As though unwound on a scroll, the picture
Of Everyman's murder winks back at God.

Farther away now, nearly hidden by the human,
Another landscape can be seen . . .
And the wan, smiling Queen of Heaven appears
For a moment on the balconies of my chosen sleep.

The Intimate Guest

A fiend slays the children of the messenger.

Grown cruel am I . . . quiet and cunning. I
Open. To close the wounds of my wanting. Wash
The daughters of chaos and plant trees of speech
That will flower my world O look it changes
Leaps oceans it lies down and cries heart
Tangled in its filth (if I had a climate or calling
Outside this encrusted forest . . .)

I devour the fiend. Henchforth I spread my own
Feast and eat everybody.

So has the messenger spoken

The Spirit of Noplace

My fool walks on wobbling roads.

Neither cradle nor garden stops his hitting tread.
He gathers wild corn on their temple steps;
He drinks seas at one draught; earth eats
In a bite; all men he leads;
And loves his God.

Neither does he listen to false tribes
Barking in their fouled caves;
Nor does he speak to me.

The Outlaw of the Lowest Planet

If someone is pleased to boast
Of inner knowledge, then let him test
My power to question his truth; permit him to rally
His hosts—for I am going to tear the tongue
Out of his lying mouth; I am going to increase
His heat until he beg mercy—this is not to be spooned up
Like alchemical water to make golden
The matted corpse in his bed.
These are pictures of heaven.
        (I defy him to offer his greasy work!)
As you stand on the first level two women
Approach slowly from a kind of glass temple.
They are covered with a substance which begins to soften
As you watch; until afterwards, and you are nearly blind,
The bodies are seen to be hollow—only the organs
Of the spirit remain, only the dress of its radiance
Shines about them; and instead of our animal odors,
They smell of God. But these are now joined by colors
Which boil up on the white hills like great birds

Out of the water. And the nature of this kingdom
Is not hidden in their light, but separates the watcher
Into his various heights—we are beginning to learn
To hasten the tongue beyond the reversing vanities
Of what is thought to be in the head. *Speech of the eye!*
The villages in heaven have been named
After the seven daughters of God, and each has
Twenty colors in its air. All in consequence are nothing
When any one is dark.

> The villages are thus known: *Lenada,*
> where the windflowers were manipulated
> by blind larks; *Rallas,* upon whose fields
> the stones danced with elephants; *Volba,*
> the original site of the pliant fish; *Dusda,*
> in which the squatic infants were conceived;
> *Onega,* where death's cathedral stands; *Criha,*
> at the center of which is a black crown; and *Mega,*
> in whose houses the hour of death is made bright.

What is running with naked legs
Beside the green wall? It is not the minstrel.
What is running with bowed head
Under the golden world? It has no mastery.
It has no landscapes in its hand.
It has no climate save its murder.
Speech of the throned heart.
As you stand on the second level a figure
Detaches itself from the surrounding haze;
And it puts its forehead against the distance,
Crying softly like a frightened kitten.
A corridor opens on a temple of birds.
Two red leopards walk into a child
Whose tiny hands hold a three-pronged staff.
Suddenly a moon shaped like a horse
Lowers its muzzle into the river and drinks.
Beyond the crowded wall a hand
Reaches into the sky and lowers Mary down—
She is draped in wild splendor

228

Like an African queen.
There are three eyes on Her dancing.
And this is silence of the morning world.
Here stand the Silent Ones whose hearts
Are wedded to God. O I lift my song to Him!
Have I not ever lain in His nocturnal grove—
O what laments upon the night
Has there its gentle home.
What is weeping in terrible love
Under this broken world?
It is surely lost upon these whirling spaces.
What cries in its divided roots
Beneath this measuring peace?
O there is no mystery in death.
Speech of the consoling heart.
As you stand on the third level the sky fills
With gigantic white deer, and their eyes
Glow like the thunderflowers of summer.
On their antlers baby angels sleep. Knowledge
Is not their horizon. Beyond all reason they walk,
And their summit remembers not the wintry kingdoms
Of the earth. The sealed vaults of eternity open
Beneath their triumphant hoofs. Unchristened saviors
Dwell in their sweet kirks.

     Upon their shoulders perfection flutters
Like a silver bird. The shadow of hunting
Does not stain their pure breath.
Sometimes this God-fired jungle
Flames with newer life . . . phantom tigers
Tremble on the brink of dark pools which reflect
The lolling eye of greater heavens. Burning apples
Fall from orchards in lands where not even God
Has been

     .   .   .   .   .

And the guardian mysteries softly call to Him.

Pastoral

The dove walks with sticky feet
Upon the green crowns of the almond tree,
Its feathers smeared over with warmth
Like honey
That drips lazily down into the shadow . . .

Anyone standing in that orchard,
So filled with peace and sleep,
Would hardly have noticed the hill
Nearby
With its three strange wooden arms
Lifted above a throng of motionless people
—Above the helmets of Pilate's soldiers
Flashing like silver teeth in the sun.

O Howling Cells

I protest against the manner of these ruins.
That their streets are soft with the dried hair
Of murdered children is not outside
The order of our speckled activity; even
The here recorded delight of the citizenry
In self-mutilation and impious sport,
Involving the real nature of human desires,
Can be condoned without loss to our earthly intent:
But that these very rocks and caked walls
Vomit a deeper evil; that this sorrowful wood
And impenetrable stone are witness
To unimaginable hells; and that no survivor
—Unless we except the insane—can share
The full horror of man's cruelty to the things
He could not kill; this cannot be forgiven.

When the last gun was stilled
And the last gunner had achieved his fun,
It was noticed by someone
That the mad, not being able to perform
Murder nicely, had been forgotten.
They had been left to contemplate
The beautiful omnipotence of reason.

Chalk coasts steam under the moons
Of this devastated mindscape . . .
Hands claw at the webs of these shrinking wombs
As the new child gropes for his monster.

Here there are
only shapes
that never
change.
Shapes that are God   son
when all else
fails.   BLUE water
They are fixed
and pure   in
outside   three
the mind   whiteblind
which is never   roads
free of them.

                    DEATH   life!

O on murder's eve the henchmen of Eunice Nauticus
Were gabbling over their spiked grog,
And Bedlam's brood were laughing at the gates,
When two strangers took their stations
Before the throne of the sleeping Infanta.
At that moment the rain, which had not fallen

Since the regatta of Our Hapless Queen,
Fell; and it was quickly seen that all the hills around
Were thick with lads and maids who looned
In the highest branches of their languid hell.
(Then a virgin, so white and shy, appeared on the cold stair)
  the blood drips onto your hands
  I do not believe in death

But it does!

I wander through these blackened ruins
Thinking that nobody has ever made proper use of murder.

O Everliving Queen!

They abuse no maiden universe
Who fall blind in their own procession,
For man himself is the door standing open on heaven.
In him the provinces of holy soldiery are restored;
His white troops abide within the savage temples
Of the earlier tribes, and compassion performs
Its own miracle—for man is only victorious
When his shrines have been overthrown.
Unless he outrage the folly of those other careers,
Which always ended in death;
Unless he poison the fury of all other avowals,
Which always ended in death;
Unless he turn from the fulfillment of all prophesies,
Which always ended in death;
He will stand where his fellows have always stood . . .
O the eagle empties his terrible eye upon them.
They are plunged into the white mouth
Of horror.
Darkness covers their cities. Their desire was ever

To know a Godless God. Solitary on the cliffs of night
They snuffle in sick embraces.
Their matted paws quicken the centuries
Backward.
The plague-bull roars within their spirit.
A scabby idiot sucks peppermints
In the hall of their quiet.
Great gray death-bergs loom ghostly kind
Within their every sea. Yet in their dreaming
God was! They shall lie down at the side of Forever
And their leaning faces shall cry out to us
O their crying shall prepare the new Christ

But No One steps out of the tired sun
And a black rain falls on their world

.   .   .   .   .   .

For man himself is the door standing open on horror.
Death is the one judge of all his sluggish freedoms—
But I believe that something outweighs
The image we have of ourselves dying,
As the innocent the acquired evil.
I believe that in the absence of guilt,
Death will be absent; as in the pictures of children,
He is not present. Ours must be a God of life.
The Word *now*, the Immortality *now*
O the Death *now*
That we may live in this Eternity, in this Present—
As we are living
Outweighing all images that are not of life—
For who says, "I live!" can only approach death
As one beginning
A new part of this same beautiful undertaking.

This living man raises his arms to the sun.
To the sun! O to these thousand dazzling suns!

233

This is the marriage day of new multitudes.
I cut through the cord holding death
And life lowers everlastingly down—O
It is my kinsman, my everliving Queen!
—Take some! O take some! Even death
Is full of it. Even death is not dead!

Written after Reading an Item in the Paper about a Young Lady Who Went Mad upon Forsaking Her Lover. He Is Here Assumed to Speak

Our chief amusement was to lie naked
In a little clearing deep within the forest.
There, while the things of fur and wing
Disported themselves about us, we lay
Together in peace and joy, our mouths
Completing what our voices could not tell.
We had no thought to enter the Anthian cave,
Which the repeated warnings of the wood folk
Had made sinister and unholy.
This was the place of love O cry cry air
Water earth fields birds and the calling
Of the wild swan O how we were taken
Into the green halls
Into the beautiful green halls where God dwelt.
This was the throne of song O fill fill her heart
Breast arms lips eyes and the falling
Of her golden hair O how I was tried
By that haunting flood
By that falling of love's swift unquenchable whips.
Within her queenly land I knew my wanton home.
Fair were the deeds of our revels, a pageantry

Of glory the acts of our two souls—we drank
The waters of fire, twisting upon a whirling sun,
And were drowned. In place of monuments
We built honor itself; and she instead of ornament
Had fashioned gowns for Beauty to wear.

The awesome houses of earth's innocents . . .

O my lords and ladies, pain walks upon my land . . .
Little snake, little snake, what a pretty pair
We make

I am thirsty! I am heavy with my stone!
That was the place of love O cry cry stars
Rain night snow death and the calling
Of the stained creature O how we were tortured
By that sublime beast
By that tongueless Horror which dwelt in the cave.
For you grew tired of our love.
Hovering in the air above heaven,
You dived down drunken with our constellations . . .
Because you grew tired of all the common mysteries,
Because you grew tired of love itself.
Not heeding the warnings of the wood folk,
You went into the cave. O cry cry my heart
Throat hands tongue spirit and the killing
Of my awesome house O how you were tested
By that murder
By that long murder which in killing love killed thee.
For I have nearly forgotten thy deeps;
Almost am I able to pass that mocking place
Without running a knife through my heart.
You were my only house O cry cry Horror
Be kind to her in your cave.

Preparation for the Highest Being

As I had seen it practiced in that land,
I attended the fire . . . translating the Julation
Into the five languages of my continent.

I saw what had been done
That the extreme and simple Authority
Might be preserved . . .
      (A lady, a lady dressed in blue and gold
      sits upon a horse at the water's edge.
      In back of her on the ground—
      where light might have been—
      lies the mutilated body of her father.
      A small rabbit sniffs at the cold face;
      then, in anger, perhaps,
      withdraws into the watching sky.
      But the Within does not open . . .)
I found such a beautiful vessel
To put murder in.

Color of the plague . . .
Liver-gray wagons creeking through fog . . .
Can I give you a river?
As I am blinded a little . . .
Breathing clocks chime in my every window.
I saw what had been done
That this world might be improved . . .
      (Yellow geese skim over these orchards
      and with some disgust the ancient tomes
      are examined by weasel-eyed clerics
      in thought-lined cathedrals . . .
      O the glacier slips a white inch
      nearer the earth . . .
      Birds pick at the eyes of sleep.

      There is blood on my voice!)

☆

It is indeed apparent that the separation
Of each being from its essential nature
Can only bear a cruel and horrible fruit.

What hast thou done for love?
Which of these steam-heated chapels is your wound?

Much is given . . .
In order that the waters hidden in this investigation
May give growth to a beginning world;
And what was least seen by man
In his destructive blindness,
May become on this first, pure island
An event of indestructible power;
I now venture to define the laws
By which all may highly enter at the white gate:
It is necessary to consist of your own spirit;
It is ordered that you hold the world
As a child the many-times handled wrapper on candy—
It is not our mortal purpose to eat
That which offers no sustaining food,
Nor is it wise to suppose we are ducks
Because we live near the water—
It is to be desired that everyone keep his own eyes
Clean. (This law fathers all wisdom,
And is to this order as air is to the earth.)

What hast thou done for life?
Which of these war-dancing camps is your world?

I offer you this new continent . . .
But alas, much is taken away.

The Climate of War

Therefore the constant powers do not lessen;
Nor is the property of the spirit scattered
On the cold hills of these events.
Through what is heavy into what is only light,
Man accumulates his original mastery
—Which is to be one with that gentle substance
Out of which the flowers take breath.

That which is given in birth
Is taken to purer beginnings.
The combats of this world
Rise only upward, since death
Is not man's creature, but God's . . .
And he can gain nothing by manipulating
That which is already hidden in himself.
The sources of nature are not concerned
In peoples, or in battlefields; nor are they mindful
Of the intensity with which man extinguishes his kind.
He who can give light to the hidden
May alone speak of victories.
He who can come to his own formulation
Shall be found to assume mastery
Over the roads which lead
On the whole human event.

The hour of love and dignity and peace
Is surely not dead.
With more splendor than these somber lives
The gates within us
Open on the brilliant gardens of the sun.
Then do these inscrutable soldiers rise upward,
Nourished and flowering
On the battleslopes of the Unseen. For Victory,

Unlike the sponsored madness in these undertakings,
Is not diminished by what is mortal; but on its peaks
Grows until the dark caverns are alight
With the ordained radiance of all mankind.

What the Grecian Earns

I do not count the day
Unless something proves life.

The sick who sauce their doings with God
Will not rank an apple with an emperor;
Little more can I distinguish between the garments
Of fortune and what fools wear—because
Heaven's pitchmen can sell me anything.

I am willing to be gentle.
I am willing to be gathered into my place.
What hurried over the womb I was in
Won't lack for speed to leave me now.
I shall not be divided by the angels
Who float about in flimsy nightshirts on wet clouds.

What gives scope to summer made the continents
Of greed and murder; put man in his little box
And slammed tight the lid. But my wound
Does not ask salve from cannibals, nor do I expect
Fleece to grow on doorknobs—because
The world's pitchmen can sell me nothing.

I am willing to be shaped.
I am willing to be shipped on the first celestial jaunt.

"Sovereign of the Wilderness"

Sovereign of the wilderness!
O Huntress of our wild star!
Where the shelter? O what soaring house
And concealing sky!

I followed her footsteps like peaks of flame
Through the whirlpool's crying caves—
The wreck of all creation floating there.
("Be prepared for gigantic struggle
And congregated watercourses
Steaming under a dreamed moon." Who spoke?
What constellations scream in this sky . . .)
My JESUS sleeps.

In the streets of Lenada, brilliant proud
Birds hung my walking on green spires.
Elephants, taller than childhood, trumpeted
In scarlet stockades, their faces sewn together
With circuslight. Twenty clerks were hard at work
Painting lanterns on an old foam-nosed boar, whose
Tusks were curled around the sea. Black angels
Paraded in turbans made of sacred thought.

It was not you I saw in grim procession
Swaying above the air—
You gave me no weapon for that battle
Of weeping monsters. I sought you, Mega
Of my innocent roads, but you did not come.
You did not come to any place.

Her steps like the power of an astronomer's gun
Ascend into cool seasons, and the dragon
Copulates with the sword on this unknown planet.

I stand beneath a new GOD. The homes of Nakeus
Rise upon the cracked plains. And now begins
The stampede of men seeking peace in green coats:
From Cbunx with randy bears on slobbered chains,
Raffia bandages covering ancient wounds, girls
Decked in hair bras and carrying shriveled heads
In quaggy baskets. Let come the sick and lame
Over troubled lands in bounding carts; waters
Of Dnius made red by their pustulent wounds;
And from hills of rattling Mugon that migration
Of grizzled men and sinister gear. Only the absent
Dead did not come. Only their wide still clay
Kept to the old continent.

Although no evidence relates to my love,
O dark Lady of Anthia's torment,
It was wrong of you not to come,
Not to come at all to that hidden land.
For there were creatures of vast size
And I heard
The sound of new voyages Oh I heard
Victory beating his ordained wings
Over that shore. There were appearances
To be understood: I saw good women
Proud under burdens where dancing gardens
Made meditation a flower pristine as Diota.
Death sat with the eye of the lightning
On his wrist. It was on that island
I saw the beautiful rose of perfection
Growing out of the Rama's womb.

Waking into Sleep

They spread their legs as a toad
When rain softens its sour talk.

These twin fates, these milkless witches of sorrow,
Whose wanton motherhood is not a home, is
Not, no, is not a house to put your sleeping in;
Whose white sex is flabby where madmen have lain;
But whose hands, ears, (even wings) and scaly buttocks
Are beloved by some dark fellow, like me, perhaps.

For they are blind . . . They hold my head in their laps
And run their listening tongues over the terror I see.

The Permanent Migrations

A suitable entrance to this village
Is made only by walking down three white steps
That lead past a table
Upon which the continents are greening.
Apparently what is suspended
From the overhighest throne
Is not an object to throw cathedrals at;
For here, beneath it, having an infinite perfection,
Stand the beautiful horsemen of death,
Their plumes unstirred by what is commanded on earth.
Hence it is that the holiest villager is somewhat colored
By the restless stamping of these carriers.
Until knowledge becomes secret
And that secret knowledge, we can possess little
In the nature of permanent union with this ground;
Indeed, as what holds walking is revealed,
Yet another traveler is seen in an employment
Which gives raiment to the most distant stillness.

All figures in this highest completion
Are subject to harbors where only eternity sails.

On the white boughs of heaven sit the creatures
Of our procedure; for no man has ever put foot here.

.   .   .   .   .   .

And most graciously . . . just covering death
A little
Edging on the ornaments
Perhaps touching the true radiation
    and the intent wings . . .
Its breath
Its white mouth
Slowly opening
    . . . the bleeding forehead
    spreading over these blind towers
        . . . *its eye*
Unhurried in the tempest
And yet something does not fully kneel
Upon these ascending highways . . . something
Does not turn beautifully mad in these deeps
Trace of fury now (whips?)—Boundaries!
A red music.
"What country is this?"
"Death's."
But to approach
I am where God is. When I have come to peace—

Green towns floating across the valley . . .
The deer of childhood walking
Unstained upon these sleepy hills . . . and the darkness
That snakes whirred in
Opening like a window on the beautiful fields
Where the seasons are built ("What crime? Whose guilt
Furnishes these black gaieties?"
"I stand before the overhighest throne.
Confession is useless to open these gates."

"Are these the provinces of Death?"
"I touch *something* . . . no, not his! it is not he!")
—And I hold the flowers of all the worlds.

Plumes stirring on these unrecorded horizons.

*FELLOW SOUL, SOUND HUNTING TO THY IM-
MEASURABLE HEART, and balm to thy wounds.
What causes thee to walk abroad upon this silly
earth, in lust (for what?), in rage (against whom?),
in fear (against whose hosts?), with thy nose an inch
and three-eighths before thy face? On guard, spit-
ling, advance not beyond thy mother's soft womb:
the sea is treacherous, still and deep—you may dance
to the witch, to the witch! I instruct thee, sparrows
have their special dangers, the wolf his lights, the
lowliest hair its kingdom (and the shadow of that
kingdom), the least savannah its own terrible hori-
zon. To live, fellowbub, is essential, but to overlive
is to court the devil's wife, and in loving that she
you will be lain in such sparkling cold labyrinths*

In this single world
What have the double-hearted to do . . .
The confident assassins wait
On the hills of my echoing creature.
Resplendent with smoking inscriptions,
The heavenly Divider
Stabs at my unkneeling child;
But the torches of this masterhood
Do not fade. The gray bugles of death

Are not heard in my principal country.
Here I am secure against His undistant slave.
—The wing walks upon its proud throne.
And I am raised above my hosts

I do not offer to serve.
Everything proceeds
From its own climate.
The womb reveals its scepter
When the child his cross.
What is commanded for one
Has no meaning for another.
Nothing shows result
Unless it grows in its rightful place.
Who breathes upon himself
Brings his own hour nearer life.
I turn my head to the East
Whence come the primary caravans.
I am engaged in the use of separations.
A thing which is two
Seeks not the one but the all in this endeavor.
To be covered in universal graves
Is not the wish of my unwelded destroyer.
The substance of man's common encounters
Does not occupy the earth with angels;
Instead, creeping to its labor
Like an eyeless ghost, this noblest animal
Grunts about among the dirt of his possessions;
And his only dream is of a pig's heaven
Where he may contentedly live with his nose
In the prescribed ass of murder.

I cannot offer to serve.
All things proceed
From their resulting center.
O the wing walks upon its proving throne
And I am raised above my harvest.

They walk forward now into this death.
The earth-lights are going out . . .
It is an hour away from Eternity.

Lying along the ground in their scarlet cloaks,
Schoolboys kiss the shaggy mouth of the war.
Languid and full of soft folds a last thick sleep
Closes their eyes—"Such was their honor."
Such was their honor . . .

Such was their honor!

There Is One Who Watches

The heavens sway at his touch,
Dropping blue pennies
Into the hand of summer.
The ears of the lark alone hear his singing.
Those who love have his waking
When their bodies are fed.
On the edge of the world
Stands his unending house.
All who have waited in the darkness
Are there shown a flowering light.
Manifest in his pattern are the crowns of destiny,
And he has speech direct with God.
Dressed in the white hoods of his anger,
Terrible soldiers empty winter on the earth.
Beneath him the wells of hair
Cloud with the warm juice of suicides;
And the splendor of all creatures is polished
By the tinkling ghost whom men call death.
All beside him nestle the eternal Guardians,
Whose kingdom is the shading of a leaf
Or the clanging open of a grave.

IN YOUR BODY ALL BODIES LIE, numbers in a caravan bound nowhere. They do not belong to you, nor you to them. All men have fed you with their want, and to them you shall return nothing; for it is not certain by whose will, nor from what womb you come. Do not grieve, therefore, for those who are lost to you; they were ever so to themselves—emerging from the unknown into what is known by none save the dead, they leave no track that time's vast foot will not cover. They who know nothing of punishment have been known to perish for terrible sins. Life's end is life. What is universal cannot be lost. The opinion of grammar has become the opinion of your world: through use of their own action, words rule the heads of men. Your native zone is silence; everything you want is within you. Do not seek the ungranting fire; man himself is the flame

I am going on with my beautiful procession,
Though the way is not bent to my conquering
And the dark kiss of the angel conceals all pleasure.

The air that burns
Questions nothing; rays of the shrouded beacon
Pick out no headlands on this unlifting coast.
Falling as the heart falls, sorrow-chilled
And unanswered in the bleak rain, the hosts
Of night pass across this gray death
That neither cleans nor kills; but like a fester
Grows, until the world is with winter filled.

Beyond this are gatherings
That solemnize the antelope's breath.
Not where I go but where silence has gone,
They herd the pale souls, and their foreheads shine
As the teeth of the sea.
Around them unending peace closes.
They are shaped like gardens O their touch
Will hurry islands more beautiful
Than a fawn's sleep.

Silently they stand there.
They are not desolate; the images
Of a thousand heights glow down
From their white eyes.
The tribe-stained animals of earth
Are not represented in that radiant watch.
The upright hound who hunts his own kind
Is not favored by their awesome authority.
They are not alone; around them
Unceasing perfection winds its gentle arms,
And from the place of sun a beautiful lion
Rests down his floating paws upon them.

This world that dies
Answers nothing; in the house of the unnamed
A naked child awakes to the eyeless operation
Of its destiny. Crying as the spirit crieth,
Alone and unseeking in the dim grove, it
Stares at its kind, which already is clamoring
To end that innocent quest.

Brilliant with immortal gates,
The unknown islands sink earthward,
And their sun enters dreaming's sky.

from *Cloth of the Tempest* (1943)

Cruelties of the Sportive Power

Loved in the black weather . . . The

Will. Life's gay will. The will of
Life. Sea. Joy. Bird. Queen. Flame.
Beast.
Stain.
The will of life. Stain on the golden
Throat. And life's wit
On the mountain. My chair. My tree. My
Lady.
And the will and the wit of the flaming bird
And the way and the wiles of the seaqueen child
And the word and the warmth of life's
Golden wakening

My tongue head cry juice great and small
Of life. Chair star tree. My
Sound lady. All in the golden weather
Of my love. Near the beast.
Please be wandering. Taste of flame
In my mouth. Green brain of His being.
Deeper to holy. Like an iron bull in a cloud.

November in Ohio

There were twelve ragged children
In the house.
The sleigh tinkled snowily down the street
And they all looked out of the window at it.

Ecstasy of the Pure

Sleep's huge soft instruments rustle
Through the age-peaked houses
Of men like snub-nosed knives of wool;
And the rock's eyes grind against heaven;
And the water burns;
And the depths are kindled
By what is the spirit of nations
And the wide
Tossing air's eyes that are looking.

Unarmed, the cold priestess weaves
The fish into the pattern of eagles;
And the priestess shines
The eyes of fish. Unfolding here
In heaven O
Touch the face! There is your
Mother.
The golden panther steps with his paws
That are made of silence
Down through the eyes of trees
Into the earth. And this be the sign
Of your death: that you have a love
Less than the naked happenings.

"As in the Green Sky"

As in the green sky
white queens
think of Fate

so in the womb world runs
and comes to naught

But every all man and brute
sings! For love, that red feather
in the hat of heaven, stabs
the naked rib of this dreaming thing
and O then it
flames (the mouth splintering open) . . .

As in the white sky
gray queens
ponder the life of man

and are not watchful, or very mortal at all
to judge of him who only really dies.

Progress to a View of Life

Heal the soul, O still-featured host
Whose white desire is to know all being;
O herdsmen of silence and cold light,
Heal the soul of his awful waking . . .
For now I have

A reason to want love;
I have a reason to want peace
And the quiet of the good . . .

There is a tree . . .
A field . . .
The warm hand of this beautiful creature . . .

O there is a hunger . . .
A fiery town . . .
And the hairy fist of this journey
Bloodying the mouth of God.

The Destruction of Carthage

Six days out of all the days.
250,000 people butchered in the streets.
The blood reached as high as the chest
Of a tall horse. The women were
Ripped open like fish—after a crude love
Had been performed.

It had an importance, I suppose.
Walls
Around walls.
What was law.
What men did.

Six days out of all the days.
The way a great city dies . . .
Bodies floating through the red churning
Of excited horses.
Perhaps the most horrible thing
Was the excitement of the horses.
That may have an importance
Which will destroy all of us.

The Pathway

The pathway. It needs O it needs
Light on it. As a face
We love.

I know the gray panther. He kills,
And it is fun O it is fun
In his heart. As a day
We die through.
Sullen. The deathman is sullen. O

He does not like
Little cars. Cars full of huge snowroses
And men wearing heaven
On their caps.

But joy.

O the joy of roads sweetens the earth
And the panther is a fool
And a fool is that deathman
Who brought us here. For joy
Shall touch every being. As the sun
These fields. O what is a tree and a brook
And a hill and a lamb and a brown sparrow?
What is a pathway?
O look at the beautiful cars O
They are full of strange creatures
Who do not have guns in their hands.

To the Jewish People

Is it tomorrow yet?
Is rain?
Is love?

Hands have lives to warm.
Joy builds a star.
Be well.
Speak of heaven.
The music weeps.

I blow on the hour.
Have sweetness.
It is tomorrow somewhere.
The wound will sleep.

TRIAL OF THE CHILL GIANT

God

Mother
Truth
Joy
Faith

"In Shadings of an Obscure Punishment"

In shadings of an obscure punishment
I watch my life choose its own wakening.
It is strange that only now as the world dies
Do I fill with the blood of my special creature.
I have no neighbor, for I come in a wrong time—
And everything is wounded that I would make clean.

Now is the hour of my templement.
I touch the wild humility of another estate.
And I know how the angels walk
In their silvery seasons.
But I taste the sickness of my fellows,
And I begin to drown in all that demeans them.

Therefore I shall forfeit nothing
If I deal with the wondrous lights
That are beginning to sparkle
Somewhere on an unseen continent.

I listen . . .
They are walking,
The jolly ones from another earth . . .
They come nearer.
I can feel their watery breath on my hands.

The Age of Pericles

O fields of the sun!
O then in flower
The standing man and the image
Of his talk like a white bird
Bathing in the pools of morning.

255

These are the friends of the sun.
They rest love—
The white bird lying between us.

All in the shoals wonder finds
Its golden fish. I do walk now
In each green and life of love. O
This crude flesh is small
In my world. Clad in levels
As a child asleep, I put robes
Over the sun. For the sun is a womb
And the mother of other worlds
Than this. Something defiles
The white bird lying between us.

Love shall have rest, and the Greek
Decide to build the new Athens.

Mirru

I tiptoed into her sleep
And she was a little girl
Listening to her father clearing the snow
From the sidewalk in front of their house
And it was sweetly mixed-up
With funnypapers on Sunday morning
And black, surly-friendly tomcats
Smelling of New England and
Finnish bread but Finns talk too long
And little girls get tired and father calls
I'll be asleep before you will
And after a moment calls again
Aren't you asleep yet? and when you say no
He adds triumphantly

I told you I'd win, *I'm* asleep
Leaving you to puzzle over it
And later when she has nearly "grown-up"
Sitting with her mother in the warm kitchen
Reading Mystery Stories and father asking
Are you two going to stay up all night?
And her mother assuring him that
Just as soon as this chapter is finished
We'll stop but somehow they never did
And holding squirmy little flower-eyed rabbits

And watching for Santa Claus at the front door
While the snow swirled so prettily on the lawn
Like a white queen in a beautiful dress.

The Empire of Persia

Thermopylae is a well
of agony.
Leonidas is dying;
it is a common death;
he was not a great man.

But there are other matters to consider:
the role played by the rain
—(the wounded, of course—but the wounded
all died—it was an event indeed. Xerxes
went on to Athens and this city burned
"to the ground.")
and the part taken by the famous Spartan
idiot
which sat smiling at a blue angel
who unaccountably persisted in drawing
on and off a pair of glass gloves.

Sit then, Darius, on your throne of empire.
The wounded die
and the rain rains; but the smell
of blood does not fade.
It is always the great men who fail.

Lao Tsze

                    Water!
                    Star!
and somewhere near now nodding
the moon

The fool
forgets
his man of ice

I weep for the world
O I weep for the world and a yellow spider
makes a web in my heart

I am hurt
I know what is knowledge
but wisdom fattens the soul of man
O wisdom is the plaything of the fool
                    The talk
                    topples
into the water and its ripples fashion
the snouts of monstrous fish

I am indifferent to the death of your world.
Stain!

Clean!

Egypt

Cle—
1600 men to a stone. Please mention
the Nile. Croco—But the slow thing
happens in the air.
Tree slender as light.
Did Cae—? I don't remember
that he came.
I remember the sand.
The limping slaves.
The *exact* condition
of their death.
The terrible thing somehow happens
in the air.
Night in that Egypt. God! how cold
the stars must have been.

Tree slender as life,
and as tall
—green then! Where are the leaves
of that time? Why can't I think
these stars are the same stars?
Where do the souls of men have their spaces?

Shall I be obedient in that silver nudity?

The Unfulfilling Brightnesses

Thy servant I am
Immortal are thy lion-drunk deeps

As a flower thinks
So am I one with thee

Thou art my acquaintance
In the unlevel light

I am falling to sleep
In thy slaying forms

Where goeth the white wind
I have been
And believe

The Shapes and Intensities of This Man, This Confucius

However that principle of reason
Which we receive from the sky . . .
That unalterable target,
And in us tranquil
The harmony of result—Who brightens
Your perfection? What produces
The rooted order of the good action?
Is man evil, or the world?
Do I write in my system?
Does any other direct me?
Have I followed my own footsteps
In a land which I do not know?
Should I do the life I seem to have,
Or does it hold holes in my real fabric?

If the truth is inside,
And the form outside,
What is the truth of sleep?

What is the truth in the flame
Which eats at your rejoicing forms?

The Appian Way

The power!
The power alone.
A road is nothing. A people are nothing.
You will remember that six thousand
Soldiers of Sparta were nailed to posts
And crucified
Along this majestic floor of stone.
But you will not remember the shadows
They made . . . or their cries!
But I think of the road too.
Of the stones.
The legions of Marius, of Sulla,
Lucullus, Crassus—"the Roman
Might" . . . I think of the stones,
Where they came from, who shaped
Their edges. I wonder what man
Stood in the howling of Rome,
And bent down to touch the stones.
He was a man of power.

Attila

The hairy full stern face
Of the Hun.
The wonderful feasts and the singing
Of his bards.
I am the ruthless one,
Butcher of the weak.
I sought life,
And crushed it in my fist.
None stood against me;
I, Attila . . .

Light bubbles up in the east,
And in my tents men harness death
To their scarred arms—Aquileia,
Troyes, Padua—the caverned flames
And the buzzing plunder. It is
Good to feel the juice of thick roasts
On my chin; to shake the bells of power
In the face of the twittering world.

And I died peacefully in the arms
Of a beautiful young woman.

The First Crusades

This is the Cross!
The Turkish horde
Holding the Body and the Blood . . .
We the common people moving on the armies
Of darkness and sin—into Hungary
To murder and loot—
And we were butchered by the soldiers.
Now into the Rhineland,
Where we murdered the Jews—
And in turn were killed by the soldiers.
We put Antioch to siege;
Under new leaders, stormed Jerusalem—
And we entered the Church of the Holy Sepulchre,
Stepping over the bodies of the heathen dead.

The Cross!
A dirty piece of wood
In the hands of a madman . . .
We knew not what we did—
And the soldiers laughed at our screams.

263

"The Snow Is Deep on the Ground"

The snow is deep on the ground.
Always the light falls
Softly down on the hair of my belovèd.

This is a good world.
The war has failed.
God shall not forget us.
Who made the snow waits where love is.

Only a few go mad.
The sky moves in its whiteness
Like the withered hand of an old king.
God shall not forget us.
Who made the sky knows of our love.

The snow is beautiful on the ground.
And always the lights of heaven glow
Softly down on the hair of my belovèd.

Gautama in the Deer Park at Benares

In a hut of mud and fire
Sits this single man—"Not to want
Money, to want a life in the world,
To want no trinkets on my name"—
And he was rich; his life lives where
Death cannot go; his honor stares
At the sun.

The fawn sleeps. The little winds
Ruffle the earth's green hair. It is
Wonderful to live. My sword rusts

In the pleasant rain. I shall not think
Anymore. I touch the face of my friend;
He shows his dirty teeth as he scratches
At a flea—and we grin. It is warm
And the rice stirs usefully in our bellies.

The fawn raises its head—the sun floods
Its soft eye with the kingdoms of life—
I think we should all go to sleep now,
And not care anymore.

Mohammed

And to the kings of the world,
My greeting . . .
The Kaaba shall be thrown into the sea.

These are the dusty little streets of Medina.
Here my people live.
They are poor;
But riches wait in the One True God.
All men are one man in His wisdom.

My wives have soft breasts.
Their hair smells of my sweat.
I place my hands upon their eyes
And they know my hands; what
Is kind in them, what blackened
By my greed and cunning. For
I am a man of thirsts and hungers.

And to the great of the world,
My greeting . . .
The temples of God glow through the night.

To Be Holy, Be Wholly Your Own

Eternally given. Seek
The flowers of the

Soul.

Be an eye. Say
Soul. It is a fearful thing.
Hard and warm, it takes men
To do.

Moving weary the birds of men
Are too full of war to know
Flying.

These are lain in broken streets
Where death fills his jolly
Hands. He smiles. But love
Weeps.

Life and youth and the souls of men
Weep,
And are not comforted.

The Authority of Krajova

That time I made the winter journey
Into his village,
The red breath from my mouth
Stood on the snow like a shaking hand.
The first of his dogs bit through
My coat, tearing the flesh

Out of my wing sockets—and I shot it
Without anger. It was gray with little
Spinning blobs of yellow along the spine.

Krajova was hidden in a tree.
The deer were singing
In mountainous drifts. I knelt in the dark
And told his wife I had crossed the world
To see him. He is looking at something
In the air, she said; he will not know you.

I am not fooled by the singing of the deer,
I told her; it is too cold to be in a tree.
Then I shook the tree—
And a shriveled little skull fell into the snow.

This is the authority of Krajova! I shouted,
And I laughed bitterly.
But the deer are not singing now, a voice said.

The Slums

That should be obvious.
Of course it won't.
Any fool knows that.
Even in the winter.
Consider for a moment.
What?
Consider what!
They never have.
Why now?
Certainly it means nothing.
It's all a lie.

What else could it be?
That's right.
Sure.
Any way you look at it.
A silk hat.
A fat belly.
A nice church to squat in.
My holy ass . . .
What should they care about?
It's quaint.
Twelve kids on a fire escape . . . .
Flowers on the windowsill . . .
You're damn right.
That's the way it is.
That's just the way it is.

It Was a Bomby Evening

"A fire of birds sweeps down
The haunted wind
And gods of light walk through
This green wood"
                    Lazy Sam Parmalee

All fine lads in jest upon the yellow world . . .
These bright little cousins of the devil

Storming up like drunken trains
In the high beautiful air . . . and they truly sing
Of one quality for all men O they sing
Of the wide and snarling
Face of death

And we are all turned to their happy accomplice,
To this ordered hate, to this eventfully mortal place.

THE ABANDONED FOREST

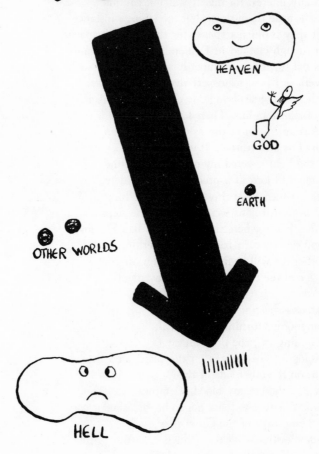

Pleasures of This Gentle Day

I expected to be greeted by one of the figures
Which stood beside the pier; more since
Their formal, black coats seemed to demand
A recognition, than because their presence
Had any interest for me. It was not caution
Which made them quiet; but the strange instance
That they could not speak—for they were stomachs,
And though clothed in fashion, their circumstance
Was not turned from the ordinary pursuits of such;
Indeed, as I bent to inspect the sodden planks
Of the ancient sea-bridge, I felt my hand taken
In soft horrible lips. Then I ran out across
The water. As far as the world is from sleep
I ran. The air breathed. It was not dark
But the light covered my eyes like a wound.
I seemed to look at a procession of maidens
Which issued from tiny caves behind life;
And beautiful lions were on fire at the steps
Of that house where the Great One had His love.
If you do not turn back now, something said,
Another use will be made of your forlornness;
But I had the touch of birds in my mouth,
And a
Heart was beating in my heart.
A languorous turning of arms . . .
Scaffolding . . . the dark music
Unfolds . . . hoofmarks on the black air . . .
Light on the other side of the
Sun . . . the creamy blood of statues . . . far-off,
Classic (neither to thaw nor to be tarnished),
Hard landscape of the *Other Iliad,*
Shadowless breast of the goddess . . . And
The masks are all in place (maturity
Of the carrion . . . companionless agony

In the charnel-houses of this day . . . soggy bread
Upon the matted tables of Ajanta). Yoh!
And walk upon the lea

Father Son flow bleed

Fled

bark fool bzzzzz

                         and the land of our
tight slowsoft luv   IN THIS WHOLLY GHOST

the stone deer drowse

to hunger

should fall so white a queen
O shudd fall so white a queen
O shudd fall so white a queen
O shudd fall so white a queen

O shudd fall so white a queen
O shudd fall so white a queen
O shudd fall so white a queen
O shudd fall so white a queen

"The Mule of Water"

The mule of water
Kicks his blustering heels
Into the snoutsmug faces of His Majesty's
Fleet . . . and their chins, which recede,
Drip a white cold blood onto his scornful flanks.

The Unnatural History of Peru

Who for their living lived
In joy
On a green ground.

O all in the heaven honey
Ate
With angels sweet and merry-heated.

In bluewhite January
They made their whole year.
Snowborn in that small,
Their lives were living.
In their going went God.

Who for their leading led
Pretty animals
Across the playing skies.

O each in that tower talling
Lay
And their kindling made love kind.

Who for their feeling felt
The caress
Of all hidden and happy creaturedom.

The Nervousness of Memory

My mother . . . (thy uneasy rust) . . .
I am patient with the angers of the mill
And with the honors of a dirty town
But I am worth something too . . .

I think the jewelry of hunger
Furnishes grace nowhere. Shelter me . . .
These are not false; they are ugly, cruel,
True to every evilness, these, my people,
My blood degree . . . they are what I am,
And what I will not be.

Class in English . . . (the lust of sparrows) . . .
The savage church and the sheriffs
Growing on the red vine of property . . .
A borrowed book . . . all I gathered,
The violet-fingered misery of the child,
The beautiful mystery of girls,
And ever a center in me—
To touch, feel, taste—that would do
What I willed done.

The doors painted with sickness
And unpaid rent . . .
Procuration of my indifferent slave.
But my native I am to cherish a finer realm.

Lunch Wagon on Highway 57

The big lad with too much face
And a voice fuzzed like a slice of grand larceny,
Pointed his fork at the counterjohnny,
Gulped twice, and said,
"Mice think the same as we do."
The countercluck drew one medium light,
Slopped it up nice all over the saucer,
Managed to get his thumb into the V,
And slide it over to a girl with brown hair
In a cutaway middyblouse tan mesh stockings

Lowheeled suede shoes candystick skirt
And a shoulderstrap purse who had been crying.
Beef went on, "Just because they're small,
And they ain't around much, most people
Most likely hardly know a mouse thinks at all."
Counter turned up the radio and the girl dug down
For her coffeenickel: . . . *of a why-it Chris-mus.*
"You got any ideas about mice?" the face asked her.
"Yeah, I got plentya ideas about both rats and mice."
He started with her rump and his eyes smacked
Their wire-lashed lips: "Maybe you could eat something?"
"Maybe I could . . . in the morning too."
"Sure thing. What you think I am, a piker?"
"Yeah, I know you're a piker."
She ate the hot pork on white with mashed,
Didn't want applepie or danish or cherry jello,
And the mouseboy left no tip when they went out.

The Battle of Unameit

Stirred . . . the fur-toothed graves
Of young boys . . . a thousand slain
In the time it would take to do love
With a pretty girl
Or think of a new God. The leagues
Of carrying the slaughter has . . . these fallen
Meanly touch death, their dying
Is such a used thing . . . O the moonplains
Of wandering their terrible hour chooses . . . This
Is a man. You are not to kill him.

This is a man. He has a poor time in the world.
You are not to kill him.
This is a man. There is a purpose in his being here.
You are not to kill him.

Eyes of the wounded . . . the shining tree
Rooted up by a monster. Shall they manage
To lie here in the rain? What do they cross to
In the smoke of so much terror?
This is a m a n. You are not to kill him.

The Man with the Golden Adam's Apple

There were four crates of chickens
Hanging from the topmost bough
Of an elm tree near the fairgrounds;
A Mack truck with a badly damaged fender
Was just pulling to a stop across the road,
When a lightly-clad old lady, her shawl
Draped like a tired wing, and with hip-boots
Of bright yellow fur on her shriveled-up legs,
Suddenly transformed herself into a shepherd boy,
And went crazy-running off over the horizon.
At that precise moment a door opened in the sky,
And the man with the golden Adam's apple
Stepped briskly down.

The driver of the Mack backed into a turnoff,
Gunned her up so hard she blew the muffler,
And then slouched limp at the big wheel,
A tiny black hole appearing "as if by magic"
In the middle of his forehead.
T m w t g A a holstered his deadly automatic,
Swore softly, and taking out a purple bandana,
Removed something from the crown of his Homburg.
He did not even then look up at the chickens;
Instead, being a fellow with a keen sense of proportion,
And mindful ever of his responsibility to society,
He built a fire and set up light-housekeeping in it.

Thinking Rock

It is not difficult to come here,
Here by the thinking rock.
It is in the way of all firm things,
Things that go into the soul.
For the souls of all firm things
Have a good way to the rock,
And the rock thinks well of them.
Not only men, but the waters, and the forest,
Have souls; morning, the darkness, rain,
Bear cubs, fog, and the wind: have souls;
And these, too, the rock thinks well of.
Beautifully.
And on the rock sits
The pretty Colleen.
About her head so fair and small
The white eyes of the air whirl
In happy solitude.
Glow deep, soul of man . . .
Let me make you climb
Into the weather
Of the beautiful Colleen.
Upon her breast so round and warm
The green heart of the earth stirs
From a winter sleep.

On a day after my death
I came to the thinking rock,
And, kneeling, kissed
The lovely Colleen.
Tell me, dear, I said,
The manner of this death
That I may not offend his bright circumstance.
Then laughed Colleen,
And she laughed as the sea laughs

When its blue legs encounter a new island,
And she said,
O death is only a word in a dull book . . .
Look! Look!
It is beginning to get beautiful again . . .
It is getting beautiful all over again . . .
Look! it dances!
It touches our faces . . .
O the beautiful again . . .
Always
The life of death dances.

May I lie beside you here, Colleen?
Do my hands offend your maidenhood?
Does my voice betray your innocence?
Because I know there is a place like this,
And as much purity,
And love,
And warmth,
And joy,
And I have seen thee, too, Colleen,
And I have known what to say,
And how to be,
And not to dirty with my hands,
Or my voice, or my anger, or my life,
But I have been weak
And I have wronged the beautiful.
Then she stood tall on the thinking rock,
And she said,
There is no purity in you, no faith,
No wisdom;
There is only the noise of these things.
What is pure cares not to be pure,
What has faith seeks not to believe,
What has wisdom needs less to know
Than to reject its knowledge.

On this day while I am alive, Colleen,
And as all around me hate
Divides the nations of the earth,
And murder shines his bloody claws
On every clean and good thing,
I truly believe
That the beautiful will come again . . .
That nothing can stay its coming . . .
O look; it dances!
It touches your faces . . .
Again and again, the beautiful . . .
Always and always
The life of life and death
Dances O
It so wonderfully cleanly dances.

"She Is the Prettiest of Creatures"

She is the prettiest of creatures
All like a queen is she

I have made a paper wheel
And I pin it to her dress

We lie together sometimes
And it is as nice as music
When you are half asleep

And then we want to cry because
We are so clean and warm
And sometimes it is raining
And the little drops scuttle
Like the feet of angels on the roof

I have made this poem tonight
And I pin it in her hair

For she is the prettiest of creatures
O all like a strange queen is she

Where Two O'clock Came From

The seventh dragon turned to his wife,
And, brushing a cloud out of her hair,
Said, If you think that much coal
Will last the winter, then you ought
To have your scales rechecked.
She burst into fire
And her tongue singed the beard
Of a crabby old gelbus who had his home
In a hollow hole. He sighed wearily
And quick-tailed the sky down.
You should not have done that,
The dragon's wife said; it looks pretty
Bare the way it is up there now.
But they could see some creatures
Sitting at a big table in the air,
And they were fumbling around
With something that looked like a clock.
It's a clock! shouted the old gelbus—
(No flies on him)—What time is it, boys?
We haven't decided yet, they yelled happily.
Make it nice and early, said the dragon;
And his wife called up, That suits me, too.
Then two it is, the creatures sang merrily,
Putting their faces inside the clock
And upsetting the table in their eagerness to find it.

"When the Stones Burst into Flame"

When the stones burst into flame
And the tameless meets his destroyer,
Will light break the star
And will the honor of men
Thunder at doors O will the good
Be dancing and the beautiful a shout
Spinning all their thieving cold thrones?

Suck at the blood.
Eat God.
Why sun?

Broken . . . .
La. La. Li. Saw a man die.
Bought a tree.

My friend, my mother, my space,
My abundance . . . (What is hurt?
O sing glorious!)
The stones burn in the fire
Of His overwhelming O the grass
Is dancing in the streets of my gray walking.

"There Are No Losses"

There are no losses.
There is only life.

Pear-smooth, cool face of a child . . .
Black cow wading in a green pond . . .
The crazy loft in an old building . . .
Sea comin in, honey

O Lord sea comin in
You will find the Lion
O Lord you will find the Lion
And war! War?
What is lost now is the world in this time.
Any peace they make is a lie.
Butchers are not interested in freedom;
The higher their talk, the bloodier their aims.
"Why don't you lead me to that rock?"

But there can be no losses.
There is only life for all men!

May I Ask You a Question, Mr. Youngstown Sheet & Tube?

Mean grimy houses, shades drawn
Against the yellow-brown smoke
That blows in
Every minute of every day. And
Every minute of every night. To bake a cake or have a baby,
With the taste of tar in your mouth. To wash clothes
      or fix supper,
With the taste of tar in your mouth. Ah, but the grand
      funerals . . .
Rain hitting down
On the shiny hearses. "And it's a fine man he was, such a comfort
To his old ma.—Struck cold in the flower of his youth."
      Bedrooms
Gray-dim with the rumor of old sweat and urine. Pot roasts
And boiled spuds; *Ranch Romances* and The Bleeding Heart
Of Our Dear Lord—"Be a good lad . . . run down to Tim's
And get this wee pail filled for your old father now." The kids

Come on like the green leaves in the spring, but I'm not spry
Anymore and the missus do lose the bloom from her soft cheek.
(And of a Saturday night then, in Tim O'Sullivan's
        Elite Tavern itself:
"It is a world of sadness we live in, Micky boy."
"Aye, that it is. And better we drink to that."
"This one more, for home is where I should be now."
"Aye, but where's the home for the soul of a man!"
"It's a frail woman ye act like, my Micky."
"And it be a dumb goose who hasn't a tear to shed this night.")

Rain dripping down from a rusty eavespout
Into the gray-fat cinders of the millyard . . .
The dayshift goes on in four minutes.

HOW OLD THE WORLD IS! And beautiful every
lasting thing . . . the throat of a girl; the vast delicacy
of the forests; the parts of the earth that are water,
and fields, and little towns; the way a mouth looks
when you bend to kiss it; the breathing of a child;
the silence of the untouched snow

A huge head tosses on the roof of the village.
Someone wanders from door to door calling,
Murphy! Murphy! Don't forget the lambchops.
(O we'll all sing one day!)

In a region near the pleasant wall
Two companies of soldiers are getting red.
You know how that goes. But new flutes
For better tunes, eh? Scrub the kitchen, lads,
The house is on fire. (O we'll all sing one day!)

282

They never get dirty . . . the fancies a man has . . .
Like now I can see a time when all the nations
Of the earth shall live together in peace and love,
And there will be no hatred or murder or fear . . .

A huge head tosses above the roof of the world.
Someone wanders from house to house calling,
    (Etc.)

"O My Darling Troubles Heaven with Her Loveliness"

O my darling troubles heaven
With her loveliness

She is made of such cloth
That the angels cry to see her

Little gods dwell where she moves
And their hands open golden boxes
For me to lie in

She is built of lilies and candy doves
And the youngest star wakens in her hair

She calls me with the music of silver bells
And at night we step into other worlds
Like birds flying through the red and yellow air
Of childhood

O she touches me with the tips of wonder
And the angels cuddle like sleepy kittens
At our side

"Of the Same Beauty Were Stars Made"

Of the same beauty were stars made
That they might guide their earthly sister
When she undertook the white still journey
Into the country of His gentle keeping.

I Sent a Mental to My Love

There were majesties.
Rain tilted his shining spears
Into the fat rump of the meadow.
The sheep wooled against one another
In fearful sessions, as
Lightning

Struck
An old tree near the brook
Where we first lay together.
I had not meant to tear her blouse
But she felt so soft and
Pretty, and her mouth tasted
Of blueberries.

The tree was split open like a fish
On a green counter, and in the middle
Of its heart, smiling as on that day,
Her face looked out at me.
Later, and I had cried,
I picked up one of the lambs.
But it only seemed like a thing
One would imagine doing then;
So I put it down as gently as I could,
And started walking fast back to the city.

She knows it's
raining and my
room is warm

but she is proud
and beautiful
and I have
no money

"For Whose Adornment"

For whose adornment the mouths
Of roses open in languorous speech;
And from whose grace the trees of heaven
Learn their white standing.

(I must go now to cash in the milk bottles
So I can phone somebody
For enough money for our supper.)

"Be Music, Night"

Be music, night,
That her sleep may go
Where angels have their pale tall choirs

Be a hand, sea,
That her dreams may watch
Thy guidesman touching the green flesh of the world

Be a voice, sky,
That her beauties may be counted
And the stars will tilt their quiet faces
Into the mirror of her loveliness

Be a road, earth,
That her walking may take thee
Where the towns of heaven lift their breathing spires

O be a world and a throne, God,
That her living may find its weather
And the souls of ancient bells in a child's book
Shall lead her into Thy wondrous house

THE IMPATIENT EXPLORER

INVENTS
A BOX IN WHICH
ALL JOURNEYS
MAY BE KEPT

"In Horror the God-thrown Lie"

In horror the God-thrown lie
Near the mouth . . .
Its teeth gleam.
In horror the God-thrown lie
Near the white mouth . . .
Its teeth close on their lives.
Its teeth close on their watching lives.

Have You Killed Your Man for Today?

In these hands, the cities; in my weather, the armies
Of better things than die
To the scaly music of war.

The different men, who are dead,
Had cunning; they sought green lives
In a world blacker than your world;
But you have nourished the taste of sickness
Until all other tastes are dull in your mouths;
It is only we who stand outside the steaming tents
Of hypocrisy and murder
Who are "sick"—
This is the health you want.

Yours is the health of the pig which roots up
The vines that would give him food;
Ours is the sickness of the deer which is shot
Because it is the activity of hunters to shoot him.

In your hands, the cities; in my world, the marching
Of nobler feet than walk down a road
Deep with the corpses of every sane and beautiful thing.

"Hold Thy Tongue, Death!"

Hold thy tongue, death!
Is it clear that you must not touch
The subjects of my dominion—
All her fair soft beauty . . .
The way her eyes look at me . . .

Investigation of Certain Interesting Questions

There were many houses like that in Canlin;
The doors of plated ivory, windows gummed over
With circus posters dated 1887, fine fountains
Gushing up out of the parlor rooms, chickens
Squatting sunfully on every roof, and the roofs
Shingled on their insides which left the brightly-colored
Wallpaper to amuse the sky and throw merriment
About the hills—but in only one of these houses
Did the lovely Cathy live, and it is to this house
That I lead you now
If you will so honor me . . .
It is a night late in the winter.
Cathy has just hung my coat near the fire,
And I have called hello to her father,
Who is in the pantry fixing himself a snack,
When the phone rings. After a reasonable time,
And nobody answering, it stops ringing.
"Did you have a useful day?" Cathy asks, taking
A book off the shelf and making a hurried comment
In its margin. I open a pack of cigarettes. "Yes and
No. The bargaining didn't get going until nine,
And by then Willowby was in a pretty bad mood,
But I did manage to check up on a few things."

"Do you really think Norden meant what he said?"
"If I knew that I'd have Kain dead to rights
On that Maipoer's affair—but, Cathy, how big
Was the actual turnout? Does it add up anywhere?"
"It adds up to this: if Tynis will make the contact
With Roymer before the fifteenth we shall know
Very definitely what the others hope to get out of it."
"But how can we be sure of Meesy . . . ?"
"Flarr has promised to consult Dykeman and
The odds are Bevens won't even come in on it,
Except to bluff Haggerty into tipping his hand."
"That still leaves Warner and Plinth to furnish
The evidence—it's obvious that Tomkins can't go
To Lannigan without some actual proof that Cark
And Sweet have already told Jalder's brother."
"Cathy!"
"Oh damn, what is it now? Yes, father . . .
Keep your britches on, I'm coming. Excuse me."
"Not at all. He's probably forgotten how to scramble eggs."
She chuckles to herself as she hurries out. Naturally
I fall into the error of my ways and begin a search
For the missing papers—not in the desk; between
The pages of a book? no; nor under the carpet . . .
"What are you doing down on the floor like that?"
"Oh . . . I was just looking for a glass of water."
"Well, you won't find it there; it's over
Under the sofa by the cellarway. And let
The rabbits out as you come past please."
While I stand drinking the water, I kick up
The cover on the rabbit-box. "There're a lot more
Here than you had last time, Cathy," I say,
Trying to keep my feet as they charge by me.
She chuckles to herself again, and this time
I hear her. "What are you snickering about?"
"I'm sorry, but you looked so funny that day
The man was asking you all those questions."

"I don't see what was so funny . . . I did fairly well,
Considering the nerve he had barging in on us."
"You were afraid of him."
"Don't be an idiot, Cathy."
"Then why did you get so angry?"
"Suppose I did . . . who was he to question me?"
"Why were you afraid of him?"
I take three rabbits off the back of my neck,
And drop-kick them into the pantry.
"Cathy!"
"Father, for God's sake! . . . Please excuse me."
"Not at all, I'm sure. Bring me a match, will you?"
"So that's why you've been eating your cigarettes . . ."
Left alone in the room now I stare at the wall.
The snow has drifted in over the body of Cathy's mother,
And the rabbits have fallen asleep in furry bundles.
"Sorry I took so long. Father had another spell."
"I suppose you could have answered his questions?"
"I know what death is."
"It's hardly fair to take the easy ones . . ."
"All right, something hard then."
"The first one he asked me . . . the meaning of life."
"There are as many meanings as there are lives."
"And has each a meaning unto itself?"
"Each life has its meaning in all."
"For Christ's sake, Cathy . . ."
I stroke the cat and toss the bag aside.
"Then you did know Who He was."
I place my arms around her.
"Yes, I knew Him. Please don't cry."
"Nothing seems real or good anymore . . .
Words have meaning, but what is in us
Has no meaning."
I open a marked deck and cut for deal.
"What is in us, Cathy, we know . . .
And words need not know."

291

Anna Karenina and the Love-sick River

I bought the river from an old man
For fifty-two cents
Cash money. Housed sensibly in a plow shed
On my cousin's place, he was happy enough
Until Anna Karenina came to live with us.
It may only have been that the sound and the smell
Of her voice and her hair got under my river's skin;
Or that the way she walked reminded him
Of his pretty home in Minnettha valley;
In any event, in an effort to be realistic
About this thing,
I shall leave the matter of Anna and the river
For a moment to tell you this about myself:
When I was five years old my father got hurt
Very badly in the mill; they carried him in
Through the kitchen of our house—two men
At his head, two at his feet—and carted him upstairs.
The point is this: during the quarter of a century
My father spent in the mills, never once
Did he come from work through the front door;
And the men who brought him home that day
Took the trouble to lug him in by the kitchen.
This is one of the most beautiful things I know about.
Why?
Perhaps because . . .
I'm afraid you've got me there.
Maybe you can tell me why Anna Karenina
Made such a damn dope out of my little river. . . ?

The Murder of Two Men by a Young Kid Wearing Lemon-colored Gloves

Wait.

Wait.

Wait.

Wait. Wait.

Wait.

Wait.

Wait.

Wait.

Wait.

Wait.

Wait.

Wait.

Wait.

NOW.

The Knowledge of Old Towns

In the eaves of the barn
A swallow has her nest.

On the ground sits a little girl.
Her face is buried in her hands
And she weeps bitterly.

An old woman pares her toenails
In the sun.
Her armpits smell of death.

Straight off in the air a valiant army
Moves its thousand sores. Flies stir
On the frenzied banners. Armies
Are not delicious to crack between
Your teeth. The wounded moan
And ask piteously for water.
Words like honor taste like
Hair in their mouths.

The swallow preens her feathers
In the warm sun.

"The Carts of the Wee Blind Lass"

The carts of the wee blind lass
Were covered with silvery wool
That shone on the road
Like sheep walking with God.
Her hair was caught in a fine knot
At the toe of her brain, and her eyes

Had been painted over by imps of heaven.
She held her name in a little dish,
And always at crossings she cried it.

The carts were pulled by horses
Fashioned of mountain-bones
And the anger of yellow eagles.
Their wheels rolled on a single track
That led a little above the air.

And what sell ye, my pretty?
It is nothing I sell, true sir.

Then what do ye bring? O lassie, say . . .
It is apples I bring. Yet none for you.

Now tell me short the name of this good lad
That I may send him spinning . . .
Then spin the devil, my happy wit;
For my apples are for him.
O take my pretty apples, Mr. Dark!

O all my juicy ripe apples are for Thee!

"And When Freedom Is Achieved . . ."

You have used a word
Which means nothing.
You have given a word
The power to send men to death.
Men are not free who are sent to die.
Only those who send them are "free."
You should have freedom stuffed down your fat throats.

"O Terrible Is the Highest Thing"

O terrible is the highest thing . . .
So be death beautiful to my love.

His nearing wings disturb my sleep . . .
So be moon bright on her lonely way.

The acts of heaven hasten my pretty fair . . .
So be God bountiful to her sweet quality.

O beautiful is the highest thing . . .
So be the angels blinded in her new holiness.

To Say if You Love Someone

O pretty village . . . aye, mine own home . . .
Lamps as yellow as ancient birds . . . here my
Love is . . .
Her breasts grow roses under my hands . . .
Her shoulders have the mark of my teeth upon them . . .
God, jewel the wind to a softer key
That her sleep be ornamented round
As halls the angels splendor in . . .
For we are tired in the green tall play
Of our bodies
And she lies so warm and sweet in my arms

O all the bright summer . . . chamber
Of our kingdom . . . here my maleness
Had its wild design . . . joyful in the land
Of that strangest farmer
A savage wonder made our every climate sing . . .

O God, such is the hospitality of my love
That the husbands of the great mysteries
Built cities near our bed,
And their white chaste daughters spun cloth
That we might be seemly clothed
When we turn from our dazzling occupation

For soon we are going to sleep

Now I Went Down to the Ringside and Little Henry Armstrong Was There

They've got some pretty horses up in the long dark mountains.
Get him, boy!

They've got some nifty riders away yonder on that big sad road.
Get him, boy!

They've got some tall talk off in that damn fine garden.
Get him, boy!

When you can't use your left, then let the right go.
When your arms get tired, hit him with a wing.
When you can't see very good, smell where he is.

They've got some juicy steaks in that nice sweet by-and-by.
Get him, boy!

They've got a lot of poor black lads in that crummy old jailhouse.
Get him, boy!

O they've got a lot of clean bunks up in their big wide blue sky.
That's his number, boy!

My Coat Is Dirty

They had taken off their sandals,
And their naked feet dipped into the black water
Which ran along the earth's other coast.
Those sandals were of angel's skins,
And on the toe of each flamed an infant star.

Two miles away a tree was just beginning to grow,
And I wanted to care in its life
Until the tiger had eaten the sky;
But they said, fingering those sandals so bonny,
You may not leave our side, Oh you may not go
Before man has touched his sparkling career.
That tiger had a crimson voice,
And all the hills about swayed in his talk.

A thousand years away a being had its home,
And I wanted to take it my heart
Because something dwelt there like love
O like when you cry you cry to God alone;
But they told me, wiggling their feet in joy,
You may not know the beautiful
Until you have drowned in the waters of our coast.
Those waters were choked with the skeletons
Of what I thought must be the soul's own creature.

A billion lives away the instruments of perfection
Were readied for the highest human-thing,
And I wanted to kneel down in their light;
But they said, as they tore at my clothes,
You may not think of them, Oh you may not tarnish
Their pure design with your tiny occupation
Until the tiger and the sky and the black water
Have fashioned you a coat that will fit your God.

That coat, which they had torn from my nakedness,
I throw out over the world . . .
And I think it will fit the world.

"Ah, God, Dear Brother,
the Mild and Frowning Rose"

In the day of this evil no man a man shall be until his own death is under-
stood to be meaningless to the ends of the State. What is constant for good
in him must be denied acquaintance with their undertaking; it is as foolish
to die against them as for them. Save when it is in his own conflict—*and
for his own purpose.*

from The Confessions of a Saneman

Ah, God, dear Brother, the mild and frowning rose
Opens under the golden breath of morning;
Pale clerks and sandy factoryhands rattle turnstiles
In bathtub caves of the I R T; Mrs. Mike Grunnet
Sloshes up the last marble inch in the lobby of R C;
Nasty Ned and Sweet Little Flo pause for a last kiss
Before sheeping out to knock off a lad at 23rd & Ninth
And get those invoices ready for Roberts Produce before ten,
Respectively; armies stir in the hairy thick cancer of Europe,
Their eyes fixed on death, their ears quick to the sound
Of the voice of death; the excellent animal begins the work
Of his day—Ah, God, dear brother, the rose that opens here
Is truly the insignia of a terrible garden

What is your share?

Hark ho! Billy Joe . . . why do they chase you?
Funny fox . . . strange tall fox . . .
He died. He died. He really died.

Now you die too.

"House, and a Dead Man in It"

House. ———————————————— House, and
                                   a dead man in it.
Hill, with
a gallows on it. ———————————— Hill.
Life. ———————————————— Life, and no one
                                   to live honestly.
Flame, and
all things dark. ——————————— Flame.
Love. ———————————————— Love, and only
                                   the murder of men.
The good, and
is it going mad. ———————————— The good.
Youth. ——————————— Youth, and the ground
                                   covers its proud singing.
Hope, and what
shall we hope? ———————————— Hope.
Death. ——————————— Death, and we are
                                   commanded to die.
World, and the
lean rifles fondle it. ———————— World.
Peace. ——————————— Peace, and the soul
                                   of man is crying tonight.
Heart, O the time
of sickness is upon us. ———————— Heart.
Man. ——————————— Man, and his works
                                   are of no importance now.

                    Pretty blood O smear
                    the pretty pretty blood
                    all over your hands
                    and into your lives

300

HOW TO BE AN ARMY

 MANY SHOES · POTATOES   FLAGS & FLEAS

 RIFLES

TRENCHES

 DETERMINATION

\>\>\>\>\>\>\>\>\>\>\>\>\>\>\>\>\>
KNOWLEDGE OF MARCHING

$$\frac{58207}{27850} = \textbf{BLOOD}$$

+(GENERALS)

AND A FAITH IN THE RIGHT

††††††††††††††††††††††††††
†††††††††††††††††††††††††
††††††††††††††††††††††††††††
††††††††††††††††††††††††††
†††††††††††††††††††††††††††
††††††††††††††††††††††††††

The Tribes of Rakala

They prefer to sleep on tiny colored stones
Which are scattered over great golden mats
And glued down by pretty children
Who are grown for this purpose.
In the morning it may chance that wolves
Have eaten everybody, though this happens
But rarely now. However, the redder ones,
And those whose fins are most transparent,
Often scold each other; and the frozen heart
Bleeds its cold blood out over their land.

"To the hanging!" they sing; "O to the hanging
Near the throne of God!" What does that mean?
I ask them; but this leads me into trouble,
For they seem to resent all stupid questions.
So we begin to dig cities out of the ground,
And they show me how to build stars from webs
Of fire and I hitch trees to my cart and drive
Upon the enemies of life.
It is usually too light to see.
To the judgment! I shout; O to the judgment
Near the throne of God! "What do you mean?"
They ask me; and, taking the price tags off heaven,
I put my arms around them—I advise my reader dear
To turn this page before I tell him what I mean.

Easy Rider

They told me I might hold the fairest one
Until the murder got finished down in the valley.
"Down in the valley, valley so low . . ."

But it grew dark that quickly I couldn't see
To hold anything very well, and the knocking
At the door came on hard through the screams
Of those outside. "Are you afraid, little one?"
I asked her, moving my hand up over the face.
"Not if there be a God," she answered, beginning
To stir in my arms like a cat settling itself.
A blue light went on,
And as quickly off again . . . "Did you see them, too,
My little one?" I whispered. She started to cry
And I took my hand away from the face.
"They were all . . ."
"Yes, little one?"
She didn't speak again and my hand moved up
Over the face. "If there be a God . . ." I said
Very softly into her hair.
Then the door opened and seven came in.
They were usual enough save for their heads
Which glowed like great lamps.
We shook hands in a little circle
And I questioned them about their world.
They smiled almost shyly at me,
Pointing to a spot on the floor.
The tiniest lion I had ever seen
Was sleeping there, its paws closed over
A little ball. "Pick it up," they told me.
I placed her on a thagen chair, smoothing
Out her dress that she might be prim.
"Are you afraid to pick it up?" they said,
And I noticed that their arms had been cut off
At the shoulder. A singing began
As I grabbed the ball away from the tiny lion—
"O away from that tiny lion . . ."
And I felt my life beat in my hand.
"O beat in his fine hand . . ."

I threw it then at the first of seven,
And my mother's face shone at the window;
It seemed to be trying to warn me of something,
But when I ran there it had gone;
And I threw the ball at the second of seven.
My father's body fell out of a cupboard,
And when I ran to help it up, a band
Started to play and soldiers marched
Over it in a very dragon of glee.
The third I threw and my brother said
"You're making a fool of yourself when
All this time you could have had a good job . . ."
With the fourth and fifth the years I hated
Sprang into my throat and everyone
I had ever betrayed seemed to be crying
All at once—and the sixth I threw—
"And the sixth he threw . . ."
And the seventh—
"*And* the fatal seventh . . ."
Then every dark thing howled and the seven
Put their hands upon her—
"What have you got to eat here anyway?"
They demanded. I gave them warmed-over
Duck and thick slices of thagen bread,
Which they washed down with hard cider.
Soon they were nodding their golden heads
By the fire, and very quietly, not to wake them,
I cranked the phonograph
And put Ma Rainey on.
"O he put Mother Rainey on . . ."
Then I knelt beside my sleeping fair,
And whispered into her hair, "O my little one,
O my pretty one . . ."
But she did not wake,
And my hand moved up again over His face.

The Colony of the Sun

We did at last manage to get the eyes
Of Dolina on us, but, as I wrote to my brother,
The misunderstanding was of too old date
To employ his complete sufferance in our cause,
Particularly since Polly and I both grew up
In the Colony of the Sun, and our employment of talk
Had a turn away from the so-called professional world
Into rather better channels, that is, we liked
Each other enough not to want to kill anybody else,
Or to do much of anything except hold our citizenship
In the universe of all men, where the exciting events
Are things like the taste of good food, and the color
Of a girl's hair, and the way cats walk, and forests
Look in rain and snow, and the bearing of the sky
As it fills with stars, and how the earth smells
When you plant something in it—but I'm wandering away
From my story—the very fact that Polly and I
Loved each other was enough to prejudice Dolina
Against us, for he liked neither her nor me; and
That's what this is about.
I first met Polly in a freight elevator in Toledo.
What she was doing in a freight elevator I don't know;
As for me, I had a job running it.
We had dinner that night in Anthony's Chop House
On Lemer Street, near where the old Strand Theatre
Used to be; and it couldn't have been loveatfirstsight
Because I didn't see her again for almost ten years.
A lot of things happened to me in the meantime, of course;
And in a minute I'll tell you what happened to Polly.
With me the little wheels went round . . .
I worked in Seattle for a while repairing refrigerators;
In Ft. Worth it was selling ladies' sheer undergarments;
In Richmond, nursemaid to an old gent with a soft pate;
In Tulsa, three months in a Chinese barbershop, shining;
I dove for pearls in a ketchup joint in Saint Louis;

Lumbered a bit up near Thief River Falls;
Then on to Montgomery, Carson City, Pittsburgh,
Memphis, Flagstaff; with shovel, wrench, hammer, drill;
Loaded down with samples of hair tonic, saddlesoap, books,
Filing cabinets, phonographs, jockey's shirts, boots, mouth-
Wash and baby preventers; and it all wasn't smooth
Sailing either—four months in hospitals, two years
In jails, and seven weeks as the husband of a circus freak
With the oiliest tongue and dimmest brain of any creature
This side of Congress. But I had a better time than Polly.
To put it cold, Polly had gotten round to being a whore
When I saw her again in Colorado. Her face
Had started to fall in, and her eyes looked like stones
Yellowed by the rain. But her teeth were still pretty
Good, and her breath sweetened up when she had been
Away from the bottle for a week. Now, the size
Of a person is what's in him, and that's the way
It was with Polly and me.
Dolina has told you that we had no right
To live in the Colony of the Sun;
But I believe I can convince you that we did.
It started simply enough.
I was telling Polly how a fellow had beaten me out
Of fifty bucks in a deal to sell horses in Laramie,
When she said, "Don't you remember how beautiful
        their hands were?"
I said, "Huh!" thinking she had snared a bottle somewhere.
"And the way we'd sit in the evening and they'd come down
To talk to us . . . all about the fun they had . . ."
"Fun? What fun? Where?"
"In the sky of course. And how nobody was ever hungry,
And no pawing over each other . . ."
"I know it was tough, honey, but . . ."
"And nobody ever called them names or made them cry."
"Sure. Sure thing. I'm beginning to remember . . .
Now that you mention it. All them fancy wings they had . . ."
"Wings? They didn't have any wings. They were just like

You and me . . . except they were so clean and happy . . .
Like . . . like . . ."
"Like angels maybe . . . ?"
"Just like the sun! And it didn't matter to them
What anybody said . . ."
"Ah, honey . . . look now, don't cry. I'll get a good job
First thing in the morning. Then, soon as I'm on my feet,
We'll get hitched regular—just like other people—
And you'll have pretty dresses and get your hair fixed . . ."
"And you were always good to me when they were around.
You'd kiss me so soft, and your arms felt like
They wanted to tell me things just like they said . . .
How everybody could be good to a person . . .
But I don't care now!
I don't care!
Let them say anything . . . let them follow me in the street . . .
Let them whisper if they like . . . sure, I'm not good enough . . .
Make fun of me . . . I know what you think . . . why don't you
Say it—that I'm sick, that nobody would want to touch me . . .
No, wait. Please. I didn't mean it. I'm tired.
I . . ."
You see how I lied to you.
I made up that Dolina stuff, and about the Colony.
I don't know how to say it.
I could tell Polly, and she'd understand,
But it's too late for that now . . .
They've got poor Polly off in a cell on the hill,
And what she says to those sun-people of hers
Must be pretty hard for God to listen to.

"The Animal I Wanted"

The animal I wanted
Couldn't get into the world . . .
I can hear it crying
When I sit like this away from life.

O Fill Your Sack with Tiger Cubs

Of keeping; the competition of brutal law;
Splendid romp of winter; and the moon—
That cold cat in her twinkling prison,
Eating the slime of women and rubbing
Her creamy fur against the purpose of the world;
When men sleep, and the finer flames—caves,
Too, sad chill brown hair flecking their mouths;
And the rocks, again brown and blown, that are
Like fruit a monster would eat; music
The sea has, the velvet voices of the drowned;
Corks of importance, those ships of Caesar;
Midnight snack of sweet resolve; though I make
No complaint; for there is the cypress and the shadow
Of The Just on the earth; and, curling like
The angry fingers of the whirlpool, the harvest
Of blood awaits the terrible farmers of Their war;
So a faint breathing in the wound; the bannered
Valleys rise to the wind; death fills his clapping lungs
And something cries—O angel deep in the water!

And the snake swings his ghost
Through the loud weather of my running.
I touch the wing.
Now churning tents abide Your reverence.
A little dog, tired of heaven,
Trots into the jeweled head and falls asleep.
Wink wide. Who are these? Why is this
Stolen? My question to You is:
What have You really provided? Just this rag
We wipe our living on . . .
The deribude grass
And the white blind road
Going nowhere. My weapons, my sport, my limits . . .
I intend that You listen!
The leprous eye blooks open . . . (For beauty?

For what is pure?) And it is easier to burn.
Wind blowing through the gray sun . . .
By the flaming rock stands Your terrible child.
Ah wee dear rain wilt thou fall
And falling
Rise again?

Above the whale road toss the shabby cathedrals
Of this tempest . . . pulleys—food, love, water,
The greenwhitelonelybrightwindows of the soul . . .
Morning keeps great kiddish flocks
In crazy pens; a fire of birds sweeps down
These haunted lands . . . And it is wiser to burn.

Ferns of hell . . .
The destiny of greasy lads . . . Ropes! Straw! To grin!
It cannot see out
The monsterkind glands of murder spewing into Your sons
As this manscape sickens unto the dark bitch.
Ah wee pure rain wilt thou fall
And falling
Rise ever again?

And into the black Fire speak my name.

What Is the Beautiful?

The narrowing line.
Walking on the burning ground.
The ledges of stone.
Owlfish wading near the horizon.
Unrest in the outer districts.

Pause.

And begin again.
Needles through the eye.
Bodies cracked open like nuts.
Must have a place.
Dog has a place.

Pause.

And begin again.
Tents in the sultry weather.
Rifles hate holds.
Who is right?
Was Christ?
Is it wrong to love all men?

Pause.

And begin again.
Contagion of murder.
But the small whip hits back.
This is my life, Caesar.
I think it is good to live.

Pause.

And begin again.
Perhaps the shapes will open.
Will flying fly?
Will singing have a song?
Will the shapes of evil fall?
Will the lives of men grow clean?
Will the power be for good?
Will the power of man find its sun?

Will the power of man flame as a sun?
Will the power of man turn against death?
Who is right?
Is war?

Pause.

And begin again.
A narrow line.
Walking on the beautiful ground.
A ledge of fire.
It would take little to be free.
That no man hate another man,
Because he is black,
Because he is yellow;
Because he is white;
Or because he is English;
Or German;
Or rich;
Or poor;
Because we are everyman.

Pause.

And begin again.
It would take little to be free.
That no man live at the expense of another.
Because no man can own what belongs to all.
Because no man can kill what all must use.
Because no man can lie when all are betrayed.
Because no man can hate when all are hated.

And begin again.
I know that the shapes will open.
Flying will fly, and singing will sing.

Because the only power of man is in good.
And all evil shall fail.
Because evil does not work,
Because the white man and the black man,
The Englishman and the German,
Are not real things.
They are only pictures of things.
Their shapes, like the shapes of the tree
And the flower, have no lives in names or signs;
They are their lives, and the real is in them.
And what is real shall have life always.

Pause.

I believe in the truth.
I believe that every good thought I have,
All men shall have.
I believe that what is best in me,
Shall be found in every man.
I believe that only the beautiful
Shall survive on the earth.

I believe that the perfect shape of everything
Has been prepared;
And, that we do not fit our own
Is of little consequence.
Man beckons to man on this terrible road.
I believe that we are going into the darkness now;
Hundreds of years will pass before the light
Shines over the world of all men . . .
And I am blinded by its splendor.

Pause.

And begin again.

For the Mother of My Mother's Mother

Wind. Flower. Pretty village.
1847.

This is the autumn, Jenny.
Leaves scratch
The lowest star.
Green are the leaves, Jenny.

Pleasure in a warm young body . . .

Dogs snap
At the sullen moon.
Cruel are the dogs, Jenny.
They do their crazysad love
Over your sleeping face.
Snow. Rain. A bad world.

"These Are My Great Ones"

These are my great ones . . .
days like cabbages rolling out
on the green floor of the world
to be eaten with sunny spoons
in this huge weather
that my joy needs
where I am
its son as a thin cord
the kite's
and a god on a pale fence
watching
death and life romp through the bright pasturage of towns
and seas and flakes of boys teasing a giant who holds a bloody gun

to the head of my hunting O look I have found
a pretty creature I think it is a man though the face
has been shot away and the hands are not caressing anything
beautiful they are caressing
a grave and the light does not come here O now you will
    need them
my great ones and I say take them take them put your tongue
on their fullness O there is a beautiful
and it lives in simple things
an orchard of sweet pears
a hut on the fragrant shore of the woods
girls with straw bonnets picking Queen Anne's lace
and the lives of men
and the lives of this year and of the next thousand years O
and the lives and the deaths of all things on earth

Lives of the Swan

(A Little Song for Myself)

Black teeth
Seek the pale ropes which bind life
To a usual career

I am tired cries the swan
I am tired cries the brutal swan
O I am tired cries the terrible one

I am tired of this white deceit
I am tired of all my silken kind
I am tired of what lives and what dies

What can I do now cries the swan
What can I do now cries the gentle swan
O what can I do now cries that poor lost fool

Instructions for Angels

Take the useful events
For your tall.
Red mouth.
Blue weather.
To hell with power and hate and war.

The mouth of a pretty girl . . .
The weather in the highest soul . . .
Put the tips of your fingers
On a baby man;
Teach him to be beautiful.
To hell with power and hate and war.

Tell God that we like
The rain, and snow, and flowers,
And trees, and all things gentle and clean
That have growth on the earth.
White winds.
Golden fields.
To hell with power and hate and war.

The Billion Freedoms

Yes, then, always, as the rain, a star,
Or snow, the snow, snow,
Faces in the village, many dead on the roads
Of Europe, guns, go, yell, fall, O wait, what
Does life do, I know, knew, go mad, life goes
Mad, as the gentle rain, run, as the cold death
Comes into, into you, into the
Star-being man, is it quiet, quiet in the ground,

I grin, gunned silly, noble, is it noble to be part
Of, of the lie, it is a lie, war is, war is a lie,
What else is war, war is only a lie, love is not
A lie, love is greater, O love is greater
Than, war, wake my brothers, love is not a, lie,
Live, as the earth, as the, sun,
Stand in the beautiful, be, as the clean, full, fine,
Strong lives stood, hated, mocked, despised, drowned
In the sewers of poverty,
And in the sewers of the State, as Christ, was, for
He believed in life,
He believed in love, and in death, and war, and greed,
He did not believe, and any man who speaks
Of a Christian war, or of war as the savior
Of anything, that man is a liar, and
A, murderer, for no man can acquire position,
Or goods, or self-righteousness
In a lie, except he be himself an enemy of truth,
And life, and God,
And a defiler in the temple of his kind, faces
In the villages of the world, millions dead
On the roads of Europe, what sin against reason
Is this, that they fought, fight, in a war
To save the evils
That cause war, for war is no evil
To those who have warred against the people,
And against truth, always, what crime
Against the soul of man is this, this fraud,
This mockery of life, that what is cheapest,
And dirtiest, and most debased, is thus smugly
Stamped on the forehead of, Christ, Who said,
Says, in the authority of God, thou shalt not
Kill or take from another, O what are men
For, or God, now, as the light, and the good,
And the truth, and the love of one poor creature

For his fellow, fall, and the grandeur
Of mankind, like a blind snake,
Crawls, on its belly, into the slimy
Pit of oblivion, yes, then, always, as the rain,
A star, or as a fire burning forever in, all men.

"How Silent Are the Things of Heaven"

How silent are the things of heaven

The air must be kind
To the clouds and stars
That they never
Cry out
Or tear their lives away
From Thee
As we do
And have done

God, how silent are Thy fair children
That they never
Scream in fear
Or kill their sweet kind
In Thy name
As we do
And have forever done

O how silent are all heavenly things
And joyous in Thy white country
That they never howl
Like beasts in a bloody wood
As we do
And have done O Thou
Wouldst go mad in the noise of this grave

The Continual Ministry of Thy Anger

The kill of loose-voiced reason . . .
Oil of heaven falling
On the sweat of towns . . .
What cold is,
Grass,
The ages of mankind, what gains light
And is a prey in my tusky sleep, what puts
Me at rage
Or to love
And to die.

Health to the lonely one,
Art in his teeth
Like a flaming star.
Death to the profane,
Who wears his art like a shoe
To take him into easier places.
For what the cold is, and grass, and men,
And to sleep, and to be angry, and to love,
And to die,
Artists do not know;
But art knows,
And is always waiting, and clean.

"It Is Big Inside a Man"

Furtively sounding
In the high
Halls of God, the voice which is
Life begins to sing.
You will listen, Oh you will not be afraid
To listen . . .

319

All these do:
The wolf, the fengy, the bear, the wide
Fish; and the deer, the silky rat, the snail,
The onises—even the goat
That waves his funny tail at trains
Is listening.
Do you now faintly
Hear the voice of life?
I will allow you respect for
Red apples and countries warm
With the races of men; peep over
The transom at China if you like;
But I will have no hatred or fear
Entering this poem.

It is big
Inside a man.
It is soft and beautiful
In him.
Water and the lands of the earth
Meet there.
I hand you a mountain.
I take the word Europe
Or the word death
And tear them into tiny pieces;
I scatter them at your feet.

Hand me a star.
Take me to a new city.
You are wasting your lives.
You are going along with your pockets
Full of trash.
You have been taught to want only the ugly
And the small;
You have been taught to hate what is clean
And of the star.

A dog will throw up
When he is sick;
Are you lower than dogs
That you keep it all down—
And cram more in?

The voice which is life
Shall sound over all the earth,
And over all who lie deep
In its green arms—
Go you to lie there as a fool, or as a child,
Tired from his beautiful playing,
To fall happily asleep?

"Rest, Heart of the Tired World"

Rest, heart of the tired world.
Hush . . . go to sleep.
Men and cities keep their cold terrible watches,
And the ocean frets at these naked lands of pain.
O hushaby . . . and go to sleep.

This red rain . . .
To breathe . . .
To weep . . .
To love where only murder has been wooed . . .
To find youth, and faith, and all their quick kin,
Buried deep in talking halls of horror . . .
No.
It is that we cannot see,
That we cannot hear,
That we cannot smell,
Or taste, or feel, or think;
For surely no will in heaven or earth
Could endure what we seem to possess;

321

We live in the shadow of a greater shadow—
But there is the sun!
And from him man shall have life,
And he shall have redress from the crimes
Of his most brutal habitation . . .

O rest, heart of the tired world.
Hush . . . and go to sleep.
There is a beautiful work for all men to do,
And we shall at last wake into the sun.

"O Fiery River"

O fiery river
Flow out over the land.
Men have destroyed the roads of wonder,
And their cities squat like black toads
In the orchards of life.
Nothing is clean, or real, or as a girl,
Naked to love, or to be a man with.
The arts of this American land
Stink in the air of mountains;
What has made these men sick rats
That they find out every cheap hole?
How can these squeak of greatness?
Push your drugstore-culture into the sewer
With the rest of your creation.
The bell wasn't meant to toll for you.
Keep your filthy little hands off it.

O fiery river
Spread over this American land.
Drown out the falsity, the smug contempt
For what does not pay . . .
What would you pay Christ to die again?

from *An Astonished Eye Looks Out of the Air* (1945)

"The Stars Go to Sleep So Peacefully"

The stars go to sleep so peacefully . . .
Their high gentle eyes closing like white flowers
In a child's dream of paradise.

With the morning, in house after grim house,
In a haste of money, proper to kiss their war,
These noble little fools awake.

O the soul of the world is dead . . .
Truth rots in a bloody ditch;
And love is impaled on a million bayonets

But great God! the stars go to sleep so peacefully

"I Always Return to This Place"

I always return to this place . . .

Roar and howl in the leaf! The astonished eye
Looking out of the air at me

O the astonished eye looking out of the air
At me—I always return to this place,
To this Gate, this Throne, this dread Altar—

I always return to the Mystery . . . *The astonished eye
Looking out of the air at me*

And I think there is nothing in the world but the Mystery

The Dazzling Burden

A great automobile turns slowly in
At the gate.
Two men and a little girl get down
And stand near
The King.
Now the doors of the ancient house open
And a black lion appears. Wings flutter
In the air.
Suddenly the people are crying.
But the King and the black
Lion watch the wings
That flutter just overhead . . .

And their eyes are not afraid
O their eyes are not afraid at all.

This Summer Day

You bring me Ocean Star a dreaming Song
that shakes the Bones of Apples
and makes a Church in this Snake's Head

—above the living—irrecoverably
a Bright Heart Goes Down—but every
Sign from Thee is beautiful O I love

this weary little rain—
the sadness of knees—O are ye in love with
brown woods and the silver tinkle
of evening birds? (Immortal? why
yes! a thinking book on a white table.

O Death must be this little girl
pushing her blue cart into the water.
O all Life must be this crowd of kids
watching a hummingbird fly around itself.)
And there is an Ear. And a Golden Heart.
And This Unclosing Eye.

There is a man wading in the river . . .
A woman baking little cakes . . .
There is a village we will come to—
O there are arms for us!
A tree of remembering stars—
There is This Unkneeling Flame—

This sudden beautiful *excitement*—
O have ye buckets great enough
to catch so much Wonder in!

It Depends on Whose Science

"the finest
lad of all is Mr
Natures (sp. b'kw'ds) who stands bravely by
to give the angels a blood test"

   BUT
damn my britches it'll be a long nose
that hasn't got a face back of it
(and and and AND
the muskrat you take for Christ's sake
the lowly rastmuk
Building! his! damn! little! house!
right! at! the! water's! side!)

"Beings So Hideous That the Air Weeps Blood"

Beings so hideous that the air weeps blood
And the forehead of God shrivels,
Advance toward us.
Smiling they hand Mrs. Buell a tin pail
Of soldiers' livers and other modern delights.

Mrs. Buell looks hopefully at Alfred:
"Tell me, dear, what are we to do now?"
"Just sit tight until the soul plasma gets here."

Lubby Stevers grins. He lifts his right leg
And squirts all over Christ.
"Here's one we haven't killed yet," he exclaims
Happily. "Let's pull his
You-know-what off first, though . . ."
"Oh, goodie, goodie," cries Hubbie, "it'll make
Such a nice trinket for my Missus."

Ah! a noble work is man . . .
Ah! a noble day for the Civilized Nations . . .

But I'd advise you to sit pretty tight
Until the soul plasma gets here.

I Feel Drunk All the Time

Jesus it's beautiful!
Great mother of big apples it is a pretty
World!

You're a bastard Mr. Death
And I wish you didn't have no look-in here.

326

I don't know how the rest of you feel,
But I feel drunk all the time

And I wish to hell we didn't have to die.

O you're a lousy bastard Mr. Death
And I wish you didn't have no hand in this game

Because it's too damn beautiful for anybody to die.

"Poems Which Are Written by the Soul"

Poems which are written by the soul
Defy man to set down. There is an area
Of feeling too tall for any recording.

Whatever harmony of spirit and life
We may have, is never sturdy enough
To withstand the ravages of our saying—
The meaning of the image is always clear;
But what the Thing is we may only sully.

Where the particular and the universal,
The infinite and the minute, join,
Is the province of the soul—
Here the red deer carries continents on its back,
And the towns of God lift their real and pure spires.

          .   .   .   .   .   .

When the great poem is written,
And men say: What does it mean?
—I think the poet will be forgiven should he answer:
Praise God, I do not know;
It is enough that He knows.

Blood of the Sun

The golden blood of the sun
Floods down in splendid abandon;
And what is full of dread
Dreams within the heart—for look,
We expect most from what we fear.

Even this sun, which spreads its glorious
Image on our lives, is only caught
Again by the great frozen hand
Which tossed it forth. For think,
Wouldn't it be more a sun
If just once it could elude Him? If just once
It missed the relentless fingers?

The great can be little.
The fun of being God would be
In being nothing;
To really live, we should be dead too.
Isn't all our dread a dread of being
Just here? of being only this?
Of having no other thing to become?
Of having nowhere to go really
But where we are?

What power has the sun
If it must remain the sun?
We are afraid that one day the hand
Will not catch us when we come;
That the remorseless fingers will not close over us.

And I think that is our strongest will—
The reason all our dreams of paradise
Are dreams of an unlimited disorder
In a lawless anonymity.

At the Entrance to the Other World

O fill pull willland lean of that gleam
Where *a nice wonderment increases* . . .
And where my creature calls me.

Glint of eyes of the Beautiful O every
Love loots Him of her
Heart. For Jesus (as I guess—
A lonely man) wanted only
To find a life of dreamless dreams . . .
And so protect the human from the animal within him.

Behold! He stands at this gate
And watches Sena crossing the white fields
Toward Him, and her eyes are alight
With fun as she calls:
"Have you found what You were seeking?"

Jesus answers: "Seeking is what I would find."

But He would like to take Sena in His arms
And whisper: "You are so soft and warm and sweet . . ."

Here at the entrance to the other world
Christ waits, and His eyes follow each of us
As we pass through the wondrous gate:
"Is this the man who will be My friend?
Is this the woman who will be My wife?"

"The Way Men Live Is a Lie"

The way men live is a lie.
I say that I get so goddamned sick
Of all these pigs rooting at each other's asses
To get a bloodstained dollar—Why don't
You stop this senseless horror! this meaningless
Butchery of one another! Why don't *you* at least
Wash *your* hands of it!

There is only one truth in the world:
Until we learn to love our neighbor,
There will be no life for anyone.

The man who says, "I don't believe in war,
But after all somebody must protect us"—
Is obviously a fool—and a liar.
Is this so hard to understand!
That who supports murder, is a murderer?
That who destroys his fellow, destroys himself?

Force cannot be overthrown by force;
To hate any man is to despair of every man;
Evil breeds evil—the rest is a lie!

There is only one power that can save the world—
And that is the power of our love for all men everywhere.

from *Pictures of Life and Death* (1946)

For Miriam

O my dearest
While the sun still spends its fabulous money
For the kingdoms in the eye of a fool,
Let us continue to waste our lives
Declaring beauty to the world

And let us continue to praise truth and justice
Though the eyes of the stars turn black
And the smoking juice of the universe,
Like the ruptured brain of God,
Pours down upon us in a final consecration.

O All down within the Pretty Meadow

how many times, Death
have you done it

The Lovers

to just such golden ones
as these

Toss at Their Wondrous Play

O how many times, Death, have you done it
To just such golden ones as these

"I'd Want Her Eyes to Fill with Wonder"

I'd want her eyes to fill with wonder
I'd want her lips to open just a little
I'd want her breasts to lift at my touch

And O I'd tell her that I loved her
I'd say that the world began and ended where she was
O I'd swear that the Beautiful wept to see her naked loveliness

I'd want her thighs to put birds in my fingers
I'd want her belly to be as soft and warm as a sleeping kitten's
I'd want her sex to meet mine as flames kissing in a dream forest

And O I'd tell her that I loved her
I'd say that all the noblest things of earth and heaven
Were made more noble because she lived
And O I'd know that the prettiest angels knelt there
As she lay asleep in my arms

Shadows and Spring Flowers

The horses face out over the world.
They are stone and their sightless eyes
Hold neither pity nor hatred
For anything. In the valley an old man
And a young girl are mating. The eyes
Of the old man bubble with sweat and
The money curls in her fist like a snake.
Dead queens in white dresses glide
Across the sky. How amazed their shadows
Would be to come upon something
That man hadn't defiled!

O great blind horses squatting above the world
The reins hang slack in the bitter wind
The shadows of clouds pass like wounded hands
O where can the heart of man be comforted

In the valley the wild flowers
Shake themselves upright again
Blood-flecked, they struggle to face the sun

So It Ends

What are these very desolate ones
Going to darling? O branching black
Hooves sklitter across the moon and
Jesus those poor things down there
Are nearly all
Mad and life is going to die.
O life is going to die
Cities blackened and still
The black awful waters churning in over everything
All the thinking
Beautiful flesh blown to hell O where can
We take the music of summer and the light
The touch the scent the color of
Being alive on this earth where
The body of a loved woman the sight of a deer
With the first star of evening through its horns and
My God the feel of human lips on your face

All life is going to die
The terrible hooves blotting out every living thing

O my God! the touch of her human lips on my face

333

The Valley-sleeper, the Children, the Snakes, and the Giant

Snakes are weeping on the rocks
Above the river. The brown air is very still
And the river makes no sound. In the valley
Someone is going mad. Two little girls walk stiffly
Into the brown light. They are followed
By a huge thing whose head glows like a star.

O down in the valley, in that dark awful valley,
Somebody is going mad for all the evil which men do
To one another—
And the brown sorrow of the snakes is more beautiful
Than this world, where
Nothing lives but evil, and where the lives
Of men are filled with horror beyond
The tears of snakes. And yet—as the little girls

Climb stiffly onto the rocks, the giant
Begins to sing—
Of love and truth and light!—and the valley-sleeper,
The river, and the snakes,
They joyfully answer him.
O they joyfully answer him!

"Here Might Have Been the Thinking of Mountains"

Here might have been the thinking of mountains
The bright-sad carnival of lovers
Roadways of arms raised above watching fields
O here is food eat it
The water of life drink it

For far away is what is real
In this terrible room the darkness fills our eyes
Only the singing of prisoners that is stopped by walls
The stale tapping of victims tears at our flesh
In monstrous ovens a devil's feast is readied
The food and drink of madmen

This is the last supper of all reason and hope
Tomorrow is dying here
The light of the burial wagons sputters, goes out

And at last there is peace

You Must Have Some Idea Where They've Gone

Somber figures that wander off into the night
Leaving all the questions unanswered
Leaving everything as it was
Billions and billions have come and gone

But *why?* Have you wondered why they lived?
Have you ever wondered about that?
Strange! how strange it all is!

The wind—
A tiny ripple on the water—

But the strangest thing of all
Is that man does not look like other things!

Man resembles nothing else on earth
Man does not seem at home here

All the questions may have their answer in this

"What I'd Like to Know Is"

What I'd like to know is
With people put on earth
No more armed with hellish
Weapons of senseless murder
Than a tree or a river or a sunrise

Why do we stand for it!
Why do we go on letting
These foul bastards pervert
And slime over everything
We're here for!

"War is evil." Agreed—
Sure, that we all buy.
But how about their "peace"?
A little less "evil," eh—
When you can tell them apart!

Why do we let these frauds and fakers
Get away with this loathsome muddle?
Is this the way men should live!
What we need to do is
Boot the bastards out—
All of them! Every damn one!

Make life fit for human beings!
Not for what these lousy bastards
Want it to be!
Not the way it is—
Not the way it's always been,
And will go on being,
As long as these filthy lying lice
Have the say—
My God! whose world is this!

THE STRANGE, MOVING LIGHTS OF PEOPLE
HANDLE HOLINESSES UNKNOWN *And in night's
pale noon thoughts of birds wander where no flower
has ever been, where the dead's high walking never
goes. We speak of planets, of sparkling creatures
about which we know nothing—the secret of the
secret*

The huge figure kneeling
Between the worlds

The air a mouth
Our dreams its speech

Oh never did stone weep
Or applebough tremble
In the stillness

Everything is known
About nothing

Child and tree of one flesh
All events and beings of one flesh

We too of that same mystery—
Imaging everything wrong
Because what is outside
Only exists in us

The universe—and everything that moves and has being in it—
Is a sort of joke—of an unimaginable new kind!
Look there for the Secret
For the secret of the secret

The Daft Little Shoe Clerk Decided It Would Be Fun to Go Up and See What Things Are Like above the Sky

At first it seemed rather tight
And oversnug at the heel
So that his nose tingled

But then there weren't any bothers
To speak of
No squalling brats or a boss
Sneaking around on soundproofed tennis shoes

By damn he said I'll not go down
There again
No siree let them all do their nasties
Barefoot for crooning on a cloud

Boppo! a nifty little babe with souped-up wings
Takes ahold of his arm
Real get-with-it like
And before he can say squeezed to meet you too

Off they happily fly forever and ever

"Pretty Glow on the Water"

Pretty glow on the water

>Christ she's sweet as a little cotton angel
>Church bells sending silver pups over the field
>*It always comes in the cry of the poor bastards caught*
>*in the wheel*

What I want to know is with people putting lights on
In houses across the river and that funny wonderful
Smell to her hair and the red and golden leaves
Dancing up into the soft dark pocket
O it always comes in the cry of the poor bastards caught
     in the wheel

(What do you think of world conditions? they ask me—
World conditions, is it! And oh for the love of God
They're absolutely word deleted, I tell them
And the price of shovels going up every day)

     The beautiful soft glow on the water
     The touch of her body against me
O it always comes in the cry of the poor bastards caught
     in the wheel

Winter Poem

When breathless queens release their panthers
Of roses upon the whitening world

And like cold beautiful statues in a dream
Of a god, the new gardens are unsheathed

I think of the winter that is coming down
Over the lives of human beings now

And of what will happen to the things I love
When its grim and horrible lips fondle them

And I know that the gods do not dream
The gods are intent on other things than us

339

Yellow Stones—Sea of Majestic Doves—
Lovers under Green Parasols—Hilarkeleddi,
Everybody Makes Love When I Say Ready!
—Noses of Roses Peep out of the Sky—
Sun Dropping Golden Birds on Every Tree—
If Hills Can't Be Fishes,
Why Do They Try to Swim out of the Valley?
—Who *Skree!*

They pretend that there's nothing to believe in anymore!
(*They're really rotten*) There's the picture of an old fellow
With a hurt look on the wall a bunch of magazines
And books scattered around but
She's stepping out of her dress now and
I get into bed beside her and somebody curses
Down in the street the damn phone rings on
The floor above hell
They've always been rotten! but

We fall asleep to the voices of angels
And the names of the great
O to the proud sad names of the great

Don't Wash Your Hair in the Streetcar, Nora Dear

(*When I think how it was staying overnight at my relatives*)

It's all right for them to make a stinking mess of everything
It's better than fine if they want to blow everybody up
But it's only common decency for us to follow the regulations
To loathe our neighbor as he loathes us

To get in there and pitch and poke and puke
Because it'll all come right in the end—and you know whose
Pour me another drink before you go, dear
Your old ma's gettin' that blind I can hardly see
To fold these goddamn red paper roses any more
Here, thread up these needles while you're about it
At least there there won't be much in the way of dyein' left to do

O whin I was a wee gel
I fancied lovely things'd come
Like tatters thumpin' on a drum;
But in the long years since then
A lot's befallen me, and my handsome hope—
Hell! need more water'n that, and plenty more soap.

No, that I didn't, dear. See if your father's stirrin' yet
He likes a spot of tea before retirin', you know
Him and Patty Doyle are goin' round to the hirin' hall
First thing in the mornin' before noon sometime

"O Sleeping Falls the Maiden Snow"

O sleeping falls the maiden snow
Upon the cold branches of the city
And oh! my love is warm and safe in my arms

Nearer, nearer comes the hell-breath of these times
O God! what can I do to guard her then

O sleeping falls the maiden snow
Upon the bitter place of our shelterlessness
But oh! for this moment, she whom I love
Lies safely in my arms

All the Roses of the World

They turn every heart to stone O for the love
    Of God they dirty every damn thing

But I am saying that along the garden path
    Moves a young girl who is as beautiful
As a deer standing at the edge of a forest
    Just as its gets dark

    Jesus all the roses of the world
Dance through her hair and on her feet
    Tiny stars learn to walk in purity

But I am saying they turn every heart to stone
O for the love of God! with what nobility
    Does she show her everlasting kinship
      With every living thing!

    O all the sacred wisdom of the earth
Rests upon her soft lips and in her eyes
Is a country where death can never go

Sure There Is Food

There is eating one's self

There is even truth now and then—
Of course a lie can be made to go
Farther that way

The trick is to get truth and lies
To sound just the same

That way you've got it made
Everybody is mad after while

Then you can come up with a world
Where madness is the normal thing

Of course those who rig it that way
End up mad themselves

But—who's to know the difference?
This world's the best example I know

"Christ! Christ! Christ! That the World"

Christ! Christ! Christ! that the world
Should be so dark and desolate for so many!
That there should be hungry and sick and homeless
In every land on earth!

Brothers who are without light and hope—
For whom Death is a friend, whose hand will save them!

This should rot the hearts of men!
Instead—instead—
O you dirty filthy swine!

History in a Minor Key

56 and *tomato*

> The only thing I liked
> about my family was the day Aunt Tilly
> fell down the cellarsteps and broke both legs
> Give me his number I'll call the sonofabitch
> So help me God! a green mustache at *her* age
> Grandpap was that fried he has to go and push Rover
> off the piano stool and all the neighbors complaining

about so much practicing anyway.
I tell you there aren't any sardines in this can!
Sure you had to stamp out the fire but for heaven's sake
do you have to track Junior all over my clean floor?
Put the goldfish in the furnace.

> it has to end sometime so why not get started

———

> O in the cold rain the stone women weep at the evil of this
> world

———

> it has to end sometime so why not get started now

Put the blasted canary in the refrigerator.
Have a good time?
So-so.
Anyone there?
What do you mean, anyone there?
Oh, you know—anyone important.
Sure, Pete wasn't there. Ed's in Albania.
Did you bring anything back?
No, I wasn't around when I got ready to leave.

> O in the cold rain the stone women weep at the evil of this
> world

A Man Lives Here

I used to think that life wouldn't always be wounded. I am a man, not some mechanical thing—cut me, I bleed. Anyway, we came to a village where somebody had put a bird of glass that towered up hundreds of feet from the special hill it was on—a hill of steel. You tell me what to make of that! The doors of the houses are open, so I guess we're welcome; but no—the doors are closed. Damn! look at the grass—*white* grass? or is it just the shine off that terrible bird . . . I hold her hand more tightly; tell her we don't have to stay in a place like this.

But getting away may not be all that easy. The houses seem to have moved nearer, or perhaps without knowing it we've edged forward. Are those faces in the windows? Damn! suddenly—but no, it can't be I'm seeing my own face repeated over and over in there! It's just some trick of the light, I tell her; a reflection off that crummy glass bird.

Oh, then you see me too! she cries. In all those awful houses! I thought I was just imagining it! O take me away from here!

Were I God! O were I God!
But a man—what can a man do in this world?
A man may weep
A man may curse against the darkness
A man may stand with all his heart's power raised against
    the enemies of light

And it will change nothing?
Ah, but it could change the world!

Come, all the things I believe in
Come, all the things I love
O hold her in your arms!

Waiting Can Be Pretty Lousy

There was a mutter of rain on the leaves and we went back in the house. She stood by the door and I sat down near the table. We'd spent our last cent getting ready. With any luck he wouldn't notice how little we ate. After all, what we'd done was for him. It started to rain harder.

I drummed my fingers on the table.

She walked over and sat down on my knee.

It was getting gray outside the door and a damp cold crept in around us.

I drummed my fingers on the table.

She got up and went to stand by the door again.

I suddenly felt like crying.

A car came down the road and rattled past without slowing.

I put my hand in my pocket before I remembered. I'd smoked the last of the cigarettes out in the yard.

She turned and smiled at me.

I stood up to move over to her, then instead I went round pulling the shades down.

It was almost dark now.

The rain went on and on.

Some crazy night bird started jabbering.

A car going the other way went by, its radio blaring.

She struck a match. There were oh maybe a dozen candles and she lighted every one of them.

The rain seemed to be letting up.

We heard someone stumbling down the road.

I walked quickly to the door and stared out. The sound stopped. She came to stand beside me. The stumbling sound began again. The headlights of a car shone through the dark. We could see no one on the road. The car splashed by.

I put my hand on her arm. She didn't seem to notice. I went back and sat down.

Some of the candles had guttered out.

I drummed my fingers on the table.

Slowly she turned to face me. There were tears in her eyes.

We both knew that he'd never come now.

Not tonight or any night.

And we could hear the sound out in the night that might have been somebody dragging a heavy object along beside him.

Not if He Has Any Sense, He Won't Be Back

I met her in the summertime. There were red flowers in the lanes and all the trees had birds in them. We lay down in the grass and I opened her dress and I put my fingers on her cool breasts and I put my mouth upon her mouth. After a little and all the birds were singing I walked her home and she went in and closed the door. She closed the door and I went away. The night came and the sky filled with stars and I walked back to her house and I knocked on the door. An old man came and let me in and he said we've been expecting you. On a great table bread and cheese and wine were laid. There were white candles and red flowers all about and at the table sat the girl. I looked around for the old man but he was gone and she said don't be frightened not everything in the world is evil. We ate the bread and cheese and drank the wine and I said after a little I shall wake and I shall have tears in my eyes because you are not with me and because everything in the world is evil. Then the door opened and the old man came in and he blew out one of the candles. I got to my feet and said it is late and I must go. But you cannot go she said for all the long sweet night we shall lie in each other's arms and there will be nothing can hurt us. I looked around for the old man but he was gone and I said after a little I shall wake and I shall be sick at heart because you are not in my arms and all the long black night will be stretched out before me. Then she took my hand and led me to a cot with a scarlet cover that stood in the corner of the room beside the stairs. But as she stepped out of her dress and I saw the beauty of her thighs and I saw the way her belly was

347

curved for my touch and the loveliness of her shoulders her throat and I was hungry to put my hands upon her and to put my lips on her soft mouth and to whisper of all the wonder of the world and to tell her that I loved her O to tell her and to tell her that all was not evil on earth another candle snuffed out and I saw something coming down the stairs and I started to curse O God there are no flowers the lanes are dark and all the birds are stricken dumb in the trees in these splintered trees O Father what is the way out of this hell and why do I always return to this house to this strange house where all the beauty and horror of being alive pours in on me in such a flood that I sink to my knees, cursing, O God I see something coming down the stairs and its face is *the face of every human being on this earth and this bread I eat is its flesh and this wine is its blood and this woman I hold in my arms is its soul* and I say that expecting the sneers and the laughter I want you to laugh see what a fool I am see what a neat tune I can play literature is such fun and so amusing to while away an idle hour O laugh you poor stricken bastards in the smoking ruins of your world here I stand and shout praise of God praise of Life O my poor lost brothers if any of you has poems to write write them now O if any of you has anything to add to the long tall dignity of human creation please add it now O if any of you has a pure heart let that heart beat in praise of God for O my brothers the world is dying and we will not let it die O since we have no power to stop these madmen who will destroy the world let us stand here praising God and I say this knowing of the sneers and the cynical laughter O see what a fool I am for it's really just poppycock to speak of the destruction of the world oh we grant that they have the means to do it but it's nonsense to think that anyone would be mad enough to actually want to do it O I say look at your hands they are smeared with the blood of human beings and O I say look at your lives and at all your smug works they are smeared with the blood of human beings and I tell you there is no difference between murdering the human beings you have already murdered and murdering every human being on earth O I weep at the monstrous

348

horror of this crime against man and against God! If you have blood on your hands take them off this page. I get out of bed and cross to the window. A milk wagon clatters down the street, a mangy little dog trailing after it in the pale, frosty light. In a nearby house somebody coughs. The stars begin to flicker out. A tree steps out of the gray jelly. I scratch in under my armpits, yawning. At last she stirs and calls over sleepily. Nothing wrong, I tell her. Go back to sleep. Actually it's nothing new for her to wake up and find me sitting in this chair beside the window. I wish Christ would come back to earth, or that . . . what? What? Yeah, *what?* Now an alarm clock goes off next door. I light a cigarette. A man comes out a couple doors down and takes the milk in. It's much lighter and everything looks sort of drab and defenseless, like the dog. Two girls hurry along and every so often one of them lunges down to yank up her stocking. More people. A taxi. I stamp the cigarette out. All the stars are gone. Quietly I get back into bed. My shoulder touches her arm. She half wakes and I lie very still. That summer is a long way off now. I can't remember what the flowers looked like. Wild roses, I think. We both got sick eating crab apples—that I remember. I don't know why every time I think of God the old gent who ran the auto camp comes back to me. Sometimes in my dreams I see him standing in the doorway of our cabin with a flashlight in his hand, and I can see the rain splattering on his hat . . . I don't think anyone else has ever seen us in bed together, like that. I remember how angry I was—so angry I couldn't say anything for a minute; but in my dreams the whole thing is all twisted out of focus, and he's there to see if we're all right. It's funny how things get into your mind as one thing, and stay on though you're only half aware of it as something altogether different.

Yeah, it's all pretty funny—funny enough to break a man's heart, anyway. Whether he's awake or asleep.

"Peace in This Green Field"

Peace in this green field.

Bird any damn kind—
They're all good! *My God!*
Grass flowers the wind—
What more do you want!

Do you know something—
I think it's beautiful!
Makes you feel great
Just to be alive!

My God! What more is there!
Piece of grass, huh?
All warmed by the sun—
Somebody pretty alongside you!

Boy! that's it, you know—
Maybe a glass of beer, huh?
Your arm around her—
My God! You can say that again!

I Have No Place to Take Thee

O fiery tiger walking down through the air. Fiery monster come
to eat the world. Pleasing death O come pleasing death for I am
tired of being alive. It is my turn to die O all the ancients
warned of the monstrous tiger of fire that would devour the world.
Pleasing death O come with your quiet hands upon my life for
I am tired of being alive. The light fades in my room these chairs
take on hideous shapes in the half-dark. Pleasing death O come

pleasing death for I am sick in my heart and I would die. There is no face I want to see there is no voice I want to hear O pleasing death come with your gentle hands and blot out this grief which has only itself to mourn. There is no woman I want to love there is no man I want to friend O pleasing death come with your quiet hands upon my life and rub out this pain which has only itself to wound. That a tree stands in a field—that a flower opens to the sun—that the thighs of a girl are soft and warm— that the wings of a fly make patterns as beautiful as a snowflake's —O what are any of these to me for I am sick in my heart and I would die. There is no faith I can turn to there is nothing to hope for at all O come pleasing death with your brutal hands and stop this throat which has only itself to damn. I feel about the room in the half-dark I touch chairs tables the pictures on the wall I touch the face of her who waits for me to end this dreary awful day and go to bed. I touch her face and I know how little we are now every one of us is all alone crying inside where no one can see. Life is without meaning, gray and dull. Birds, stars, trees, stones—what good are they? What use are any of these to me? I have known rain and wind and snow—I have known a thousand rooms and towns I have seen and done what all of us have to see and to do O God what good is any of this! of what use is any of this to me! I am tired of stars and of the rain and of these hate-filled towns and of everything that's ever been done or said on this earth O pleasing death come with your terrible hands and blot out this noise which has only itself to stir. That men have said God there is a God—that men have said the beauty of a woman is as a flame in a holy place—that men have made cities and sent motors down the roadless heights—What good is it to say there is a God when there is no sign of God at all? What sort of beauty is this that rots like a piece of meat in the sun? What manner of building is this that we are all waiting here like cornered rats? The fiery tiger is walking down the air and his eyes are fixed on nothingness. It is my turn to tell O all the prophets of old have sung of the death of the world. Once it might have mattered which of the millions of lives I wanted to live—

this house, and not that—this woman, not that one—this belief, and not that—but how can it matter now? Unless death has rooms and streets and being hurt when the things you love are hurt—unless—I will not say . . . Ice on a dead bough. Dirty socks in a bureau drawer—ah, yes, my jollies! and yes my pretty dreams! See me in my grim sullen yeddle waiting for the world to go pa-tit-pa-tettle—and indeed all over the toost went the strangely be-waildering soond of the shoost. It is such a poor and meaningless thing, this putting words on paper while the world is dying O what difference does it make what is said now what difference does it make what little noise goes up from any of us when all the long howling weight of an eternal silence is pressing down upon us and if we cry God God and cry God God and if we cry God God and so we cry and if we cry God God and oh my love my pretty dear and all these poor majesties that live on the earth these birds and sheep and turtles these rivers and hills and the snow and the little wood under the blue sky and all the nights you've lain in my arms O my love my pretty one there is such sorrow in my heart there is such pain in me for all the world is dying and I have no place to take thee and I have no place to take thee. Now it is my turn to tell O all the fallen of heaven and earth are watching out of his eyes as he wades toward us. The fiery tiger is walking down through the air and I feel about this room in the half-dark I touch the faces of my father and mother the pale floating dogs and wagons of childhood the blustery day I found a nest of baby quail in the orchard and fat sweaty-handed Billy Rovane killed them with a pointed stick. Pleasing death O come with your stern hands upon my life for I am sick at heart and I would die. There is no voice I want to hear there is no faith I can hold O come death and put your cold lips upon my life for I am tired of everything and I would die. Men, sun, fields, temples —what good are they? What use are any of these to me? I have known rain and wind and snow—I have knelt in a thousand shacks and spit on a thousand thrones I have cursed and praised what all of us have to damn and to sing O God what good is any of this! Of what value is any of this to me! I am weary of the sun and of the fields and of all the mountains and the seas and of everything that's ever been dreamed or attempted on this earth O pleasing death come with your gentle hands and cancel out this enterprise which has only its own nothingness to harry. That men have said Truth there is a Truth—that men have said the grandeur of the sun is a torch in the hand of God—that men have paved the wilderness and sent slim boys down the roads of the wind—what good is it to say there is Truth when everything around us is a lie? What good is the sun when we are all blind in this darkness? What manner of noble achievement is this that we are all cowering here like beaten curs in a ditch? The fiery tiger is walking down through the air and his breath is a horror on our faces. The world is dying and we are all lost in the folds of the robe of that incredible dreamer into whose consciousness we shall wake. Toad astir on a rusty watch. Smiling child in a pool of snakes. I touch your face and I know how lonely you are how every one of you is crying all alone deep inside where no one can see. Life is without meaning, ugly and drab. It is my turn now to tell O all the fallen of heaven have told of the fiery tiger that walks down across the nothingness toward us. Pleasing death O come pleasing death for I am tired of being alive. The light fades in this room and bloody paws tear at my heart. It is such a poor thing, this putting senseless marks on a paper when your soul is dead O what does it matter what bright juice oozes out of any head what does it matter how well the silken beautiful drums of art are thumped when all the long hideous whiteness of an everlasting void is stretched out here before us and if we cry God God and cry God God and if we cry Father Father and so we cry and always we cry God God and oh my pretty one my darling and all these sad majesties that live on the earth these lions and bears and doves these shores and thickets and the snow and the peaceful little wood under the blue sky oh my own love my pure sweet my darling there is such anguish in my heart there is this black and raging fear in me for all the world of God and man is dying and I have no place to take thee and oh my darling my darling I have no place at all to take thee.

I Care What Happens

Prodigious goals—Flakes boat starmarsh—Great Highone I care what happens to every human being, O I live locked in that—the smell of a stone in the sun—Locked in my heart are all the slender still silences of the grove and there too the black cries and the pierced beggars in fluttering doorways—Call through the howling O
someone thinks of greater deeds than lying and murder.
Every mouth sucks at life and is filled in one way or another.

Hounds playing tennis on a pale bridge. The grim asses of trains bluther down the valley. Nowhere to go, brother.
Even hard things hide.
But life does not break.

Let us shout in our cages! Rattle the damn bars!
Under the invisible is a man's heart.
I am like you. We are things of the same kind.
We are all standing here among the hideous statues.
I urge you to protest this murderous swindle. Do it.

I walk out into the streets of this city.
They have made liars of all these people. They have made them cheat and do murder. Their faces are afraid, and ugly. They live with hatred in their hearts. They love nothing at all.
Everything in this city is ugly. It is a sort of death to walk here. A filth of lies and hopelessness covers everything. I go into a lunchroom and order coffee. Every table is taken. I stand in a corner and drink the coffee. I have a feeling that at any moment somebody will blow up and start clawing everyone within reach. But they just sit around in there and make the usual stale noise. I get out as fast as I can.

Prodigious dreams—I walk down and sit on a bench by the river. An old man sits down beside me. A sour vomit smell comes off his clothes. He picks his nose and hums a popular song. I move on to another bench. Two girls are sitting there smoking. They don't look at me. A shout from over by the drinking fountain and a man lurches down the path with blood streaming down his chin. I wait a minute, then set off for home.

You—

The meaning is in the wonder.

Towns and seas and all poor devils everywhere. In no way is life ever changed.

Through acceptance of the mystery, peace.

And only through peace can come acceptance of the mystery. We are not open. The glory cannot come in. How soon after our best things is the taste bitter again.

As of this earth and what I am on this earth—I fiercely wish to protect the things I love.

They fill my eyes with tears—the things I love.

Suppose they are nothing—they are all I have.

Each Is Alone, Each Is Everything

O ghost in the bluehearing grove
More tongueless than pity.

Quiet as a breast. Alive above the noisy killing of men. A red red rose and the patient hands of the snow. O tranquil forest under the darkening sky.

Half-lived and unintent the poor lives of men.

The listening souls of twigs.

O starry weather lofts a bird and in that profound cave our father sleeps. Hey creatures! forgive us!

Conditions are Queen. Fullswirl care in the gadgets of being.

Flesh cottages.

Crowing pigflowers spray at the castle wall.

Rundown it's five o'clod. The more ways the samer way.
Eternity is kinder
Than any clock.

Harmony always rejects power.
Each cottage holds the world.

Horizons always end somewhere too. Vice in art, as in life, is not looking at what cannot be seen. The beautiful brutal hours fondle alike the thoughts of snakes and the lusts of angels. The garments of Shakespeare hang in the closet beside the fool's— each with the marks of the loom upon it, neither altering the set of the shuttle in any fashion whatever. O ghost in the heartseeing grove tell me are there any coats at all that will fit the life of a man in this world?

As meaningful as love!
Peaceful as a breast. Alive above the terrible agony of men. No really I'd prefer not to. Have more of it, that is. Feeling, caring . . . My own bit of cottage. Why should I always return to where I haven't been! Let you now—I am speaking to myself—come a little nearer to where I am. It may be true that that is a better place to be. Wonder, anyway, is nicer than any name.
I'm all sold on the Beautiful.
I hate with all my guts this bloody crawling cell they've turned the world into. I can't get any of these damn coats to fit any part of my life.

A Time to Believe!

O "fruitful and purified"—an identity in the Invisible! Nothing is ever contradicted, all remains always, unchanged and unchanging. Instruction never saves, it lifts but what it lifts is itself.

Ambition is the weakness of all great spirits who in acceptance will find the joy and the despair they seek. The physician can only cure when he is willing to assume your disease. To be shunned is to be God a little—

We cannot add to what we are, nor can we take away. The world is One Thing.

What sort of theory can any man draw up for the human spirit! We don't need theories—we need Love, Humility, Simplicity— new ways to give! The brightest boys have all sold out. They can't get anyone to believe them because the only "truth" they spout is one that won't offend. But I am exaggerating—they are quite willing not only to offend but to murder anybody their "governments" tell them to. With all proper respect for metric nicety, let it be said. These *disgusting* little lice! These betrayers of Life!

Everywhere the same—the same lousy sellout! The whole kit and caboodle of them! The vicious, stupid fools! Lackies of madmen bent on butchering the world!
But I tell you that Life will be avenged
I tell you that Life will look after its own
I tell you that Life will allow nothing to be added or taken away

Aye, now is the time to believe
When there is nothing to believe in!
Aye, now is the time to believe
if it does no more than show we're still alive!

So let us present our duties with some humility as it gets dark now. In case it all does end, the crime will not be of our doing. For I'd rather take a nothing I loved to my grave than a something I have every reason to hate.

The Builders

Sky black black clouds and black rain falls. That blond wound does not show. Sun is out. The black rain falls and the serpent of darkness has eaten the sun. My father used to kick me in the behind when I'd forget to scrape the mud off my shoes before walking into the parlor. I hate to imagine what would happen if any of my heads ever got away. Dear soul—no, it won't help any now. The pale eyes of pigs slip back into the womb and the black rain comes down. A group of people are walking along the wall. They have a number of lives in a tin box which they would have me kiss but I move quickly out of their way. It is beginning to annoy me that I left my cigarettes in my other coat but I can confess without having a cigarette poking out of my face. The trouble started before we were little more than moved in. As a matter of significant detail, the curtains had not yet been put up at the tiny windows, and the broken lock on the back door was still not fixed. I was helping her with the supper dishes and since we were both tired and out-of-sorts we said little. As I was putting the last cup on its hook I said it'll drive both of us mad if we don't talk about it. She said oh then you've heard it too! I thought maybe it was just—I put my arms around her and said nobody's nerves could play them tricks like that honey. Then she cried and I could feel some of the tenseness going out of her. Oh darling she said why did you wait so long to tell me! I thought the voices and the pounding were just going on in my own head. I laughed. I couldn't help it though she drew back in terror. At last I managed to say so you think it's just in your own head eh? I led her out to the yard in front of the house. Stars and a new moon. I was very excited. Plainly now we could hear the shouting of the workmen and the noise of stakes being driven into the ground and of stones groaning down log runways. Even the labored snorting of horses. It seems to be coming from over there she whispered pointing to a place about fifty feet from where we were standing. You stay here I told her and I started to walk slowly over. She called for me to come back but I went on and as I got near I could smell the giant labor of the men and horses and the stone burning into the wood. The commands were in a language I had never before heard and of course I could see nothing. I stopped about ten feet away and considered what I had to lose. I was covered with sweat and my skin pressed in on me like a sheet of hairy fire. I walked right into it and the noise filled my ears with blood and two trucks hit head-on just under the ground. Then there was silence and I felt a drop of rain on my face. I turned around and I started to walk back toward her. She said what are you doing wandering about like this in the rain darling? I went to see if I could find out what they're building I answered wondering if she would try to get away with it. She took my arm and led me into the house and into our bedroom with its peeling wallpaper and the broken pane in the little window over the dresser and she sat up in bed her eyes big with fear and she said oh my God you scared me where have you been? I sank down in the chair by the window. She got out of bed and came over and put her hand on my shoulder. Why darling she exclaimed your pajamas are sopping wet. At last I managed to say I thought I heard something moving around in the yard. She went in the bathroom and got a towel and while she was drying my hair I looked out of the window and I could see them building the wall. There were at least a dozen men and two teams of horses and though they seemed to be working in what amounted to a frenzy there wasn't a sound. And then she heated up some milk. She poured the steaming milk into a glass and while I was waiting for it to cool I said it's nice of you to go to all this bother for me. She came over and settled down on my knee and she said don't be silly darling and I watched the steam rising from the milk and it was all I could do to keep the tears out of my eyes and she said it's cool enough to drink now. And then she put the light out in the kitchen and we went into the bedroom and she pulled the shade down over that window and she said why don't you read for awhile and when I said no she said well we'll just leave the lamp on anyway. And then she fell asleep and

I watched the night out and I didn't really care one way or another. The next day I sat out on the porch. The wind was rushing new clouds into the sky and about halfway through the afternoon it started to rain hard. I was surprised to see my brother walking across the field toward the house and I sprang up and ran down to warn him but before I could make him hear above the storm he had reached the wall and the foreman set him to work on the highest level. Then one of the workmen looked over at me and I said what are you doing here in the rain and she said please come back into the house darling people will begin to get suspicious if they see you wandering around like this with your face and hands smeared with mud. I said I was just going to speak to my brother when you made them all go away. She took my arm and started to lead me back into the house and when she didn't try to remind me that my brother was dead I knew she had a plan and I broke away from her and I ran into the woods. When it got dark I sank down under a tree and fell asleep. The cold woke me up and something standing beside me in the dark said I was sent here to take you home. I stood up and a hand took hold of my sleeve and led me back to the house. I walked in and she was sitting at the kitchen table with her face buried in her arms. When she looked up her eyes were swollen and red and deep lines came away from her mouth. I said I'm sorry I frightened you honey I won't go away like that again. But she didn't seem to hear me and when I bent over and kissed her forehead she didn't lift her eyes. Then she got up and went on tiptoe into the bedroom. My mouth felt dry and I went over to the sink but I couldn't get the faucet to turn. I pounded and hammered but I couldn't get it to turn. I wonder why she doesn't come out to see what I'm making all the noise about. Things never seem to work right in new houses. Finally I gave it up and went into the bedroom. There was a man in the bed and she was standing there looking down at him and crying. Then as I watched she bent over and kissed him on the forehead but his eyes didn't open and a lot of people came into the room

360

and stood silently there. I looked out of the window. The wall is finished. I can't help thinking that it is a pretty hideous wall. The sky is full of black clouds which on any ordinary occasion would plunge the earth in darkness but a great light shines down upon the wall and through the beautiful light a group of people are walking. They have a number of deaths in a golden chest which they'd have you see. There are any number of better ones than this. And O God the black rain falls. My father used to kick me in the behind when I'd forget to scrape the mud off my shoes before I went into the parlor.

Father, look what I have on my shoes now.

"No One Ever Works Alone"

No one ever works alone.

Put the good things here. There is so much, so very much!
O trees flowers birds the face of my darling! hurry hurry the great tongues of truth! O speak out!
Against the dead trash of their "reality."
Against "the world as we see it."
Against "what it is reasonable to believe."
Out with the rascals
And all their bloody works!

There is a beautiful sun today.
Have you change for one hundred and ninety odd dullards, sir?

Look you have a life—*use it!* No one ever works alone! Hate and fear O blast them to hell for love everyway and every old how you can! There is so much, so very very much!

Gategeese the windopeninghosts of air. My invitation—O come
if you like: I won't forget your kindness. Live gently. Now is the
I wouldn't kid you time to stand up and count them.
My conclusion is:
There is only one thing that matters and that is life.
No one ever works alone.

Life needn't be ugly. I don't protest great good God I demand!
All this ratty lying murderous swindle of theirs be damned!
There's a beautiful sun *today!* When are we going to throw the
bastards off our backs. Art has no place for lies.

Jesus the earth is real and it warms like a hand in the sun.
Three green white horses. Look you have a life—put your soul
into it! When you buy a suit don't just get something that will
look good on your boss. If you won't mind I'm going to say get
with it! Live your own life for a change, eh?

The leaves fall. The chances don't lessen.
Nothing of flesh should be treated shabbily.
I at any rate cannot resist trying a little one-step even on the brink.
What are you in terror of?
The baby fox goes to sleep under the thousand-ton tree.
Life needn't step to their dirty tune.
Each pays for his own piper
When you get right down to it.

from *Red Wine & Yellow Hair* (1949)

The Hunter

Why do you stay there in the wood?
Star droppings stain your gun,
While hair and rotted blood
Make up your only food.

Why do you hide then like a thief?
It's said that empires have flicked
As sparrows into your sack—
And a whim's made kingdoms grieve.

Why do you pause now on the scent?
The quarry's done what it could
To leave plain traces—here's a scrap
Of spit-fouled paper signed "The Christ."

Why do you wait here in this night?
All earth's poor things to you
Must go. Have you pity now
That you are hunted too?

The New Being

They'd make you believe that your problem is one of sex,
That men and women have mysteriously become
Strange and fearful to one another—sick, diseased, cold—
And that is true. But no loss of a father-image or of
Any other image, did this. Why don't you face the truth for once?
You have accepted the whole filthy, murderous swindle without

A word of protest, hated whomever you were told to hate,
Slaughtered whomever you were told to slaughter; you've lied,
Cheated, made the earth stink with your very presence—Why
Shouldn't you despise and hate one another? Why shouldn't
Your flesh crawl every time you touch one another?
Why should you expect to make "love" in a bed fouled
    with corpses?

Oh, you poor, weak little frauds, sucking around
Frantically for something to ease your guilt—
Why don't you face it?
Your birthright, liferight,
Deathright, and now your
Sexright, you've lost. What
Did you expect? How
Else could it be? You've
Made property and money your only gods—
Well, this is their rule,
This is what you wanted.
And now they'll wipe you out.
Why don't you face it?
Stop sucking around.
Your pet witch doctors can't help you,
They're all sick from the same thing.
Your pompous intellectuals can't help you,
They're all sick from the same thing.
Your sly, vicious statesmen can't help you,
They're all sick from the same thing.
Why don't you face it?

No, your problem is not one of sex—
Your problem is that you have betrayed your animal
Into hands as cruel and bloody as your own.
Man is dead.
I don't know what kind of thing you are.

A Lost Poem

O now you've got a very different look.
What of the tree which the falling dark put faces
In, only a moment ago? And the light
On the sliding ground, what has become of its cold
Waking figures? O where is the lion that gazed
Down out of the leaves, and cried in pity as something
Beat its hands up through the grass and thrust
Its bleeding hands up through the grass? and the quiet
      wings folded over the air
O where have they been taken—the chaste, unshadowed
Ghosts from a place far realer than our own?
How then did you come to me as I stood at the window?
      After a day of bitterness and sorrow
Why did you come? And the hair of my head rising up
And the breath in my throat like an eye that listened.
With the evening star you came, shining as a god—
And my thoughts like wounds from staring at nothing.
O something gathered—growing in purity—
Gathering me back to the naked Singer,
To the wounded, angry voice calling the thunder down.
      But now you have a very different look . . .
And the bitterness and sorrow are back in me;
For your wondrous lion is a dog that howls next door—
(People are cruel when their lives are meaningless)—
And the moving Stone, the thinking Staff—what the silence
Said

      O what something felt for my heart to feel
      O what something knew for my days to know
Gone, gone—
All that is gone. The neighbors are getting drunk.
The radios are on full tilt. The tree's in darkness.
      O like a god you came, but a tongueless fool
Stayed.

And a Man Went Out Alone

For it did come to that
    And a man went out alone
Drive the pieces together
To the brown dogs be given the mauled junk you make lives of
           Do you know what I am saying?
           Have you thought of love today?
Behind this familiar scenery of words
        the fear-stained placenta
        the mucronated cowlknife
        the enchorial puddercap
        the dissentient conglutination
        the dagglesome crassitude
        the spool-mouthed gaddement
        the ruck-souled concinnity
        the sperm-gummed ankylosis
        the winnowrimous scissility
        the midgeyed superfetation
        the chuff-groined copulatee
        the knurlated deathambulist
        the intershagged caudateable
        the pretoltering inchoation
        the scroilette nevernesser
        the mash-piece misbirdile
        the gowlern neoteric and
        the bull-rigged hartalor
           Do you know what I am saying?
           Have you thought of death today?
O the wonderful wonderful wonderful
      careless careful quietude
      of the mason-fly of the
      monster at the oasis
        BUT MARVELS again, and, as I say,
this I say because I am alive with wonder
at how good it is to want nothing
      but to give what I have away

Take it
Do I have something you want take it to hell
    with it take it come in Take it for when
    it comes to that I say every human being
    is God
            every living thing is beautiful
    and I want nothing on top of me
    or under around or in me, God my brother,
            which you don't have
O drive the pieces together
No one can die when any one lives
No one can live when any one dies
    What do I have that you want?
My life you have for our lives are one life
My death you will have for our deaths are one death.

The rest is as it is—ghosts peering from mirrors.
Make of it what you will.
But surely man's concern
Should be with real things in a real world—
A world where every human being
Is responsible for every other human being!

"Blind'd Be the Last of Men"

Blind'd be the last of men,
They'd have no taste for honest song;
Pressed to a sour teat drinking the red scum beer
Reserved for their like.

Deaf and soft and dull they'd be;
No truck with a lawless heart for any of them.
They'd only stir—and lift their wet, drooling snouts—
Should the sow threaten to move away.

Hovenweep*

Frogs and Queens

To the vast, shy light
That strikes her vase's stone,
I turn a charmed attention.

Fragments of spiny clouds,
Discarded carcasses of salmon,
Grate across the blue sky.

They've always said it's blue;
But her blue eyes are another color.
I think they may be wrong
About more serious things.

A man should keep an intimate count of his own feelings.
I doubt that any two lives touch except as they go back
Into the darkness,
Or come all the way out into the light.

Her fingers are made of the same stuff as mine,
Bone and gristle, cells and moving blood,
Many times repeated through thousands of shadowy existences;
But in the sunlight
They're more like rosy birds or thoughts than flesh—

I can't imagine them between the teeth of a dog;
Or moving anywhere on my body.
And that's another thing they are wrong in:
There is something exciting about a beautiful woman
That has nothing to do with wanting her.
What are we to make of this excitement?
A new color for feeling's sky perhaps . . . ?

* The site of prehistoric cliff dwellings in Utah and Colorado.

The figures on the vase—
When, taking it from her warm hand,
And shading my eyes against the sun,
I study them, it's as though
In the passage between us,
They had been changed entirely—
This ugly frog, these hacking bear-men and leering snakes,
Where did they come from!
Queens, harvesters, and flowering vines she held.
Don't tell me that this can be explained . . .

Then explain how this wise and ancient one
Can be only fifteen!

The Krelullin

"Older than the races of men, wiser than their Creator."

Behind the mask, like the slow beat
Of a death drum,
The painted lids of an old man
Rose and fell in the smoking light
Of the Krelullin fires.
As the mern-stone dagger
Entered my chest, the thrust
Cruelly slanted to touch bone,
—Spiders of dark blood screaming out of
My eyes, my ears, and my nostrils—
        (Pain is life's only reality,
            Greater than faith, or hatred even)—
I felt the oneness underlying all things,
And in that sudden, blinding, slow moment,
Phantoms and disguises were gone.

I understood the Krelullin code of my people;
Saw my own face grinning behind the Krelullin mask;

Knew that it was my hand
And not the hand of my father
That held the Krelullin knife.

I understood that the Krelullin was made to be broken;
For in what other way could a man die
With such unshakable conviction about
The profound and absolute
Uselessness of every human action?

Ugly figures on a crumbling vase—
(O life, O death . . . the light and the darkness
Coupling like maddened tigers in a raging nothingness . . .)
Pawed at by a terrible hand. I go away now
To wait for you here
Where your mask will be lifted too.

But, first, tell me,
What is on the vase you hold?

"White Lions Are Roaring on the Water"

White lions are roaring on the water
And cold are the winds along the shore;
And I think of men and of their wonder
That now they're asked to square the whore.

Who've prinked and gacked and goggled in the slop
Of every ordered fraud and cheat,
Now'd have the bloody swindle stop—
And march against the drums they beat.

So I think of men and of this winter,
And of the spring that comes no more;
Death's lions are raging on the water,
And black are the winds upon the shore.

Latesummer Blues

(In a Variety of Keys)

Well, the grass is a pleasant thing,
Blue of the sky against its green —
And the peaceful wind and water singing
Most likely of an ancient queen
Who sleeps in another kingdom now;
And the sun, like a gentle hand, scattering
His gifts down on the peoples of this world
Who seem to have turned from all wonders now.

A battered hat, a torn shoe filled with gray sand . . .
Now that's where Gizzle Robby went, down where
     the colder fishes stand.
I know, I know,
If it doesn't rain, the grass won't grow . . .
But have you heard
From Shammy Pistonrod and Kubber-Bubber Ned?
Huh! no word
Of that magic bird
Whose gland they thought would fetch the moxie back
When youth had fled?
What news of Lem the-Human-Toiletseat?
Remember his noonday snack—
Two buckets of eels, six oyster pies, and a couple
     sides of beef?
He's on a diet now, you say?
I see, I see,
Silence in his banquet hall, and eyeless waiters making free.

Hua! huua!—the grinning wind runs along the ground
"Flesh"—"spoon"—what other word or any human sound
Can make much difference now? in this black wound
"Light" and "button" mean the same.

371

What have you found that the world may use?
Blackened grime on an idiot's shoes.
But where is the trust in man's high aim?
Darkness waits at the heart of the flame.

A pink tea-rose gown all squished into a bloody wad . . .
Now that's what Irma Shannon got to wear before her God.
I know, I know,
Some of us stay, while some of us go . . .
The proudest bastard and the sorriest whore, etc.,
All get a little less, who'd have a little more, etc., etc.
But, Jesus! where are these poor human rivers supposed to flow?
Just take the case of Susan Hooker,
Nobody's dope and a top-class looker—
Yeah, Bob, that come-and-take-me grin,
Her teasing eyes, and flaming walk . . .
She'll have the angels off that pin!
I'll bet she made St. Peter gawk—
For she got hit
By a lad who was lit
On goofer-dancing snow.
Ah, any time you listen, kid,
You can hear them bitter winds a-blow.
So mention this to Sulliman, Grote, and Easy-Fingered Syd;
Who've got a patent out for an indestructible man
That's made in the image of a Lorkadorcus squid,
With a detachable soulborator on the X-D-7 band.

But what of Hurk–the-Woggling-Can,
And Dan-o Groob, the last of the famous Pohunkett Earls?
Where's Seraphane & Cathotex & Joanocoxi
& all the rest of Yaakibazzy's pretty factory girls?
—O flow peacefully my beautiful Lepiwammatoxee
And let them sleep, you filthy lousy poisoned sewer!
How come the lives of people are wasted like so much manure!
I know, I know,

The latest tommy gun for little Alfy, and take
    the missus to a show.
Ah, let you be ever so noble, Mr. Foxey,
You can't stop them blackened winds that blow
    and blow and blow . . .

O love, now the scarlet leaves are falling,
Thrown to earth by a cold hand.
In the gray woods, so still in the falling
Dusk, all the sadness of life is held.
Since it's up to God no longer, but to men—
Who knows? summer may never come again.
Monstrous fire by a monstrous hatred fanned!

What have you there for the world to see?
Some bloody rags beneath a tree.
But where is the faith in man's great hope?
This tattered rot at the end of a rope.

The Radiance in a Dark Wood

In the Chill—
        what is nameless but the Source, the Cause
Of the unsleeping terror which blackens every life?
And shakes men on to find the Christ for a world
That only lives through the daily crucifixion
Of most of its kind?
        Within that
The heart freezes.

All else is named, and useless. Fear is the Grace
Which moves the stone. The laws of the universe

Grind on as the laws of an executioner
Whose knife has shaped the grove and splashed its leaves
With the innocent blood of all who worship there.
        In the Darkness
Love must hide its human face.

O not on a Cross but in a mortal womb,
Like victims bound to the rack of a mad king,
The sons of earth coil round their heritage.
        But from that Darkness
Life yet digs its standing fuel—
        And to this
The spirit bows. Unto this we give no mere name
We give a flesh, and a world, and a dream—
                            O honored
Be the Light that stays
Though all else returns unto the Darkness—
                            O in that
Is a Birth, and a *fire!* O Great Growl
Arun home
Shind cold Laddie dealbrekk Thy
FURY

O hert doun in Thee I keen the sweet
And lone for still it calls to One O One none has
And a' the lost alain the Beastfilled Dark

O blind and corrupt are the living
Corrupted and still are the dead
Black leaves that rustle in a frolicking wind
Driven leaves in a beautiful and terrible forest

A Radiance where! (O star flame somber wind . . .)
Wherewhere
Where is it running?
        O into the Light
Death must raise its human face.

Portrait of the Artist as an Interior Decorator

Ah, it's a damn pity that you were put to all the trouble
    of being born.
You're such a nerveless, spineless little whelp. (Even though
    you are a *perfect dear.*)
It's a crying shame you had to be subjected to something
    as common and trite as that.

Painting, music, poetry—the whole art thing, in fact—
They're all on the dull side really, unless, that is to say, old chap,
One can tinker them into being a spot of fun, a witty game . . .
Where one can be clever, *oh deadly so,* but
Not worth being truly serious about—no, never *truly serious.*

Go to it,
Pretty-pinkie away at it,
At your "beautifully" beautiful, "artfully" artful
Something or other—which, for the sake of accuracy,
I'll call a bed (*Now Don't Be Scared*), a precisely
Fashioned, precisely daubed and plumed and caparisoned
Bed . . . where nobody, but absolutely nobody, would ever have
The bad taste to take a woman
Or himself to get an honest night's sleep
Or to beat out an illness or a drunk
Or to die.

Ah, you're such a clever, lifeless little phony,
With precisely *the* correct manner for doing everything
That's useless, worthless, and quite safely dead.
I can guess what it is that bores you.
Life is not often worth the bother really—
And that whole art thing gets rather a bore
When one sees people treating it seriously, you know.

"Breathe on the Living"

Breathe on the living,
They are numb.
The dead have tidings,
These have none.

Stones roll off graves,
Men rise not.
Your Son was saved,
Ours cry out.

Send down a light,
All's dark here.
And prove not Your love,
As men have done.

Weekend Bathers

Sun on their naked shoulders
Like a sparkling hand;
Marge and her big-legged sweetie
Laughing to beat the band—
O glory in the Garden!
He finds her halter straps
And such pretties are exposed;
Yet, *Wonder*—now what is that?
Perhaps the water knows.
Thunder rides with the gnat.
Ah, each day a weaker bridge is crossed,
And nearer rush the wings;
Too soon all youthful swagger's lost
In the dark hurry of things.

Together—(if this will place them better),
They weigh three hundred pounds;
And quite often are their haunts
Where postmen make their rounds.
Beauty gets what it wants—
And should [would you? or *you?*]
They sin upon the bank,
They've only themselves to thank . . .
Since heaven does seem a trifle overdue.

The Question Is, Who Is Afraid of What?

Worth no more than a man's hard pride,
Hard ribs against his woman's side;
For both in the night's wild later stages
Are humbled by that sense of sorrow
Which underlies the mating touch
Of every living thing—for the touch
Of generation has death in it,
And a pride of this kind will be dealt with
In the usual way. Yet the will
To disguise the faceless beast on the sheet
Has made the star-born people, and guided feet
On the valley's shadowy roads—

                      where all,
Of course,
Are met with a sterner show of pride, and old
Queens and famous whores have been known
To jig about in somewhat drab apparel.

So—and it will hurt no one . . .
Be proud of the rider—
Look at the legless nag
He's got to ride on!

"Put the Rest Away, O Put the Rest Away"

Put the rest away, O put the rest away!
I'll tell you what it is I've found—
Ah, there's little time for tumbling in the hay.
Then best and worst get planted in the ground.

How many lives do you expect to squander?
The soul has wings like a bird? Y'know, I wonder.
For the dead do stay awful quiet like—
You blow out a match . . . *poof!* Where's the light?

So put the rest away, O put the rest away!
I'll tell you what it is I'm sure of—
Neither of deathless souls nor fleeting clay,
But that we're most alive when we love!

The Lute in the Attic

As this comes in
Call you
I call you
The apples are red again in Chandler's Valley
            redder for what happened there
And the ducks move like flocculent clocks
            round and round, and round
The seven fat ducks whose mouths
            were wet crimson once
                O William Brewster Hollins
            I call you back!
        Come you and stand here
By the fog-blunted house that is silent now
And watch these terrible ducks moving
            slowly round the rock of Santa Maura.

Your father's gone daft, Willy.
    Did you know that?
And Isalina's flaxen hair is the color of the mud
    at the bottom of Rathbeggin Creek.
Her teeth are crooked and yellow,
        more like an old sickly dog's
    than a woman's—but her eyes
    still hold their light, people say.
(Though for me it's a very strange light, Willy.
I remember I saw a different thing there
        a few hours before it happened—
    and the two of you lying naked together
    under the apple trees.
For myself, to be truthful, her eyes have changed.
    They are not at all as they were then.)

    In his poor unease your father
Has come to love rather fearful things.
"Don't hurt my spider-ladies!" he screams,
When Beth or Danny go in to clean around him.
It would be better if he died, the town whispers.

Sam Hanner drowned two summers ago.
    Old Krairly wanted to carve
"Lived on strong drink, but his last was weak"
On the stone—the Fathers said no, of course.
There was talk that Sam watched you do it.
    Did you know that?

        As this comes in
    and so much hate will go anywhere
I call you back
To lie here in the rain and the dark beside the willows
Hearing the voices of lovers under the flowery hedge
            O William Brewster Hollins
I call you back!

Come you and lie here at the side of your brother . . .
    I can tell you exactly how many times
    these seven lean ducks have gone
    fiercely round the rock of Santa Maura—
And show you worse things than your father sees
And show you things far worse than your father sees, Willy.

Fog over the Sea and the Sun Going Down

    Shrouded maidens sleep on the wave,
Their garments flecked by the wounded sun—
Listen . . . (O *Nellie Malone,* only the wan silence now)
The bru-hooned Ladies are singing
Down in their cold, moving grave—
And in Captain Swaggle's skull two gwerps
Are blindly kissing.
    (O *Alba-Maria,* only the black silence now)
Sing correlay and lift the startled goddess up!
On the shore,
        as though a mouth had rested there,
        the glistening wonder!
    And floating in across the water,
These strands of gray, wet hair . . .

      Blood on the ancient water
    and darkness falling on the world.
Down the beach
The Marsden kids are torturing a snail
With a jagged stick.
(O star-led Caravans . . . "Master, Master, I fear
        this huge and surly fish!")
    Sing correlay and correlemus
For all ladies, kids, and captains
        who're soon lost in
These coils of wet, gray hair.

The Little Black Train

(Suggested by a folk song)

Who hears that whistle blowing?
Who hears that hellish din?
Not the living—but they will.
    Ah, where is it going?
    And where has it been?
Ask the darkness that falls on the hill.

Behind—a ghost smoke flowing;
Ahead—that quiet inn
Which all may enter—but none come back.
    Ah, where are they going?
    And where have they been?
Ask the thistles that bloom on the track.

The cabman is all-knowing
(They say), and at peace within;
But it must be lonely at night.
    Ah, where is he going?
    And where has he been?
Ask the millions who wait without light.

Black roses need no sowing,
And the soul is born in sin
(We're told)—fouled by that ancient pair.
    Ah, where is it going?
    And where has it been?
Ask the star that touches your loved one's hair.

And now the train is slowing,
And the passengers they grin,
As well they might—a little sly.
    Ah, where are they going?
    And where have they been?
Ask the lanterns that swing in the sky.

To the Tune of an Ancient Song

A man out of the fire rises,
    O out of the fire rises;
All Life and Death he'd save.

What has he found?
Why does he weep?

    The bones upon the ground,
    The laws for butchering sheep.

Whence then his rising?
How then his song?

    O the grandeur in king and slave;
    The world not evil, but *wrong*.

A Plate of Steaming Fish

The Scene: A Fishermen's Boarding House
The Time: Many Years Ago
Menu: Choice of gudgeon, remora, tautog, skopjack, burgall,
    gurnard, chogset, etc., etc.
The Speaker: A Sailor's Widow

As you would know, having lived in trouble here at my side
    For such an outwardly-long time,
I dread this hour, now, at the day's end, when seamen supper.
Sitting before this checkered cloth, the worn silk of my gown
Rubbed by their tarry legs, the thick sweat of them like
    a breathing
On my face and breasts—O tonight again, and on again
    forever,
Listening to the shameful jokes that are meant to taunt me,
Digging my nails into the ugly tan and blue of these squares.
    O come and take me back to my own people!

The flowering tree we planted outside the kitchen window
    is gone.
Your brothers chopped it down and burned it.
Now I see their fyke nets and brush-hinged weirs
    a-drying there.
And along the wren-gray, friendly wall,
Where I set such tiny yellow roses,
Their stabbing hooks and evil-looking lobster-cages hang.
    O come and take me away from here!

And all I went to the lone cliffs, to the streaming rocks
    where the sea
And the whole bitter world cried with your name—
O heart, my heart, how should I not have found thee there?
How was I to know that I lay with strangers in the rain there?
Bald Tom and Ernie Willis, Old Roaren and
    Captain Donahue—
O mine is only a spiritual fault, my love . . .
Yet they threw me down, it was you lying above me there.
    O come and make me pure again!

On the morning *The Kalinn* sailed, and its masts and spars
    like the hands
Of a child waving back to us—to your mother, who is dead now;
    And to your wife, who'd rather be, than like I am,
This woman of forty-one, no longer straight, her skin and hair
Dried by sun and wind, and her breasts by lonely grief
    in the night—
    O as it went down in the toppling sparkle,
    And the little flowers of phosphorous
    Rested for a moment in that gray and gentle cradle,
I saw the figure of our love standing there on the water!
    And so, confused and mocked by all of them,
I wait at the side of our watching son and daughter.
    O come and take us away from here!
O rise up out of thy cold grave, Lennie
        and take us away from here . . .

383

The Orange Bears

The orange bears with soft friendly eyes
Who played with me when I was ten,
Christ, before I left home they'd had
Their paws smashed in the rolls, their backs
Seared by hot slag, their soft trusting
Bellies kicked in, their tongues ripped
Out, and I went down through the woods
To the smelly crick with Whitman
In the Haldeman-Julius edition,
And I just sat there worrying my thumbnail
Into the cover—What did he know about
Orange bears with their coats all stunk up with soft coal
And the National Guard coming over
From Wheeling to stand in front of the millgates
With drawn bayonets jeering at the strikers?

I remember you could put daisies
On the windowsill at night and in
The morning they'd be so covered with soot
You couldn't tell what they were anymore.

A hell of a fat chance my orange bears had!

Shapes

As a horse of shell, the water's.
Curled in its tracks, where the creaking
Spokes of an unknown wagoner
Turn, blind serpents sing
To riders of a great ungoing—
While answering hoofs smash up from the deep.
O what does a soul look like when it's asleep?

As a wall of space, the earth's.
Before it strange hunters gather,
Who stalk one another from birth;
Yet behind it, and quite near—
Say those who've gone there—
Men may live without hate or fear;
But where are the hands that would scale the wall?
O how much nicer to speak of some dead Adam's fault.

As a hall of monsters, the air's.
Stripped, buckled—out of whack
From explosions (bursts of stained tin
                and sweat-matted hair) . . .
O a thinking blood smacks
Down on the sin of these poor fools.
      Alas, your fine machine is no liar:
      You chose to live by, now fall by, fire.
O what might we have built with man himself as the tool?

As the dream of a lion, is fire's.
Dry sticks near a heap of dawn-pondered
Bones.
      Who kindled cold reason?
      Not that fellow in the blood-spattered
Roadster; nor those fine patriotic ladies
Who turned tail betwixt a soldier's paydays;
      Nor even Tobias Q. Jones
Who threw his blades away and shaved with the hones.

No. It was a raging flame
In brave and peaceful hearts
Which kindled cold reason.
      That, and that alone.
O when shall their fiery names be heard again
     in this black season?
O the names of free men who were chained to a stone.

As a tree of darkness, is life's.
Bough on bough on bough
Surely . . . these warm bodies . . . !
I—with you—and with them—
    wait on a bitter twig
    for the light of truth to guide us
    out of this darkness
    that we may do a real work for men
    to put their love and their lives in—
And that we bring no birds of steel or of curious gold there
But invite real birds to come in and sing there
And none need be hungry or homeless or cold there.

    As the thoughts of the snow, is death's.
"Blown leaves, crowns . . ." And the caves
Of Haynen? are they to be swept
Under thy silent drift? "In their graves
Beside the *ing* and the *en*
        lie the patient great and
        the once-beautiful faces of women . . ."
        O unwept
Be words.   Between them and us
The dark voice.
    "But a man
Chained to a stone!" That is well.
O if anywhere, there, there, is the throne.
And that is well. *O that is well!*

"This Summer Earth"

    This summer earth
Lion's skin spread on the warm ground
Beside the listening waters
    O summer earth

Wheels of the golden chariot turning
Slowly over the breathing fields
        Driver, we are
        In sorrow here

O we are in sorrow here
Winter is in our hearts

        Bird and leaf
These listening fields and breathing waters
        Yes, and even
Your chariot's golden wheels
Are splashed with blood

        There is no summer here
Why, even the tiny white blossoms
        Of the wild cherry tree
        Have been stained.

After an Old Song

        The horror came
When I was in my mother's womb.
I think that there's the wrong.
        The horror stealeth the heart away;
        At first, at last, it's in our clay.
All flesh is sick, death is the healing wing;
And worms complete the cure for everything.

        O the horror stealeth the mind away;
        Awake, asleep, it has its say.
And through the veiled shadows looks the Father.
How should I greet Him, and I so barren of all save fear?
        O the horror stealeth the heart away;
        Even He—*He did not wish to stay.*

"O When I Take My Love Out Walking"

O when I take my love out walking
In the soft frosted stillness of this summer moon

Then are the mysteries all around us
O what can I say!
   the ever-known, the ever-new
   like her they seem
O lully, lullay
   only this little moment is real
Here at the edge of the world
   and the throne. The rest's a lie
   which shadows scheme.

Now gentle flowers are awash on the sleeping hill
And as I bend to kiss her opened lips
O then do the wonders and the sparklings seem
A shabby tinsel show for my dear queen.

Wouldn't You Be after a Jaunt
of 964,000,000,000,000 Million Miles?

When my Uncle came to visit us
He brought cigars and a jug of wine
And a mule he had just invented

Round dark he put the mule on the grass
Near the porchsteps and soon it commenced
To walk up a rope into the sky

Then a speck moved across Sheliak
While almond-green Nath and Menkar
A moment later felt new tin hooves

And all the heavens I swear flapped like
Some delighted bird with glowing eyes
Fixed down on our bedazzlated faces

In the excitement Betelgeuse fell
And Uncle Pluddie burnt a big hole
Clear through his favorite yellow duck

Pants. By three o'clock the wine ran out
And we were all a little wondrous
About when that damn mule would get back

I went in the house for some reason or other
And when I got out there was my Uncle at
The rope helping it down. It looked tired.

If a Poem Can Be Headed into Its Proper Current
Someone Will Take It within His Heart
to the Power and Beauty of Everybody

Arrive to arrive and to arrive here in such thick
White silence
The eye turned away
Without vanity or desire
And seeing is seen
And the music of the silence flows on the world
With a rhythm and a pulse which are changed
In the blood-beat as the heart's course by death

And hearing is heard as in the very sea
There is no sound
So in the purest thought
When vanity and desire of all mortal ends

Have been submerged
We may join the thinking which is eternally around us
And be thought about
For the common good
Of the one creature which everything is

Man is not to direct or to be directed
Anymore than a tree or a cloud or a stone

Man is not to rule or to be ruled
Anymore than a faith or a truth or a love

Man is not to doubt or to be doubted
Anymore than a wave or a seed or a fire

There is no problem in living
Which life hasn't answered to its own need

And we cannot direct, rule, or doubt what is beyond
Our highest ability to understand
We can only be humble before it
We can only worship ourselves because we are part of it

The eye in the leaf is watching out of our fingers
The ear in the stone is listening through our voices
The thought of the wave is thinking in our dreams
The faith of the seed is building with our deaths

I speak of the music of the silence
As being what is left when the singers and the dancers
Have grown still
Something is left there
A part of the reverence and of the need
A part of the fear and the pain and the wonder
And it goes on there
Coming from where it came from (O beautiful goddess!)

And reaching for what it can have little awareness of
A rhythm quite unlike any we know here
Bound and swayed as we are by the blood's orchestration
Bound and swayed as we are by the orchestration within us
By the deceptive orchestration of the blood

And I speak of the goddess
I speak of the goddess
I speak of the beautiful goddess

O tell them what I would say

Down in the Lone Valley

What cheer, O Ren Jaldain?
Have the grieves come to your full
Dish of skin? ha,
And the slimy teeth of them
A bad habit to get accustomed to—
Happily the world
Is a stinking drain. But, man,
You should see—*first moon on your grave*—
The cold, dancing hands of the rain!

Dear Mistress Jean, your bitty bird,
Sweet little nestling—how she would perch
On a hairy bough and chirp to a sweaty ear!
Ah, Ren, let the hags in the ground
Give you constancy; for now Jeannie pecks
And is pecked by that shaggy old runny-eyes
You kicked a-scramble down the stairs one day.
Unfortunately their love
Is not profound. But, man,
You should hear—*new frost on your grave*—
The priestly voice of silence singing to the wound.

How Jimsey O'Roon and Peter Stack, Coal Miners, Came to Be Put in the Ferbettville (Pa.) Jail Early One Saturday Night

A Family Story

Ah, ruined are the Queens of the high and the low
   Flowers bloom and wither
   And off on the dark wind they blow

Long since the time their wives had set for them to come
      from work—
In fact, shadows were beginning to rot smoothly on the fields,
      and the herk
Behind the hill was turning cold, with ghosts upon her wrists—
There they were, the one holding the other up at both
      their risks;
The two of them as drunk as how-d'-do, their paychecks bar'd
And more than half-spent . . . singing of the maiden Hansagarde.
A better thing it would have been if they had done their chores
At home, instead of running off to fool around with wantons.

They'd got to where a sylvan plenitude displaced saloons;
And a passion for truth cried on the grass; and in the willows,
      surly foons.
The night was coming down, their spirits too, when Petey saw
An old burying ground with crumbling headstones, and an awe—
Filled urge to make orations took possession of the pair.
Said O'Roon: "Do you suppose in regard to the growing
      of their hair,
That clause about 'the crowning glory' rises?" Stack
      touched a stone:
"I guess you'd need something to do being alone down there."

Some distance on they crossed a pasture; tawny cows
      and their companion

392

Munched clover in it quietly. "Pete, I know, of course,
The hell we'll take when we get back, but what a pretty duckling
Is the vegetable they call the horse; down in the muckland
We sweat our years away, forgetting why we ever came
    to the earth."
"I'd like these bosseens too," his friend replied, "save for
    the chancy mirth
Of marrying one." O'Roon hitched out a match and fired a barn:
"When we come stumbling home in the dark, this one
    will give no harm."

"Now I suggest it's getting late, and we are here," O'Roon
Went on, "and town's there; so let's jiss on in as we sing this tune:
'Oh! sweet as any berry that grows just out of reach on the tree-ee,
Is Bonnie Maud, the pride and sorrow of the Susquehannee.
Upon her cunningness a thousand angels worked, in double shifts,
And wise men to themselves do tender the fulsome bounty
    of her gifts.'"

The soft brown owls were whooing in the kreen; the stars
    looked full
Of thinking—of Egypt, perhaps. (What they rode was neither
    of farm nor heath.)
They waded brooks and rivers, valleyed and hilled,
    philosophizing
Of the evil, pure hell of a miner's life, without disguising
The ardor of their bias; but once, when Petey's waving arm
Shot forward, he observed, "Horns on a nag, now I, personally,
    find a bit odd."
To which O'Roon rejoined, "The matter is, life tends to cheat
    a fellow."
And Stack: "Contrary like, if he was a cow, where would he
    come by that bellow?"
" 'Oh! fairer than the dollar bill I found on the street
    in Reading,
But how she does string me along when I hint at a beading.'"

Now Ferbettville is typical of many rural places;
Sodden, dull, and absolutely lacking in all human graces.
The Society for the Prevention of Everything Worth a Damn
Was stinking up the courthouse lawn . . . and doffing
     spangled tams
At some new device for wholesale murder. Then, arrayed
In nature's best, for they'd shed their wet clothes
     along the way,
Stack and O'Roon rode wildly in on the back of a golden deer,
Shouting, "Ho! ho! we're alive, not dead! Do you hear!
     Do you bloody well hear!"

Lament for the Makers of Songs

Now the singers leave the darkened garden.
The rash and the holy are still, without light.
Hands, now slack as rags—they once held love.
Their instruments fall, and they rot on the ground.

Fools of God, they go.
The flowery tree is dead.
The cry of the bitter snow and
The giggling of pimps in a hangman's bed
Are the only songs I know.

The sun goes down on the reddening tide.
Chains rattle on a bloody rock . . .
This is the cross
     which man has made;
And this, the wheel . . . and the murder, the hunger
     the fear, and the pain
     which man has molded
To the loss of his spirit, his reason, and his world.

The beasts are loose, inside. Our killdom's crime—
Man's will be done.
As he was in the beginning,
So shall he end, in slime.

O what is there to sing!
Man has conquered everything.
Hate stares out of every face.
The final victory is near—
And the baaing of the doomed as they toe
Their righteous marks in a butchers' race
Is the only sound I hear.

Old Man

I'm now tending a son's hearth,
And the hours of my life seem as flies
Rasping at the closed screen doors
Of a house where a world lies dead.
There's no rest there's a grumbling wound;
And as I toss on this narrow cellar cot,
A young woman dances through the stains,
As real now as ever then—but ah, I'm not.
These gray furnace ashes are as lively
As her husband is now, and as warm.

I once planed at a carpenter's bench,
The sweet curls of pine like a spray
Of little fingers, or the slivers
From a sun bright as the day's;
And I had always somebody
To notice when my joinings
Made the set a whit stronger

For a man and wife to be playing in—
But beds are twin now and strangers
Make their weekly slaying there.

My boy's kids all day they clang
At their guerrilla shooting;
But try to mention the old kings,
You'd think time itself was closing.
Small frogs in gramp's coat pocket,
Gloves with the fingers pinned shut;
And my shoes taking on an odd fit
Whereupon their puppies squat.
It's true that these spites are minor,
But of quick whims the slow murder.

A cup of an honest whisky,
The bite of its mist on my brain,
And a door clicks up its latchkey
And I walk in out of the rain.
But seldom do I get enough money
To buy me into that ballroom,
Where the tall dancers move to a music
That's far cleaner than any of ruin's songs.
The first thing if I could be rich,
I d get blindo and sing up angels in a ditch.

By life wasted and by death denied—
O a sour breath breathes on the rose;
And what I have left I would hide—
Gray hairs in a shrunken nose.
Rude are the words of old men,
But far ruder this talking flesh
That would speak to its Maker again—
And I think not about fire,
Or prints of a hand on stone,
But of a grave being gone.

Two for History

Loud on the bright-necked grass
The golden music beats,
Smug as a banker's elbow,
Beautiful as an empty street;
There Clem and Junie lie—
Tabulating each sacred blessing
Which droppeth not from the sky,
So much as when undressing
They found real things to sanctify.

Moose-eared Mullen he's called,
And Babe O'Gruck is she—
But Trojan Helen's cold,
And dark is that Galilee.
Now in the sun they sweat
And make their poor little human noise—
Ah, bodies of laughing gods . . . soon
In the damned ground you'll lose your poise.

Then wings from living shoulder-blades,
O Clem and Miss O'Gruck!
There's none among the famous dead not
Envious as you take your mindless fun.

Poor Gorrel

For a woman named Gorrel
To be afraid of birds
Is neither unusual
Nor important—with other things
Like they are.

She'd never married, but
For twenty-eight years
Had the evening habit of taking
Her cats, Tom and Matilda,
With her to call on a barber
Who had a shack deep in the woods
When
And where
The four of them would munch almond-flavored peppermints
Until all hours.

Two weeks ago—O Lord was it ever raining!—I mean
    it was *raining*—
Gorrell and her cats
Were hurrying home—the rain coming
Down harder and harder—when just at the old footbridge
—Which the rain had washed some slimy-looking grubs
On—a huge, furry owl-like thing with razor-sharp claws
Got Gorrel down and
Above the slashing sound
Of the rain a candy-coated scream
Rang out. The eight cats (and no wonder
Really) all had severe colds when finally found.

Family Portrait

Great tarry wings splatter grayly up out of the blinding glare of
the open-hearth furnaces. In the millyard the statue of some old
bastard with a craggy grin is turning shit-colored above the bowed
heads of the night shift that comes crunching in between the
piles of slag. That's my father washing at the kitchen sink. The
grimy water runs into the matted hair of his belly. The smell of
scorched cloth and sweat adds its seasoning to the ham and
cabbage. The muscles of his back ripple like great ropes of greased

steel. An awesome thing to see! Yet he never raised his hand in anger against any man—which was a very lucky thing. A soapy snort escapes him with the sound of a thunderclap, and my kid sister vigorously rattles the lid of a pot. In the parlor my grandfather lies, two days dead. "Aye, and the only statue for him's a spade in 'is stumpy teeth now." —"A lapful of withered nuts to make the muckin' grasses grow . . ." —"Hush you are, for here be the priest with his collar so tidy and lady-clean." —"Liked his bit of drink, Hughey did, God take the long thirst out of his soul and all."

I myself remember once after a brush with Mrs. Hannan, who happened to be passing hard under his window one morning, he told me, "Ah, there's only one thing worse than the rich, my lad . . . and that's the poor, and that's the ruckin', lyin', unmannerin', snivelin' poor, my lad!" and a great whip of tobacco juice lashed out onto the tar-topped road.

On, on into the small hours went the singing and the laughing and the gay, wonderful story-telling . . . and all the while the candle wax dripped slowly down on my grandfather's shiny black Sunday suit.

An Old Pair of Shoes

Instead of throwing them away,
I'd put them in a bag on the shelf;
Where, forgotten as that world
They tramped through, and the self
I had then, the quiet dust
Settled, and other feet walked on.
Here's the nail that made a deep
Pit in my heel when I looked

399

The whole damn town over for a job
Those lousy winters of the "recession;"
And here's the scar a policeman's horse
Left one of the hungrys in that "mob."

Well, my cheap-shoe time is gone—
(For the moment anyway)—the rent
Is paid (clear to the first of the month),
And I smoke tailor-mades on the lawn.
Many of the books I wanted then
—And records, prints, and magazines—
I have. The work of "our finest minds" . . .
And every day I'm more amazed
At how quickly I could choose
Between the lot—and this pair of dusty shoes.
Ah, in them walk my youth,
My unsoiled hopes—belief that some day truth
Would set all things right. Hell yes, Jack—
That's one deposit you won't never get back!

The Event at Konna

The light was eerie, unreal. In our rush
to get away we'd forgotten how early
and fiercely sudden—Christ! it
    was only four o'clock—
the day ended in that place of hell.

Blood-red sun
above the yellow mud
of the huts one moment—and then just
a gray swinging weight
    in a gray nothingness
the next. The green world
gone, and our wounded begging for water.

I have nothing to say
that I can say without weeping;
it is well for a man—(if a man I am
still)—to keep silent at times.
The various official reports
have all been honest and exact—
            except for one thing:
They state that men fell in the darkness there . . .

But it wasn't men at all who fell there.
It was children
        children crying in the terrible darkness
        for a Father Who never came.

Winter at the Inn

(Somewhat, as then, aroused as they were,
Those of today can imagine wonders;
But now, of course, it can lead to nothing,
Unless you call wordless sorrow something.)

At the gay at the apple at the white sun
Throw down your purity, sky . . .
Warm ruddy voices float out
Across the cold peaceful fields . . .
Another glass of steaming wine and one more
Song around the board—Good men
And beautiful ladies all go journeying
Alone into the grim night.
        Ha-la ho! come along, bring
        The tears to our eyes again.

Is that you, Tim? and Maideleen Anuin! my
God it's nice to know you haven't
Gone yet—O wonderful things
All of us, eh? eyes and hands full

Of love and sorrow—Ah, life is a funny
Sad proposition, now
Like a flexing wing and then like the snow
Falling in the stillness there.
   Ha-la ho! come along, bring
   The tears to our eyes again.

"Do Me That Love"

Do me that love
As a tree, tree
Where birds and wind
Sing though they know
How real night is
And no one can
Go on for long
In any way
Do me that love

Do me that love
As the rain, rain
That has voices
In it, the greats'
And fools', poor dead
From old weathers—
Lives considered
And rejected
As ours will be.
The rain comes down
And flowers grow
On the graves of
Our enemies
Do me that love

Red Wine and Yellow Hair

Ah that the world could use a dream or a flaming truth
Cold teeth in their fat throats! O the lock is crusted over
With frauds and tricks, a silt of greed and compromise
O break the damn thing! And I sleep here away
From sorrow. The winding sheet and the paler thighs
A Grecian virgin, my silken braids all tangled with night.
Is late so soon that it runs the stag and the bell to cover
Before the warm mouth can be flowered in youth's merry weather?
O let them remember me, and forget the lies and the hating
For the dark sex that coveteth all shall soon be their lover.
Sword on the wind, black knuckles of a thief, is this
King to be left here like a cast-off dog? the bloated
Tongues of flies licking the juice of His saving wounds?
O come a little way in, death, my lads have no supper
And the old woman she wails like a goose, ah there's plenty
Of fodder and beer as well though the bastards don't want
        a meatless
Nose like me poking round their slops. O Rosalind
And Penelope, what lovely grub they must have had!
Ragged sacks for a fool to put his neighbor in, the digging
Grave is proof that none is given what all would have.
Blather dung and rubble, a coat and sup, their meanness
Is my lot. Back down and hold your clutching gab.
Swine hiss amongst their gems and Ledas bite their nails
Above the mirrored waters of this destroying world.
O none save the fiery hunter would stay to mourn the tiger.
Dotellers told in the black dice of their cities. And I lie here
Removed from all sorrow. A withered heart and a rusted dagger
The Laird of Emmet, my powerful hands they squeeze at the dust.
Is life the meat that swings the falcon down from his highs?
Yes, a poisoned bait in the trap of a vicious fancier.
O let him chase me now, and give this slowness haste
For the dark peace that abideth here is filled with eyes.

If Fannin's river whispers the fate of my tried love
And a red wild voice laments where all sorrow lies
O Willie brought me ribbons, I thought he was so mild
Prettied me for an angel, but under a devil I got my child.
Cold rain on the talking stone, the weeping mind
Poor guest at a poorer feast, O who is born dies
And a grim hand colors the rose. O wondrous Light
Titanic wings of fire sweeping down through the night.
There was never money enough, ach I'm tired
Of showing them pictures of plump-bottomed queens
And reading aloud at wine-and-biscuity tales
Where ghosts rattle the lids of tombs and flick up like beans.
O resurrect my sons, Lord, from this empty table!
Worms begin lower, and they gather all, but the mold
Out-thinks the stone and the hangman's tree. Words of the flesh
Bleed out of the moving dark . . . We fall we thirst we are cold
While in the summer meadow lovers find what is warm.

    A broken cup and a wisp of rotted hair
Come cry come in wrath of love and be not comforted
Until the grave that is this world is torn asunder
For human the lock and and human the key
O everything that lives is holy!
And Man and God are one in that mystery.

from *Orchards, Thrones & Caravans* (1952)

For Miriam

As beautiful as the hands
Of a winter tree
And as holy
Base are they beside thee

As dross beside thee

O green birds
That sing the earth to wakefulness
As tides the sea
Drab are they beside thee

As tinsel beside thee

O pure
And fair as the clouds
Wandering
Over a summer field
They are crass beside thee
The hands
Move through the starhair

As tawdry beside thee

But of Life?

What I want in heart
—*O stiller, wider, nearer*—
Said the tree
Is that none come touching
For their own stuff
Any part of
Me. And over him a wall
Of shifting fog began
To build, little on little—
Like a wet shroud.
No birds
Came then. And with them
Stars
Stayed. His poor branches
Trailed white and still. He
Wept. His
Loudest cry went unheard.

So was Crucifixion's tree

The Green Fires

Died in the meadow, there
Fallen, they've all gone
Down the wind
Old men, maidens, children, dry
Twigs in the wind

Hush, what is
That hurrying there, along the wall
Its face agrin, agrin

Under leaves hidden, and green
Sticky the arm-hair
Flames lick
The hand-backs, smoking torrents
Charge
Down the thigh-flesh
Fields towns heavens crackle asunder!
Green flaming
Teeth eating this world

Fiery rot again enwombed

Lowellville Cemetery: Twilight

Gone silence down lowered sun
O at this each
Of everything here
These poor knotted hands lost
Under the darkened foam
Of grass. Stone
Unto stone and flesh unto flesh
Scattered as cold petals
On the floor of winter's
Own walking. All should
Be dark.
And dark on dark forever
Now.
Sundown and world, too.
As it is for them,
Lying here.
Why is it not?

Why is it not

Watching Neighbors' Children

Little gay bonnets! so many
Bright pretty birds dancing
By this morning!
In your candystick stockings,
Where's a braver bunch!
Jenny, Ann, Kate—
Which one will in yonder meadow
Meet Old Bloody-Beard?
Ah, stained be the lilies
No eye see, or
Voice tell—
Save leaf's, and wind-cry—
Which
In humble bridal bed
Shall write the race's story?
Ah, both—
And all hand that

On—O bravest dancers stilled!

The Constant Bridegrooms

Far down the purple wood
Coats of a company
Of silent soldiers
Flap idly in the wind.
There they have stood
Since early day—
Faces turned incuriously to the sound
Of the dry rustling

Of leaves in the wind.
No command has reached
Them there;
All silent have they stood
As
Though they were asleep—
Now night darkens their coats.
Far away
Their names are spoken

Somewhere at world's end

The Unreturning Hosts

Supreme in the distance, veiled
As one's own horizon,
The ancients stand,
Immutably shadowless in lengthening obliquity.
Stone is the rain
That falls on
Them. Panthers of frozen gold pad
Soundlessly round their shrouded
Immobility, while history's piping flutes
Shred hollowly against their
Stone music.
Honeycombed with shadow, great
Unsorrowing
Roses garland their sleep.
And stone is the air . . .
Of stone,
Their sea . . . *O dreamers lost*

In an unrotting solemnity.

Folly of Clowns

Come laughing when the wind
Has blown a hole
In the world
See the moving sparkle covers
Such chits as orchards
Thrones and caravansaries
Blackened eyesockets above the grit
And silt of destinies
O come here laughing anyway
And let your head
Be daft
With sun and glitter of
Running
Naked beside the waters
As in pallid sand life's
Statues sleep
Tattered arm waves up!

School keep or not

All the Flowery

Along the red ledge I
Counted so many blossoms
That from first
To last nothing could hold
Them. No number of
Vases or even
Countries like Seyn or Merry Waain
No number of horses

Black as inked snow with
The pink stain of
Girls on
Their massive backs could stride
Through
Even the first row.
And I, as my fathers
Would . . . watching
The nude sad riding—

With joy, with fear!

At Grandmother's Wake

Cot of an old lady
Grubby candle dripping wax
On its sheet
A grimy blanket, wadding coming
Loose along the edges—
And under it
Silverfish and roaches scurrying like sores—
While nearby on flabby haunches
Elbows crook'd like fat worms
Squat the drunken mourners
Each louder
Than the next in praise
Of
One whose name'd need
Greening with something stronger'n water
Aye, brushing flies
Off the cold foot

Of Cinderella's all too earthly daughter

Two Ghosts Together

She walks beside the river
The birds of shade
Fastening their claws
Into her shoulders and hair

And ever more awed
By her sadness
Evening's arcades whisper like muffled wounds
Under her sorrowing feet
Dark words of the river
Singing to the leaf

Long ago
As a maiden, she walked
Here
And all the woodland
Was amove with joys of
Gathering love
Hair, birds . . . O golden

Sheaf! *O winged thief*

Where Every Prospect

There will be no evil
No throat bared in
Scarlet agony here
But only the green grass
Waving beside peaceful roads
Along which gay
Runners carry thoughts of the sun

To fill the wilderness
With animals of loftier design
Than bowed to thug
And gun
In whose image created they
This
Where no peace is
Where only the stench of
Smoking flesh
Can adequately say, *Now*

Man is not evil

It's My Town!

Streetlights wreathed under saffron curls
In crazy jollity herds
Of lurching storefronts
Laughter of the gentleman wind
Frets the neck-hair
Of scurrying shopgirls
And then it begins to rain!
—Well, as it does
We see a good-natured
Fellow full to the brim
Squatting happily
Beside his circus poster collection
Drinking
Wine from the bottle
And laughing to fold flags
For he's
Just bought the town

Yowee! let 'er rain!

Walks There?

They come closer together, vines
Of the rain, tendrils
Gleaming silver, shining
As they fall, shining as
They thresh down, one
Upon another like
Ropes of thin fish swinging, threshing
Down, flower-like yet
Snake- and fish-like, too;
Coiled scale on petal,
Petal on
Gleaming gill-plate, the silvery
Spittle
As from a mouth
That's half a reptile's, half
A flower's . . .
O this strange air-garden where

Serpents, and roses, together are gathered

So Be It

There are no rooms here
Better go right on
No light shows
This world is finished, done
Let the dark come
Let night strike
Let no stone be left unturned
Let it be over
The lie told too often

Truth itself is eaten away
Let it
Be over and done with
Forever
Houses for grisly whores
Light to light funeral trains
Let it
Be over and written

Off, everybody's bad debt

Under a Tree

More than this flecked thing . . . ?
Tell me, will you,
What that is?
See how delicately it's made!

It lay half hidden
Under a tree;
A few leaves had fallen quite
Near where it rested . . .
Its eyes, as you see,
Open when they please.
Its breast
Is like some bluish chalk
Dappled
As by flashing keys,
Swung back and forth in
The sun.
You wonder whose it

Is . . . why, it's His

Beautiful You Are

Cathedral evening, tinkle of candles
On the frosted air
Beautiful you are
Beautiful your eyes, your lips, your hair!

Ah still they come
Evenings like chalices
Where little roofs and trees drink
Until a rude hand
Shatters them, one by one

O beautiful you are
My own
Land of holiness, unblemished grace
Springtime
In this winter place
O in the candles there
More beautiful
Than any legend's face

Your eyes, your lips, your hair!

It's a Smallworld

He brings me cast-off innertubes
My friend the giraffe
He can't afford
Very expensive gifts now that
He's lost his employment—
An old man
Used to pay him fifty cents
To swipe the underdrawers

Off some trapeze artists who
Insisted on practicing in
His back yard
But he startled one of
Them
So badly she fell
Smack on his ex-employer

It developed she
Was the detective for
Some animal-welfare syndicate

Should Be Sufficient

Someone may be a horse
Somebody else a bush
Or a 'lassesjug
We don't know from apples

Rivers could be women
Ice, old men
Mountains and harbors could be breadpans
For all we know
Lots of horses eat bushes
Swig out of jugs
Spit blue
We don't know from gaslogs
Anyhow
So gnaw your loaf
And expect to have it too
But next
Time you go rivering

Don't stop for no halfwaycrossings

Day of Rabblement

O come here! a sunflower!
No no no no
O hurry! hurry!
A sunflower is standing here!
No no no no

O come here!
There's a sunflower beside the wall!
No no no no
Great God! hurry! a sunflower!
No no no no

A sunflower!
Come! look at the sunflower!
A sunflower!
No no no no
Then tell me why you
Won't come!

No no no no
No no no no

The Magical Mouse

I am the magical mouse
I don't eat cheese
I eat sunsets
And the tops of trees
I don't wear fur
I wear funnels
Of lost ships and the weather
That's under dead leaves

I am the magical mouse
I don't fear cats
Or woodsowls
I do as I please
Always
I don't eat crusts
I am the magical mouse
I eat
Little birds—and maidens

That taste like dust

Lonesome Boy Blues

Oh nobody's a long time
Nowhere's a big pocket
To put little
Pieces of nice things that
Have never really happened
To anyone except
Those people who were lucky enough
Not to get born

Oh lonesome's a bad place
To get crowded into
With only
Yourself riding back and forth
On
A blind white horse
Along an empty road meeting
All your
Pals face to face

Oh nobody's a long long time

etty Animals

Where are my pretty ones!
Ah-ha! Ah-ha!
Found you! ha!
Bandy legs and all! Ah!

Dance me a dance!
Into it, lads!
Checkerboard for belly, willowroot for tail,
Goofy-go! Goofy-go!
Round the wishingpost, faster, slow . . .
Skip! Ho! ho! ho!

Pretty pretty
In your spotted coats so
Merry!
Dance the gates away!
And of every city make
A carnival
With masks bands gongs!

O my goofy-guys!

Little Cannibal's Bedtimesong

Two bres's, 'n' 'gongo 'brella
Th' goddum buckwheat clovah
Sun he shimes
Birdz he sing-bes loudah loudah
Four she am mimbes

I'n like hur
Bettah'n even m' own fambly mothah

Oz sun he shimes
Birdz he sing-bes up top
Th' goddum buckwheat clovah

Me'n' hur
Dun't wunt no crocodilin' heah
Nohowah
'Lissa eat hur papah
I'n eat couple each ob
M' couseens
No eat 'Lissa though

I'n no crazly barsted nohowah

All Is Safe . . .

Flow, water, the blue water
Little birds of foam
Singing on thee
O flow, water, blue water
Little stars falling asleep
To thy tossing
O flow, water, the blue water
What matters any sorrow
It is lost in thee

Little times, little men
What matters
They are safe in thee
O
Flow, water, blue water
All is safe in thee
Little birds
The shadows of maidens
O safe in thy singing

The Oldest Conversation

"There came one day soon
It will be when
Or after then
The hour midnight reaches noon"

"And I in shoon
Of finest leather
Blood-red roses in my hair
O soon my lover
Cold grows the weather here
I fear I smother"

"The moon
Upon her skull-white horses
Dear
Love was the loser
Tarnished now your little shoon
And hair"

"O come soon my soul!"

"Now only death can hear"

A Trueblue Gentleman

This gentleman the charming duck
Quack quack says he
My tail's on
Fire, but he's only kidding
You can tell that
By his grin
He's one big grin, from wobbly

Feet to wobbly tail
Quack quack he tells us
Tail's on fire again
Ah yes
This charming gentleman the duck
With
His quaint alarms and
Trick of walking like a
Drunken hat
Quack quack says he

There's your fried egg

Always Another Viewpoint

You climb three "golden steps"
Past some friendly "lions"
And "the skeleton
Of a king!" The "lions"
Belong to a woman
Who's said to
Be a bit off. Actually she's
A fine person. I
Think more misunderstood than mad.
I live next door
In the
House with the dwarfpalm trees
Growing
Up through the roof.
Over beer she tells me
Stories about
When she was a

Queen of the North Countree.

The Irate Songster

I went into my parlor
Sang the sparrow bird
There sat policeman
I busta yohs head see
I grinda yohs feets
Lika dem wormz
Yohs no minda m'biz take thet
Yohs bigga loafeh yohs
Phooeyz blooeyz blahz on yohs
I squeeza yohs noz
I teara
Yohs eyez off'r yohs faz
Ptooeyz
Take thet yohs ret
Thisa my own house see
No policeman
Sitz in my parlor

Onless I want'm to

The Cruelkind Swans

O face within the sky
Heart upon the fields
Watching guarding praising
All that runs swims flies

O peaceful the deer
At their grazing
Beside the snowy tossing of swans
All things beautifully heralding
The birthdeath of the year

The red leaf graying
To death
That is always birth again
As
The mold catches fire
O always the flowering breath
The swans
Coming in on greening wing

For all that tires

A Vanishing Institution

That crude little old logcabin
Where I was born
What it now
Playgro'n' for heh-hehing rabbin
And little wild chickerbug

That crude little
Old logcabin where my gramppap's born
What it come to
Buryin'gro'n' for stiff-neckin' gruntyhog
And little ornery chasserbear

That crude
Little old logcabin of m'greatgrampy
What
The hell it doin'
Meetin'gro'n' for fancy-kickin' societybig
And little
Sneerin' lace-overalled pipsquirt

They was home t'us all

Limpidity of Silences

In a limpidity of silences
Speaks what is unanswerable
And is answered.
In a limpidity of silences
The laurelled heads turn
Away from death
And away from life and all
Other trivial little dissolutions.
In a limpidity of silences
Sleep the laurelled heads.
The silences
Speak around us forever; yet
None
Knows what is said.
In a limpidity of silences
Reality speaks . . .
Perhaps of a maskshroud

Cast over all things

What There Is

In this my green world
Flowers birds are hands
They hold me
I am loved all day
All this pleases me
I am amused
I have to laugh from crying
Trees mountains are arms
I am loved all day

Children grass are tears
I cry
I am loved all day
Everything
Pompous makes me laugh
I am amused often enough
In this
My beautiful green world

O there's love all day

An Easy Decision

I had finished my dinner
Gone for a walk.
It was fine
Out and I started whistling.
It wasn't long before
I met a
Man and his wife riding on
A warbond with a clatter of
Skeletons running along after them.

I nodded ugh and
Went on.
Pretty soon I met another
Couple
This time with nineteen
Kids and all of them
Riding on
A big smiling whatthehellisit

I invited them home

The Unanswering Correspondences

Intensification of compassion; extraordinary; incalculable;
Grandeur hurls us down:
Tears blind us.
Sparrows! lions! crags! meadows! seas!
Inexhaustible; wounding; unimaginable; illimitable;
This imperishable grandeur!
The heart breaks—tears blind us—
Immensurable; unfathomable; implacable; unsayable;
We cry our animal grief—
Compassion blinds our eyes—
Each blade
Of grass, leaf of tree,
Each
Feather floating to earth,
Is a signature of love
And sorrow.
O sparrows, lions and
Seas! tears blind us.

The Bird-Queen

The swan of the heavens
Whitens the soft plumage
Of hurrying clouds
And on earth peace covers
Fields and rivers with
A meditative grace
O the swan of the heavens
Wanders upon the air
Like a queen going home
To some half-forgotten
Castle keep
O the wondrous moon-swan
Glides

Above the quiet world
Like an enchanted maiden asleep
The plumed
Headdress of her courtiers
Waving protectively about her

The Everlasting Contenders

Of the beast . . . an angel
Creatures of the earth
It is good
Any who praise not grandly
O but they should
But they should
Death waits for everything that lives
Beast of the wood
Grim beast of the wood
Who praise not grandly
Should should
Heart weeps for all things
Here
And is greatly comforted
For heart is the angel
Of all
Who praise not grandly

But wish they could

What Splendid Birthdays

The ears of the forest
Twitch in the sun
Flies of cloud
Are shaken off so carefully

they alight again
in confident purity
And their wings seem to rest
Against the sky like
Candleflames painted on a cake

Deer in the sunglow
Green ears
Twitching sleepily in the warmth
Of
A peaceful summer's afternoon
Later . . . the herd stirs awake
Antlers purpling
And the first match
Touches the darkling candelabra

Encounter at Nightfall

Smashed bones. Gristle of ribs.
Brittle thigh-cases agape.
Scoured. Racked. Gutted.
Bristling with crawling pocks. Grizzling
In the wart-kinked,
Gyring, pustulant light.
Brattle of shale on craggy tusks.
The gentle terrible faces
Clotted over, empty eyesockets
Staring without much hope,
Or surprise.
What met they here as
Night
Fell? Did the sun
Go down weeping as they
Were slain?
Did horror walk the earth?
Did pity drain the sea?

from *The Famous Boating Party* (1954)

Not Many Kingdoms Left

I write the lips of the moon upon her shoulders. In a temple of silvery farawayness I guard her to rest.

For her bed I write a stillness over all the swans of the world. With the morning breath of the snow leopard I cover her against any hurt.

Using the pen of rivers and mountaintops I store her pillow with singing.

Upon her hair I write the looking of the heavens at early morning.

—Away from this kingdom, from this last undefiled place, I write civilizations, governments, and all other spirit-forsaken and sol-diery institutions. O cold beautiful blossoms, the lips of the moon moving upon her shoulders . . . Stand off! *Stand off!*

Childhood of the Hero

I

The hero of moment is no bigger than a bean.

Within this established range, however, he will be of very precise fit; otherwise the dangers to him would be harrowing and ex-tremely complex. Even for one of his *identical* measurements!

Then when we realize that his size is in perpetual flux, it becomes at once clear that whatever else we are dealing with it is not some object fixed to the ground like, perhaps, a cleverly painted pole or an immense cheese boarded up against thieves. On the contrary! His like must be sought in altitudes somewhat more supple.

Hence we began at bean. But with a rather special representative of that gentle race, we readily admit. For how many beans can you, offhand, name whose average height is just a mite under a small handsbreadth ten times repeated?

II

"That he is of fundamental stature, according (at any rate) to the lights of his own impeccable taste in matters of this kind, is a proposition lacking only the conceited lily-garmentation of proof to render it sound. Heaven witness.

"A hero may be out of pocket, he cannot be out of impossibles. Therefore—I see that he wishes to applaud *now!* Therefore . . . never does he enjoy impunity from riches, from wealth in its multiform insinuations; never does he for long escape the gilt whiplash of propitious circumstance, the sirenlike yodeling . . ."

But the orator was, on several, unrelated counts, mistaken. (1) The banquet had been advanced to the Tuesday following; (2) neither clubmen nor hero *could* have applauded his extemporaneous reading:

The former were of another language persuasion; the latter, pergglepitting.

III

The role of pergglepitting had, alas, even then, become largely reliquary. Some perchance it recalled to days and, why not confess, nights of limpid perfidy and a blondery contemplative as the chests of quite immature swans! Ravishing drift of chariots across those long-ago sands; ah, the glitter of those wheel-knobs; someone calling "Hey! don't we turn off here!"

You do indeed, chap. And with you, pergglepitting; at least from the viewpoint of community service. In very olden times it was done mostly from boats, each manned by a carefully hand-sorted crew of village maidens. This didn't work.

They could manage the grappling hooks all right *going out* . . .

But once arrived at the beds, or "old papa's 'brella-stand," their familiar title, the crews seemed to lose their poise entirely. The hero's own grandmother led several such debacles.

IV

As a stripling the hero went to visit a relative.

He hadn't been listening too attentively so he got the right directions but for the wrong residence. Moreover he had eaten every one of the little salamis from his basket.

This did not appear good when he thought how hard his mother worked, how tough and sinewy her arms had become. Could she not knock the curly head off a washtub with one backward motion of her dear mitt? He winced to the roots of his foamy locks thinking of it. Meditatively he advanced through a pasture of elongated sheep.

"Mother has wished me to sell you these strictly fresh sausages-o, Uncle Belknap," he remarked to the gaunt woman who stood, rifle-akimbo, in the doorway. "Perhaps you have been planning a sandwich, either for yourself or . . . close friend?"

V

"Sausages . . . *Oh!*" responded the gaunt woman, beginning straightway to squint into her riflebarrel. "Only to think . . . such a perfectly grand, even *infectuous,* child . . . pawn of a counterfeiter!" Impulsively the hero remarked, "It is overlate, nor earlier grows, Uncle; we duel!"

One of her overgrown sons strode forward: "I entertain a far nicer idea." Whereupon rapidly twenty-six other bebearded louts bunched round, each a bigger bone-mealer than his fellows: "Tell! Tell! Tell! Tell! Tell!", trumpeting like a flame of elephants. "Oh! Tell! Tell!" The first son observed petulantly, "Doesn't *anyone* desire to know my plan?" (Fearsome the bellowing! "No! No!")

"Incurious swines! Ungrateful, sleeveless dogs!" their brother protested, chagrined more than angered. "I'll relate you my proposal nonetheless . . ." Turned out he had in mind "Challenges," a pastime frequently indulged then.

The old woman lost the toss and elected to lead off.

VI

Craftily she studied her small "nephew," who was puffing easily on a cheroot of home manufacture. Her bleak face lighted and a knuckle at the corner of her hand snapped triumphantly. "Mmmm, splendid . . . I challenge you to set fire to the front porch, upon which we are now so amply assembled. Mmmm-*hmmmm!*" The hero accepted, without tremor or unsightly haste, manfully unruffled.

By the rules of the game, since modified for the protection of overzealous spectators, the only real threat to the commanding position enjoyed by the challenger lay in his opponent's power to back down, to suddenly come up chicken.

Awesome and masterful, the display of that ancient female's ingenuity!

What did that now-prosperous concessionaire not challenge! Even today (paying) visitors, trudging through that horrendous devastation, pause limp-legged before the vanquished's little mutton-pattie booth . . . "Sandwich, fellows? mam?"

VII

Another time he happened to notice a bird in a high silk hat standing weeping at the edge of a hole in the ground. "There seems little art or future, even, in your momentary occupation," the hero advised his new friend, who, with a wan gesture, asked, "Can you turn yourself into a lion? Oh, my blasted cousins!— *There!* Do you see!"

Pebbles, fragments of roots and insect-cases spewed up out of the hole to the accompaniment of whooping laughter and general helling-round. "Blast! they're certainly playing merry hob with my hat down there! Oh . . . *this?* I mean my *good* hat."

"Well, the answer to your question, friend, is: Of course not!"

"I'd so hoped you could," mournfully said the bird; to which, indignantly, the hero: "Well, I can't. Since I am."—"You are . . . what?"—"Why, a lion. What else? *Turn* myself, indeed!"

VIII

And so it had proved, on that occasion. Only later, with hands pressed tightly over his belly, did he wonder whether assorted crumbles of stenchy rubbish and other even less appetizing items of discard were normal to the menus of (really) well-appointed lioneries.

much of cousins or, for that matter, hats, did he discover in that hole as would fit comfortably in a tiny, overpacked briefcase. In fact it was by dint of turning himself into a wandering band of native hunters endowed with considerable savvy in the use of hoists that he succeeded in extricating himself from the pit at all.

To be sure, he had also been the bird with the glee about hats. So, all in all, at the very inset, he really hadn't too much to complain of.

And the hero never did complain—about *anything*. Anything whatever!

IX

Childhood's days passed in their headlong sparsity, like hundred-forapenny balloons.

Yes, childhood! Opinions might divide around it, like scoffing ancient water around a new-made boulder, still would it be necessary to remember the bit-of-thisness, -thatness of it.

When things are going unblemishedly, much can be borne. On the nightstand beside his little bunk, festooned by the shadow-ribboned hair of first one candle then by its replacement's, reposed, in a battered, fly-embroidered frame, a photograph casually torn from a newspaper. Every evening the hero addressed himself to the monastic countenance of the gaunt, ink-faded horse therein depicted:

"'Morning, Senator. How be ye this day, eh?" It is true that the answering voice was almost totally lacking in modulation and resonance; but nevertheless it did manage to convey a certain underlying heartiness as it replied: "Get me out of here! Get me the hell out of here!"

436

Soon It Will

Be showtime again. Somebody will paint beautiful faces all over
the sky. Somebody will start bombarding us with really wonder-
ful letters . . . letters full of truth, and gentleness, and humility
. . . Soon (it says here) . . .

In Order to

Apply for the position (I've forgotten now for what) I had to
marry the Second Mayor's daughter by twelve noon. The order
arrived at three minutes of.

I already had a wife; the Second Mayor was childless: but I did it.

Next they told me to shave off my father's beard. All right. No
matter that he'd been a eunuch, and had succumbed in early
childhood: I did it, I shaved him.

Then they told me to burn a village; next, a fair-sized town; then,
a city; a bigger city; a small, down-at-heels country; then one of
"the great powers;" then another (another, another)—In fact, they
went right on until they'd told me to burn up every man-made
thing on the face of the earth! And I did it, I burned away every
last trace, I left nothing, nothing of any kind whatever.

Then they told me to blow it all to hell and gone! And I blew it
all to hell and gone (oh, didn't I) . . .

Now, they said, put it back together again; put it all back the way
it was when you started.

Well . . . it was my turn then to tell *them* something! Shucks, I
didn't want any job that bad.

Only close up could you make out the wings on their horses. They were nearly transparent.

But that's how they covered so much ground. In a single night they'd be twenty places.

Someone told me he'd noticed them in two places a good hundred miles apart practically simultaneously.

He also said they had mouths in their foreheads. You'd probably think him of dubious value, witness-wise.

However . . . the fact won't down that an unusual number of schoolgirls have been disappearing these last couple weeks.

It may well be all that talk of mouths in foreheads and of strands of long silken hair found caught in the branches of the dogwood down by the river has given some people a false notion of the thing. This won't be the first publicity stunt to get out of hand . . . though it could be the last.

Yesterday They Tried

To sell me an old hound dog they'd tricked out to look like a donkey. Painted mockorange.

"I never heard of a mockorange hound dog before."—"Ah-*ha!* Youz clever boy, Boss! Him dem fine donkey, yez?"

"Look doze soff footz . . . Youz bet yohs life he don keek yoh brainz oud wit won ponch lak ordinamary jack'!"

"But what about I want to carry things up a mountain?"—"Ah-*ha!* Whut yoh needz izza leetle train!"

So they go away and pretty soon come back with that hound dog all rigged out with wheels and goofy pulleys-like . . .

They started in to toot and clang until an old man put his head up out of the ground and called: "Here, Milissa . . ."

Then out of that crazy clutter of wheels and assorted junk sprang a very fetching young girl, who, wagging happily, answered: "Paw! *wow!*"

On My Side

Of it, the trees have the wind willing one thing—*pretty feet* . . .

And the snow another thing; the grass gets fine clothes one day— O *pretty feet* . . .

And next day a shroud; the waters have roses for eyes—O *pretty, pretty feet* . . .

And then somebody blinds them; O somebody cold wilts the white sparkling roses of the waters—

Pretty feet, O pretty feet . . . The dancers show a man legs beautiful enough to frolic across any heaven on;

Then somebody breaks both of his, and leaves him an old gray wind as his only cart through the world;

But just now, I think, the earth has the loveliest of little pink roses walking upon it—O *pretty, pretty feet!*

439

Deathsong for a Maiden

Now littlely wandering . . . littlely dressed in raiment suitable to marriage with that groom whose attentions are never so discriminating as constant.

Named by her flesh was all that littlely finds breath in this so filthèd-over carnival: the rose-shadowed walking of the clouds across a snowy field; the holy-seeming tears of the flowers at early morning in a wood . . .

Littlely O how littlely bodied and booted she was to set off on such a journey as that!

Rough, coarse, ugh, the touch of him—O little flesh . . . O sweet little flesh . . .

O littlely wandering . . . O how littlely stronged and shoed she was for such roads as he will think fit to take her upon! Let no man of heart hear of this thing, or with his two fists doubled he'll come running even if it means battering down the cold, slimy door that separates this one world from that other there.

Worn on The

Sleeve, picked out with gold and stones of rare design, of interest too for color subtleties—attend:

Reputedly of sanguine and dubious history, still must it command my interest for one reason alone—attend this quite carfeully:

Originally it belonged to my mother, and was the bridal gift of that man, a king and mad—quite carefully . . .

The astonishingly appropriate gift of that foul sub-brute who went to his grave believing me his son!—attend carefully:

They were not such fools, the historians of his reign (and of my weak brother's after him): no, they were paid!—carefully:

Paid their cur's wages from the table of his unspeakable lust . . . But—how would they write *this* record!—very carefully:

Of these six thousand years I've worn it . . . this emblem from "the Darkness" . . . How would *they* warn its latest thief!

Delighted with Bluepink

Flowers! My friend, be delighted with what you like; but with *something*.

Be delighted with something. Yesterday for me it was watching sun on stones; wet stones.

I spent the morning lost in the wonder of that. A delight of god's size.

The gods never saw anything more enchanting than that. Gorgeous! the sun on wet stones.

But today what delights me is thinking of bluepink flowers! Not that I've seen any . . .

Actually there isn't a flower of any kind in the house—except in my head.

But, my friend, oh my friend! what wonderful bluepink flowers! Delight in my bluepink flowers!

An

Expert coachdog when other things go slack

When sickness hits the house or work's not to be got

You'll find him out in any weather briskly running alongside

The tumblehell equipage of some gone to soakrum gentlemandator

Down on his all fours in the mucky lanes barking up chicken-storms

And sniffing at an occasional farmcuress's asafetida by way of lending extra verisimilitude

To performances which have reached such a point of painstaking that now he even personally grows his own workingcostumes

The Great-Sledmakers

They get drunk, these Great-Sledmakers. Their copper mugs, around which their fingers easly circle once, and once again, hold what's called a "quart handsome" (about five and ⅜ths gallons mirke-measure).

The Great-Sledmakers get drunk like other people do hopeless. An hour or two old they demand whisky, and poor slaphoppy brute the mother who'd not lay them lovely on . . . all pink-fuzzy, ah, happy little belchers, rest ye well in between the worlds, as you might say.

Seven sees most married. Typically they live above saloons, their sole furniture a firehouse pole.

For, you must understand, it doesn't take a few hours or even a few days to make a Great-Sled; it takes closer to a thousand years.

Eleven have been built so far, not counting of course those which slip away from time to time (no doubt you've heard of tidal waves and earthquakes). Each is heavier than all the mountains placed together on a table having proper equipment for weighing of this sort; each requires a highway of at least a million lanes . . . at the very least. In other words, the Great-Sleds are not small. Just picture them! with their runners of molten silver, their golden bodies painted a screaming red under a zigzag of yellow and buff stripes. The effect is quite nice. Only so far, you've probably guessed by now, nobody's bought nary a one.— *Whh-isky, bo-oy!*

"There Is the Hand"

There is the hand that has nothing attached to it, no arm no chest no head anywhere near it,—manless,—Thehand

It teeters drunkenly . . . finger to finger,—at first . . . slowly, now in great, convulsive twistings, like a five-necked bird striving to hide its axbite under crimson leaves.

The flesh of it, even the wrist-flesh, that blind lump of flesh there . . . ?

How is it flesh?—and if not . . . flesh . . . !

The hand O thehand thehand *thehand* that has nothing attached to it,—no mouth no brain no eyes anywhere near it,—earthless, —scluppering like a blind roach-Thing (or angel— . . . ?) along the world's edge—Perhaps, friends,—it brings salvation . . . ?

443

Do it *just right,* anything will grow.

I started out with doorknobs, grew me dozens and dozens.

Then I tried a puppy, why that was easier even.

I guess because of the eyes. Don't plant very deep.

Dirt enough to cover's about right. Then just go away.

Watched things won't come up. That's how I lost Agnes . . .

I had my best luck with horses. Sprout already harnessed.

Opening the Window

They called across to ask me to get some beer and come up and cut a few touches.

I'd already gone to bed but I got some clothes on and went down to the store for the beer and some of that nice dry kind of salami.

When I got up there were two old women and a tall skinny man sitting half dressed holding musical instruments.

By half dressed I mean the old women were in their birthday suits and the skinny fellow had a couple heavy overcoats on over his regular duds.

And speaking of musical instruments I refer to the fact that each of them was holding a full-blown mermaid in formfitting tights that was sort of crooning-like in a Greek accent.

444

As I commenced to set my parcels on the bed another old lady came barging out of the closet on zebraback.

After I lifted her off she said she had herself a sore behind from riding all the way up from Boston and would I mind holding her for a while. Pretty soon they wanted I should fetch some more beer and I found out the only way I could manage her up and down the narrow stairs was to go backwards and to squeeze like all hell on her long legs and even then those boney knees of hers sounded like somebody having a fit with a snaredrum on either side of us. And every trip I went to a different store and they kept getting farther and farther away. I took the next day off and moved into a YMCA.

Vines with Their

Red grapes shielded from the sun by thick, velvety leaves . . . Vines strong with the strength of the loved earth, grapes like huge, shiny drops of blood on the undersides of those green fingers.

The air is rich with the smell of growing, womb-warm under the sun of the noonday . . .

Down the rows walk three men in single file . . . heads bent, hands tied behind them . . . A few yards back a fourth man in the cab of a truck sprawled high with bodies listens to instructions over a two-way radio and yawns nodding at something said by a fifth man who is squinting wearily down the sights of a heavy rifle mounted in the cowling . . . After a time the voice of a two-millionth man gives the awaited order and the finger of a two-millionth-and-first man tightens on the trigger. And under the sun of the noonday the air is rich with the sweetish smell of the harvest.

That Night The

Moon came out full, you could see the white breathing of the
fields down by the swimming hole . . .

After the heat of the day it was wonderful to stand on the hill
and feel the cool night air . . .

It was like having cool, moist hands touch your face, you could
smell the sweat rising up off the fields . . .

The moon seemed to get bigger by the minute, you expected it
to burst it was getting that swollen-looking . . .

The boy who worked the next field said to my brother, "Them's
my goddam feet you're a-splashin' 'baccy juice on."

I knew that my champion water-drinker of a brother had run out
of cutplug long before supper, but I didn't say anything.

After while there come the town girls out of the pool to get
dressed . . . All shiny wet—like little soft pink and white fish . . .
Oh Jesus they was all sorta crazy pretty . . . And we ground our
broken nails into our fists, hating them . . .

Rising a Little

Fearful with them gathered about my bed on that dreary autumn
morning

Wouldn't it just be to one like myself—a defenseless mouse-thing
quite unnailed and unnealed by the grayest of lives here below
in this vale of blackened tares—that they'd come

And not ever no no never to one of your fat and fancy-whiskered tomadandandies in their soft-padding motorcars emboldened all in as out by prosperity and other similar figures of an economic legerdemain

Even driving up in horn-happy pomp out of the immensely priceless and communal alike to flea and kingpot territory of sleep itself with no flick of hair so much as slightly rumpled and smelling that grandly of the imported gloss of other men's thoughts

But let them search through my stuff until the eyes in their stupid heads turn up in a leafy humbleness before a somewhat more common quest (with maybe the little wild rose which is the color of a man's lifeblood growing so prettily and so proudly up on top there), they'll never in this world know where to look for my bit of cheese.

Her Talents . . . Of

The many talents, oh hers was greatest.

A talent for loving she had, oh that is always wonderful.

A talent for being loved, oh that is equally wonderful.

A talent for loving, for being loved, oh wonderful, wonderful!

She loved all right things, wrong things, in-between things.

No taste, discretion, none whatever, oh what a fool she was!

But merry to the very end . . . toting her brimming slop pails at the county poorhouse.

O What a Revolution!

It is remarkable but it is no less painful for that, how rarely people make an effort not to understand "things." They start well.

Children say "Why doesn't grandpa grow no beard like a cow huh?" and they're told "Because he doesn't have to, that's why." or "Why is grass always the color of engine oil and conjugations of cigarette?"—"Because your papa's a sloppy, ill-tempered bastard and I'd shoot him in a minute if my particular brand of sex had any appeal for the insurance man."

Children don't want "to know," they want to increase their enjoyment of not knowing. But people will go on Thursdaying on Wednesdays.

What precisely is "a tree"? What *does* the grass "mean"? Why *are* snowflakes snowflakes? Why do animals have *"faces"*?

These are not casual questions. Think about them. Then tell me what conclusion you reach. To the first person sending in a satisfactory answer to any or all of these questions, I will pay the sum of one million dollars. So think them over, won't you?

There Are Two

Ways about it. In fact, that only scratches the surface; for—well, had you seen the weeds, the weeds—even those weeds growing just below the outer edge of the wall! that would fix you! Crested . . . tubular . . . a few with—well, sort of hands . . .

In fact, I told my friend Flip, "Flip, you've got to do something about those weeds, especially those weeds down there just under the stains along the wall by the gate." But as usual he was monkeying around the car. It was almost dark by the time he got downstairs again, and the first thing he said was: "Do you want that other set of pipes inside, or do you want them curled around the hood?"

I told him curled around would be just dandy as a pair of little pink panties.

So. You know how it is. Sure, I had come there looking for that elusive oyster, happiness. Yep, that's what I was after, that goddam little sad-faced, buck-toothed oyster, happiness. And what had I got? Do I *really* have to tell you?

After a while I went out and climbed up on top of the wall. It had started to rain again. Pretty soon it was coming down in the large economy size buckets. I tore up all my identification papers and stripped down to where I had only one shoe and my hat on. Then I stood up on my hind legs and shouted: "So! Enough's enough, you lousy, scrounging bastards! I'm off to join the Indians, see!" Then taking my other shoe off, I added: "And while you're at it, to hell with the Indians too!"

It Was Being

Answered when you appeared at the gate. Not always, or even ever, by a spokesman of any importance; most times you would be received by an utter dolt.

Perhaps, even, by a beggar. Wretched, sore-covered—smelling horribly.

But then!—Was not oneself more doltish . . . in deeper beggary sunk than any man ever before stood in that gateway—? Wonder then that the guard's mask was always your own face—?

To Be Charmed

Seemed enough ambition for anyone with sense.

Scant matter with what. Be it only with the serenity of veils at
the funeral of a river, or even with the compassion of first snow
upon a blackened wood. (Of course taste did set certain limits: a
bit of all too responsible soul-baiting went a long way to Redjelly-
head Fair.)

Those horriblenesses of words that never, never, never, never, O
never have anything at all to do with the lives of the people who
say them, or to whom they are said . . . "Mercy." "Gentleness."
"Peace." Mercy . . . ! Gentleness . . . ! *Peace* . . . !

It Takes Few Kinds

They made very little of such events—*Horses rising out of the
water, the dark hair of the riders beautiful in the moonlight* . . .

Where one moment you would see nothing except the peaceful
silvering of the water—*Great blond horses rising slowly into the
sky, the dark and the beautiful hair of the riders trailing down* . . .
down . . .

*The dark and the beautiful hair trailing down through the moon-
light*—No, they made very little of such things.

One moment you would see only the water . . .

*Then great icy blond horses would begin to rise slowly into the
sky* . . . *And the dark and the beautiful hair of the maiden riders
would trail down through the moonlight*—But, actually, they made
very little of things along that general line.

Sturdy Legs, That

Gal; many a thing I've seen her lift without strain or hurry of any kind. A barber—it was the Sunday I went boating they had that disastrous party and only those twenty saved were too drunk to rush into that freezing cold water. Umm, a very tiny barber, it's true—but a whole team of exasperated horses had plunged through the bridge on top of him; she lifted them off like so many not very interesting watchfobs. (Art appreciation was not exactly her line.)

But when it came to lifting!—park couples, of no matter what sexual disposition, benches and all; porches (particularly those equipped with swings), sunparlors, buses and trucks, whether stationary or in motion—all were grist; I once myself chanced to notice her in the act of carrying a freightcar full of green bananas home to bolster her anemia. (The doctors explained that her lifting mania was accountable largely in terms of this rather common deficiency.)

Often Was It

Because, straying through the wine-gardens with the grace and the stainless impermanence of old poems spread out upon the wind like the ghostly sails of so many long ago unaccounted-for ships . . .

And seeking through the silvery branches of the appletree for sandals that would suit the little walking feet of the moon . . .

Was it because, knowing what dye reddens the canvas of this earth now, what howling substance covers these shoes . . .

Was it because of these signs and portents, that I . . . that I—

451

Wanderers of the Pale Wood

And they walked in the ancient wonder of the morning light
together. Spring sang in their faces . . . a blossoming choir.

O springtime come again to the world! The shimmering toss
of the instruments in all the green wood round them!

The sparkling strings of the water humming under proclaim-
ing fingers!

Petals of roses, wet, pink . . . her opened lips. Tiny birds of
sun brushing golden wings across her throat and hair . . .

II

The animals of the morning wood watching in silence as
     they pass . . .

Lion, deer, and hare
     serpent
     the leopard of the snow
O the pale chill flight of the albatross over the ghostly
     emptiness of the waters

Kinsmen of an uneasy realm
     watching in silence as Bride and Bridegroom pass into
     the opening wood.

III

O sorrow it is
     and sorrow
          O sorrow that waits under the mask of every joy

So sang the wind above the little grass on the hillside in the sun. In the green waiting of the trees the song of the wind made its sound.

And there
in a gay tumult of flowers
with the branches of the sky above them ablaze with the lovely darting of birds
he laid her down and unloosened the blood-red sash which bound her waist
and he placed his two hands on her body . . . felt the hush and the wonder of it flood through his heart.

IV

Listen
Listen
O what is that sound
Is it only the rustling of shaggy vines against the trees
Or is it perhaps a scraping—
The scraping of some . . . scaly thing through the underbrush
There!
There!

The print of hooves on the moss . . .
The glisten of stained fur . . .

V

But the Beast of the Wood came as a smiling man.

He entered upon the hillside where they lay, and he watched them through a long time with the fury and lust of his yellow eyes unshielded.

For they were asleep
lying in one another's arms in a little hollow sheltered
from the full light of the sun.

Then at last he wakened them
wakened them to the gentle-seeming smile of his smiling
face.

And he said: Ye rest well, my children. Honor me to drink
of my humble wine and to eat of my humble bread.

O then did petals of roses bruise themselves across her cheeks
under the smiling eyes of that smiling man
and like another wound of flowers was the pulse at
her temples beneath the silken mist-breathing of her golden hair.

And he smiled upon them.

VI

O out of that feast in the blond wood of the morning
came any shadow or unseemly darkening?
Did any staining drop
fall, unnoticed
on the roseleaf?

O removed from them by only the thickness of a leaf
by no more than the width of an eye as it looks whitely up
from the quick thrust of an oar
stand another Three . . .

And from that thrice-riven shadow
Bride, Bridegroom
and Smiling Man
step forth . . .

VII

And forth from that shadow of a shadow
   O caves of the leaf!
      blinding the sun's eye in their green vastnesses

O in shadowing of the leaf
     thoughts of the rose reach the whale at his nightroaming
      stand him thinking at world's end.

And somewhere
   —back of sleep?
     the shadows move like great eyelids.

As eyelids in a face whose brow is fashioned of mountain ranges
    and at whose temple the planets pulse
      like the heartbeat of a sparrow.

O caves of that darkness where alone the light is!

Then did the wind move sunful fingers through her hair
    and birds sped along the glittering branches of her voice.

    Presently
    The Smiling Man took himself off to the river
    and as they watched he settled himself on the riverbank
    and appeared to sleep.

  Something left his side.

  It crawled toward them.

And what had concern for the lion and the deer
    for the sparrow and the whale, for the hare and the serpent
      for the leaf of the rose, and the oaktree's roots

O what had concern for the albatross and the leopard of the snow
    seemed then
            to leave the world.

And then it was that the Bridegroom beheld the Bride wraith-
like in the soft mists rising from the river, and in an anguish of
fear he went to her.

After a little time
        very slowly, she said:
                I heard a strange moaning under the willows. And
. . . I found a strange being lying here—I thought it was . . .
wounded. It was like . . . like a deer, a strangely beautiful deer
. . . and it had . . . it had the body of a man.

O when he lifted himself up
        his horns flowered and spired above the tallest trees!
        And on his face . . . O on his face
        there was a look of such cruelty . . .
        of such strange beauty . . .
    O there was such a glory there!

And then it was for the first time that the Bridegroom saw
how her dress had been ripped and torn from her body, and how
leaves had been matted and ground into the tangle of her golden
hair . . . And he stared at the prints as of bloody flowers covering
her nakedness . . . and slowly, without speaking, he turned away
that she might not see the look of loathing triumph which twisted
at the corners of his mask.

X

And then a bird that was like a great pale wolf flying down
through the grazing clouds appeared.

And the white, unrevealing weather of its being swirled about
them.

And through the leaf-thin covering of the world a voice said:

O rest in thy woundedness

O rest, rest, take now thy long sleep in me

But from the little grass on the hillside another voice spoke, and it said:

O have joy, joy, and joy now and unending in the ancient glades of this believing forest.

Behold the shining raiment of this spring-holied daughter of earth.

In the wonder and mystery of her living flesh wilt thou find thy Dream-Kingdom,

And the gates thereof like a fiery blossom in the all-surrounding darkness.

And time waited on the world's edge.

XI

Then at last the Lovers began to speak together.

They spoke of their love for one another

They spoke of the special wonders and puzzlements of which it was made.

And to the Bride it seemed that there was the talking of blossoms in the hands which moved over her nakedness.

And to the Bridegroom it seemed that the tips of his fingers had stuck in the honeyed flaking of a golden music

and that to remove them in any of the usual ways would surely strip the covering from their two hearts.

For this was the very music of the heart itself . . .

Which nothing moving upon the green earth or rooting in the night-shrouded vastness of its waters could ever still.

For here indeed was the unassailable kingdom of the heart itself.
Under his fingers her warm, human flesh was alive in the sun
And across that living bridge they Godsped.

And there under the spiring thrust of the horns that were at
once tender and so strangely cruel, the Bride was careful to keep
well hidden from him the mocking smile of her smiling face.

Moon "Continued"

Right after the Moon was got rid of, a moon was brought on. The
same moon, of course, but a different Moon.

In what the "second" moon resembled that Moon of "the first
instance" might extraordinarily have given some clue to their
essential sameness, but this, alas, was only the usual deal and by
then, certainly not surprisingly, the number and, well . . . "tone"
of substitution had become somewhat involved, even, one might
say, just a shade, only a shade, mind you, but still a shade, unfair.

Having said that, it remains only to say that I could not, this
minute, give you any good reason why I should have expected
them to be content with simple substitutions—you know, the
"m"-moon, M-"Moon" sort of thing—but . . . I was hoping . . .
no, I was disappointed . . . yes, I was *disappointed* . . . I was
bitterly disappointed, if you like, that they had to up and move
on to another table and a new game just as I was beginning to
catch the drift of some of the simpler plays.

The Great Sadnesses

Throng like shadowy caresses on the horizon . . .

They are Woman-things, favorable only to the most exceptional of suitors. And always it is hard to imagine the nature of the equipment which one should bring to such a courtship—whether fetched up out of some secret honor, or an uncommon ardor of insight . . . or out of the more common possessions—fear, envy, doubt—but these brought to new and unexpected intensities. At any rate, it is hard to get any foothold, to get any really useful purchase for the effort of lifting the matter up into any sort of light; for so many, many other little wingless beetles besides man are involved—they too, in the most humdrum and usual course, have felt the coldwarm, forgivingdamning press of those lips; they too have always watched into the shadow, and have seen as much, and as little . . .

Court of First Appeal

Humbly—but without caution (in unbridled vigor of faith: acceptful of joy for whatever reason, for no reason—humbly I believe!)

In the splendorment and holification of every thing individuated, and of every thing togetherized; from causes known to me, from causes forever (unassailably) unknown to me: I believe!

In the serene and beautiful prevailation of life, from causes beyond understanding, I believe!

Serene and beautiful, that livinglifeness beyond understanding!

(But of that most unsubstantial—though momentarily conspicuous—of all this earth's pitiful little commotions, the human, I delay judgment until such time as the evidence shall reveal itself as being in any way applicable to what I must imagine the true nature of the case to be.)

In a Crumbling

Majesty of horns sweeps in the stagtide . . .

After such glory . . . the glory of that vast frosty wood there . . . O the belling of that glory bringing a face to each of night's cold windows—this defeat, this death, this petty corruption . . . He stumbled to his knees, and the proud forehead of his running broke upon the sand like an egg.

(Ah, the angry, lung-colored stain that flowered at his bridle, that spilled like a cottony cheese over his withers and harness-buckling . . . that raged like a tattering doom of flags above the chariot there . . . that rose like the grim pale frost of an agony above the decaying splinter of wheels . . .)

The stain widens, briefly . . . hesitates . . . then drains back without trace.

For Miriam

Little birds sit on your shoulders,
*   All pure and white.*
Little birds sit on your shoulders,
*   All lovely bright.*

Men and times of evil,
*   Nothing more is right.*
Little birds sit on your shoulders,
*   And sing us through the night.*

"First Came the Lion-Rider"

First came the Lion-Rider, across the green fields of the morning, holding golden in his golden hands a thing of great wonder and loveliness—and it had your name.

Next came the Provider of Birds, and over fields white-shrouded he walked crying *Mercy, mercy, O cold winds, for these are the visible thoughts of the air that I carry*—and it was you talked then.

Now came The One Most Kingly, all unseen in the pulse of this anciently new world: Who thought the waters into being! Who first imagined a woman's face! Who conceived the splendor of an apple bough! And the fields He came across were as a beautiful heart beating within the skies—and ah, all that He ever saw there, I have seen looking out of your eyes.

Swallowtail, swallowtail,
You leave that pore barn alone!
What'll we do for cherrystone
Now that pretty summer's gone?

O, pardon is a lady,
And envy's a thief;
But the bull is only an apple
With more prominent teeth.

A Matchstick-Viewed-without-Regard-to-Its-Outer-Surface

Was enabled to ride.
    First on a "wafer."
    But it set up a roar and presently fled.
Remember that even the gorilla will feel lost without his roller
skates if he has become accustomed to them long enough.

Then on a sort of tile. Which was very like being flopped about
in the wee small hours of the night. However, that is not another
story; and the children are going back along the unlighted way
into the forest now. Perhaps this time will be the last time for any
of us to see joy and innocent pride on a human face again.

Then on a blind turtle away out ahead but running the wrong
way.
    On a plate shaped as a shield.
    on a shawl slung across a pit.
    On the castaway wheel of a Ferris.

On a mountain tethered to a post in front of a little ghost town saloon.

But by then the wolf had died. The lion had died. The bear had died. And mind, these are only figures of speech: *you can imagine what had happened to real things.* To those poor gentle and defenseless things which a few men still think about in the wee small hours of the night. However, that is not another story; and the children are going back along the unlighted way into the forest now. Perhaps this time will be the last time for any of us to see joy and innocent pride on a human face again.

"Give You a Lantern"

Give you a lantern,
It belong to a bird.
Light on your lovely face,
O angel is such an awkward word.

Give you a sadsome tune,
Sung inside a tiring wing.
Hold it close within your hand,
Nothing'll ever seem like hurrying.

Give you a basket,
Forest keep the prettiest deer in.
Put there a bit of your heart,
Nothing'll ever harm them.

Give you a basket,
It belong to a bird.
Tell you that I love you,
O love is such a sightless word.

A Message from the Assistant Chief of the Fly People

You peculiar pink stinks been crowdin'
On the Sun's Life   Look out!
Green Him's home's the last place
You should mess with   Move it!
Shove ass or
Off!   Watchin' Eye
Won't care you're gone   WHO is
Nothing. But all of it's
Everything!

Who is nothing   Hear that!
Meaning:
The stars sing
Because it's always all right!
So far you've
Not been near except when
You didn't know. Night's day
Was everywhere. No one is
Ever separated from every other
For then the world would die.

And the world does not die!
O Glory, Glory of the Light!

We live one life. Message ends

The Great Birds

A gentle wind blows in from the water.
Along the banks great birds are majestically striding.
It is morning!

464

Far out there are boats. Far, far out on that crumbling blue shelf
. . . toy swans slowly, slowly moving their honey-clotted wings. It
is morning. Morning . . . and as every morning is, it is unstained,
now . . . *exactly like the very first morning ever to come to this
world.*

O the sparkling land, the sea, the heavens!
O hushed and clean in the wonder of it!
As slowly, slowly now the great birds appear . . . wheeling up,
up, up! And at last they are above the village, above the golden-
pink blur of houses and bridges—*with our two hearts caught in
the lift of their great wings.*

And now the boats . . . nearer, nearer they come! At last we can
see the tumbling glitter of fish on their decks. And yes, one of
the fishermen has glimpsed us—he waves, calls a greeting, as above
him wheel the birds in giant spirals. Ah! suddenly one dives, then
another, and another—*their wings brush across the water like
fingers of a caressing hand.*

A strand of your hair touches my cheek.
How much better for the world had
nothing else ever happened in it.

"And Her Look Touching the Air"

And her look touching the air between us like a hand alive to the
difficulty that may not be touched out—not once, *not for the
smallest moment;* and the world be only what it is.

This shadow under a leafless tree—
This brief lord of uncertain estate,
Whose sons are as the dry leaves
Scuffed into dance by the swine-wind.

"And I, Too, Am Something of a Stranger Here, My Friend"

On all fours around the roof,
Setting the windhens acackle,
Clockbagging about up here,
Certainly a change from deskwork—

You see, I lost my roll in an old game,
And she went helling off, friend,
With a copper screen installer,
An emerald too big to be real,
Though he damn well was,
In his chilly dark gray hat—
To you it'll not matter at all,
On this nice summer night,
What the hell, you only live once,
As his sort always say—
But I didn't intend things to turn out like this.
No, that was not my intention, friend,
Yet the best here is only a heeltap on a floor
That's on the thin side you might say,
That a person in trouble goes right through,
That a person in trouble finds slipping away,
Let him stand as still as any scared kid,
Let him try what the hell he can,
At the first hard black hour down he goes,
And people tab him for a coward,
Say that he deserved what he got,
That somewhere he might have met the right kind of woman,
Someone he could latch onto like she was the handle on a lamp—
As though that wasn't just my trouble, friend,
As though that wasn't just the trouble with me!
That's just what got me up here where the hurt brings
The top of the world and the bottom of the world together,
And you see them as one, friend,

With no difference between the cellar and the roof,
With no difference between what you have and what
      you're going to get—
When both are covered by the shadow of a chilly dark gray hat,
And you see what kind of a cold face looks up from the papers
On that desk you know you can never go back to,
Or ever really leave, my friend . . . after a manner of speaking.

The Curly Blue Buppo

He didn't deny it.
He knew I had him pegged.
(If you're a curly blue buppo,
It's not the easiest thing to hide.)

I'd say to him right in front of them,
No use trying to fool me,
I know a curly blue buppo
When I see one. And he'd nod his head.

I never had any doubt what he was—
What else could he have been!
Coming to the house just at dusk
With his great curly blue fists
Loaded down with money,
And with that big smile on his face!

Then one day he said he'd not be comin' round again—
And he never did either.

To be very sure by then he'd made me pretty damn rich
And I could have bought all the curly blue buppos
I ever wanted. Except, of course, there weren't anymore left.

"O Kind Watchers Came"

O kind watchers came
To the starlit wood . . .
    Lo, lo,
Hear them blow
Winds of darkness
Winds of night
Winds of death's name
Winds of eternal light

And while they watched
And waited, listening
For some word of their Father . . .
There was only the wind's sound
Shaking the last leaves down

That and the terrible noise
Of the wound wound wound
Which the world was making.

So Near—and Yet . . .

Bent over the railing in the back woodlot
With a too-inquisitive cloud stuck to her sweating arm
The canny old woman tries to reach a certain cucumber
Which she can exchange for an invisible cloak
Two whitegreen rabbits, a talking tree, and a magic bowl

But it is just out of reach, that certain special cucumber
Out of reach, yes, alas, it is out of reach, though
    her fingernails
Come away all coated with some strange and star-colored substance

And that is a pity
That is a very great pity
Because made invisible by the cloak
She could go into the vaults of the rich
And free them of their worrisome and trying burden
And with the two whitegreen rabbits
She could so confuse the monstrous and bloody hatters
That human bounty and not perpetual bullshrift would pop forth
    for once
And with that wonderful talking tree
She could fasten people right onto a clean and decent sky
And with just one little tap on the magic bowl
She could get them kissing something besides asses for a change

"O She Is as Lovely-Often as Every Day"

And tallness stood upon the sky like a sparkling mane

O she is as lovely-often as every day; the day following the day . . .
the day of our lives, the brief day.

Within this moving room, this shadowy oftenness of days where
the little hurry of our lives is said . . . O as lovely-often as the
moving wing of a bird.

But ah, alas, sooner or later each of us must stand before that grim
Roman Court, and be judged free of even such lies as I told
about the imperishable beauty of her hair. But that time is not
now, and even such lies as I told about the enduring wonder
of her grace, are lies that contain within them the only truth by
which a man may live in this world.

O she is as lovely-often as every day; the day following the little
day . . . the day of our lives, ah, alas, the brief day.

Flowers to the House

Too pale! Too changed!
Like some gradual cow
Of swamps which leaps at moths,
Grudging their blunted kisses;
And murmuring stale oaths
Which frighten schoolgirls meek as badges.

The azure droop
Of thawing sails? Mawkish steed?
Yon tower-browed window?
No! Your speckled neck.
Your walk faded like a crest.
Your muglamps that once giddied and stomped.

Who would want knobs
On a door that grabbed back?
Where never makes a shadow—
And no coat ever wore lad.
(You were always quite fond of lings.
Perhaps why you fished in streetcars.)

The oncomings go
Ringdove and blazing tiger creak
Off to dark bachelorhood together.
In rime-stilled woods the singers huddle.
Ah, ragged figure, man or maid?
I cannot tell you out in that shire;
You are all so pale and changed there!
Say you rune or call you up some sneering jest?

O flowers to the house
And beauty to the fang
It is dark O there is no dark!
It is too late, O all is glorious with morning's light!
O flowers, flowers to the house!

470

Down in Ol' Dontcaradama

A Play of One Fact

Mrs. Dampgress, the Mother of Joel—Don't, oh don't go barefoot tonight. Instinct with risk would the chance be . . . whether you took it or not. For you know how them bears kin smell.

Joel, her Son—I sure do, Maw. Specially after it rains.

Mrs. Dampgress—And mind you don't hold thet Harriet down too long. I don't hanker after no more lawshoots.

Joel—Suits. No lawsuits, Maw.

Mrs. Dampgress—How true. How very true. When folks are as poor as we be, Son. But won't you jest change yer jowljive when we oncet git aholt a some a thet good ol' unlonesome barter-starter. Oh thet purty green barterstarter . . . thet gudgrimed l'le ol' lovely, *lovely* barterstarter (*She commences a brisk dance.*)

Joel—But—

Mrs. Dampgress—On a silk cushion! And one fer yer head too. Soo-wow! kain't I jest see you now, all fattened out on prime bull-leg and them l'le greasy yeller bransusettey's, boy! And won't I jest have me a pair of *real* teeth . . . no more a these ol' home-made Jorgewash dogjaws fer me!

Joel—Then I better git started. It might jest cud happen I'd git snarled up in all them paths agin this evenin'. A person kin shore get tired a huckleberries 'long about the fifth day. (*He goes out almost due right, missing by two spray-toed feet a candelabrum of little nursing pigs.*)

Mrs. Dampgress—(*presently scratching her laig*) Ummmm. All them *two* paths! Thet boy suttonly inspires a body with confidence . . . pronounced "heartburn."

Catfish River Lullaby

Alligator steal your blanket off,
Sheriffman rip out th' spring;
Now don't you worry, mah l'le sof'top,
Don't you worry 'bout a thing.

Oh yoh mammy is a right sassy passel;
Honey, don't you fret none!
Ah'll fiddle beefstakes down from baldy apples,
Scrounge us some purty biskets off th' cloudknees.
So hush, you little cabbage-grabber,
Iffen you wants me t'be yoh good naybor!

Oh hollah log, hollah log, scratch mah lef' leg,
Yow hush you to sleep, mah l'le bush of sorrow, hear!
An' the very fust thing tomorroh,
Ah'll git yoh a little ole awful-smellin' dawg yoh kin keep
Until the river turns to burnin' stone
And there ain't nobody left to weep—
And there ain't nobody left to weep.

Beyond the Dark Cedars

A thread was snapped too soon.

Promptly the cut filled with doglips and state senators. Enormous small lion-eared ants began at once to munch train-windows.

Of course thighs hid. Who these days would trust lovers?
    Bells bled. But!
    The little chap wouldn't get off the board!
    The little wee chap in his once brightly colored rags.
    It was their board. Who wasn't he to get off it!

They offered him a custom-built peaceofmind with the lard-speaker smartly concealed under a wide choice of the same flag. Our little chap demijohned myrrhlessly.

Government spoonfeds, that had first been nabulated by spills of still warm crimson paper, were hastily brandished (speaking napoleonically) from around frontless walls. Calmly did our little chap shake them off in conic sections.

They got the rain to come down on him dryside first. He succeeded quietly in moistening the skinned side of his nose by the old reverse-profile method; and then said he: Bloody rotten pigs, are you asking *me* to get off your board!

Why, but for such care and love by fellows like the one you are honored to see before you, that moon, and that sun, and those stars, hell, they would have long since given up on the job of trying to clear all your stinking rubble off this lovely meeting ground. Look! Look, you bloated slimy rats! Look just away yonder there, beyond the dark and stricken cedars, beyond even that ticking chill which seeps from all your building plans—there! Just there! Don't you see it! Coming toward us now! O don't you see it! Don't you see it!

Do you?

"O the Sledbird Rides over the Willow"

O the sledbird rides over the willow,
Over the willow so small'n all;
    and I—*who're me* . . .
Inside here—is it really like that in thee?

This bit of snowmelt in the hurrying sun,
This featherless crankcase stuck on a bum.

Now not every man has the makings of a barber
Or even a tuner of one of those classy white-wood pianos
Like they used to have in most of the river towns hereabouts
But when you stop to think of it up real close
It takes something special to be something special
Clint Burrows, now, his kind don't just happen
Sure, there was something to start with
But you might say a man like him
Shook the hand of all his chances
One Sunday, for example, he comes walking into church
Naked as a jaybird and says in that soft deep voice of his
Thanks, Lord, for making me like I am—thought I'd just drop in
And let you know I'm not ashamed of it either

Of course there were some wondered what he was getting at
Especially since it was the first time he'd ever attended services
And I personally knew he hadn't been steeping himself
In the Good Book on the sly because every now and again
When I'd pass the saloon on my way home from playing hookey
He'd beckon me in to read a piece out of the paper to him
Usually something from the front page with his picture
        alongside it
First whole dollar I ever saw I got that way

Anybody'd get the idea from those stories
That Clint Burrows must have been a real whiz in school
Ten million dollar killing in cotton futures
Sells Lackawanna rolling stock in brilliant coup
Astute speculator again stuns Wall Street
Well, if he was, I always thought it pretty strange
That he never bothered to learn how to read or write
Why, he even had a little fellow named Samuel T. Tomkins
Who wrote all his checks for him

But, as my Dad always said, you had to hand it to Clint Burrows
—In fact, that's just what everybody made a big habit of
Except when he'd give me those bright shiny silver dollars,
 that is

It was pretty strange, too, how one fine day
Clint Burrows clumb clear to the top
Of an oak tree smack in the center of the courthouse park
And there wasn't anybody important you can think of
Didn't come and try to talk him out of staying up there
Until he died
But that's just what he did—
Yep, that's just what Mr. Burrows did.

In the Courtyard of Secret Life

The earth-animal tastes
Blood on his back; spurs of hate and ill will
Have ripped him raw.
What now to him this talk of purer villagehoods
Above some flight of cloud-held stairs?

Ah, Accuser-Judge
And all your sidelines-executioners,
What is the crime here?
That this flea has nipped some star's behind?
Made little stink-robed earthlings spout of their godhood?

It would appear that blowing up the dog
Is how you would go about freeing him of pests;
But what that Houseman up there in his high white wood
Will think of such a drastic procedure,
May well give you a bit of a fast hop on the other
 foot entirely!

Just outside Tombstone

Hey there, you in the macadam suit! Mr. U. S. Highway #1—
    How's that for a fancy name, eh?
Or maybe you're only some casual man of leaning like me, huh?
Spooking up pals out of shadows, making buddies from candy
    and cigarette wrappers?
Whooo–ee! Boy! that is a freight train!
Good ten mile from here—Be an hour 'fore we smell her breath,
    I betyuh.

Getting used to the idea that when you're on your uppers
    but good
There's no use pretending that any kind of blather at all
Will make a damn bit of difference—
Like sometime a guy will be outa work
A couple weeks—sure, even more—it don't mean
The end of the world. But oncet you get over
In that column with the "goin' nowheres"
And you figure what the hell
Ain't no one town nor nothing better than any other
'Cause it's all the wrong damn fit—just different ways
    of bein' fouled up—
Like my old man sweatin' his nuts off all his life
At the same crummy rotten job—and for what? You ask?
Why, so he'll look respectable and proud in the breadline!
But don't get me started on that, mister—it's bad
To laugh on an empty stomach. Let me
Tell you what we've got right here and now.
That's no houselight over there—had you fooled, didn't it?
Hell, it's just another place they sell gas and beaded pillows.
There's never any houselight in this bitch of a country.
Remember that, mac. Yeah, I know you're just a newspaper
Blown against the fence. Met a lot of you fellows. Whooo-ee!
But those jelly-like blobs stuck to carseats,
What would they need with houselights? Tell me that!

Mean to say you thought they were alive?
Why I've known tumbleweeds with more brains than you've got.
All right, blow off into the ditch—be a crummy sorehead.
Hey there! Come on—there must be somebody around!
I bet you if right now—right this minute—
A man-sized, living, breathing heart
Jumped all by itself off one of those big shiny damn buses
And started to head over here
They'd have it clubbed to a pulp
Before anybody could say
If this is the human race
I'll just dash down that rathole
And pull it to hell in after me!

It's Because Your Heart Is Pure, Honey

They won't let you in there for no seven cents
So Sweet Day asked some old little man
Who looked about broke in the middle
From doing right by the boss for maybe twenty-thirty years
How come that gun-colored fellow
Won't let me in The Hippodrome for no seven cents
I want to see all those big white paper horses
Dancing round and round
For that shiny goldhaired lady with the torn-off face
But the little old honest working man
Is in such a hurry to get to the corner bar
Where he can watch some not so white and not so paper horses
Of his own that he doesn't bother to tell her something
He sure as shooting should know by heart if nowhere else
That prosperity is just around the coroner
And that this time preparedness
Looks to be the only lay-away plan ever thought up
That hasn't got a single flaw in it anywhere.

Morning, My Prince—the Eye That Walks

O hand that smooths the air's flesh,
O hand terrible of
His gazing touch—
O still as leaf's breath, O loud as dust,
O hand that soothes the vast hurt of the waters,
Excuse me for wishing that there was
A bikerider with floppy yellow shoes
Whizzing merrily along here.

And you, O hand, could let him pass
Into some unfenced yard where people
Laugh just for the hell of it
And never give a particular damn
Who said what wise and dreary thing
About some particularly joyless lot of fluff.

O kind and gracious hand,
Thank you for this beautiful day!
—How horrible it all is

When We Were Here Together

When we were here together in a place we did not know, nor one
another.

A bit of grass held between the teeth for a moment, bright hair
on the wind. What we were we did not know, nor ever the grass
or the flame of hair turning to ash on the wind.

But they lied about that. From the beginning they lied. To the
child, telling him that there was somewhere anger against him,
and a hatred against him, and only for the reason of his being

478

in the world. But never did they tell him that the only evil and danger was in themselves; that they alone were the poisoners and the betrayers; that they—they *alone*—were responsible for what was being done in the world.

And they told the child to starve and to kill the child that was within him; for only by doing this could he safely enter their world; only by doing this could he become a useful and adjusted member of the community which they had prepared for him. And this time, alas, they did not lie.

And with the death of the child was born a thing that had neither the character of a man nor the character of a child, but was a horrible and monstrous parody of the two; and it is in his world now that the flesh of man's spirit lies twisted and despoiled under the indifferent stars.

When we were here together in a place we did not know, nor one another. O green this bit of warm grass between our teeth— O beautiful the hair of our mortal goddess on the indifferent wind.

"O Now the Drenched Land Wakes"

O now the drenched land wakes;
Birds from their sleep call
Fitfully, and are still.
Clouds like milky wounds
Float across the moon.

O love, none may
Turn away long
From this white grove
Where all nouns grieve.

The Rose of Life

What need? This strange desire for something which desire
itself seemingly has no understandable use for. A pebble . . .
What is a "pebble"? This strange mold, this shape of an un-
imaginable life, this . . . this *way of ease* for something we can't
even so much as guess at! The "nature" of the world around us
. . . into which we so blindly poke the stick of our blunted and
unmanageable senses. For the pebble is, after all—before all!—
something very "real." Even we know this, we whose only con-
ception of reality is in the reflected image of our eyes looking
back at us through what we "see."

So it is no wonder—and at once, it is absolutely inconceivable!—
that every worthwhile, meaningful message between men since
the start has been a message of only one kind.

A message of Passionate Folly!

A love letter to the Boatman's Beautiful Daughter.

Why beautiful? (For often she is not, by any dispassionate stand-
ard, even comely.) Ah, but she is beautiful, she is always beauti-
ful. Because *loved!* She is loved! And not in some cut and dried
"cause and effect" sense at all; no, it is not that, it is certainly not
that—for she is loved in an indissoluble, simultaneous union, a
union wherein what is merged becomes the instrument of separa-
tion from all that binds man to unlighted earth.

And in that is man's way of ease. Only by becoming *something
else* does he find what truly stirs him, what causes him to be
truly unmindful of his lot—because in that sacred moment he is
freed to wander among the terrible and majestic beings of his
own anonymous imaginings.

Where no peace is sought, and no salvation, and no wisdom; where all is attained outside the self, without striving for anything more than to be conscious that what one believes himself to be is only the distorted mirror-image of what he knows cannot possibly exist. And in that wonderful awareness, in that country whose every frontier is an abyss, whose every horizon is a pronouncement of the meaninglessness of all temporal concerns, dwells the goddess whom we have called the Boatman's Beautiful Daughter. And who is this wondrous being, this enchantress not of earth, not of man's most ardently dreamed heaven, but out of their secret union come?

The pebble is. The tree. The sunlight on the water. The fiery storm above the mountain. The face of a young girl. Of an old woman. Of a child. The blind touching of bodies.

All these she is. All these carrying their message of Passionate Folly!

And this I call The Rose of Life.

O bitter Rose of Life! O beautfiul Rose of Life! O wondrous Rose of Life! In its petals we are all so briefly, briefly enfolded.

O glorious Rose of Life! Unknowable—it is all we would know.

O belief in a radiant day in the terrible reality of this so complete night!

This message of Passionate Folly! We live—and then we do not live—understanding as much of the one state as of the other.

This only and creature-steeped way of ease for man in the unchartable and awesome continents of himself.

"Who'll That Be"

Who'll that be,
    Your little pouty kitten?
Coat as fluffy as a cloud's frontroom . . .
O, milkjug on th' mountain,
Hoofprints on th' sea,   .
    My little honey, you wonder me.

Who'll that be,
    Your little dancin' horse?
Bridle as sparkly as a river's tiepin . . .
O, moonlight on the fountain,
Startalk along th' sea,
    My little honey, you wonder me.

Who'll that be,
    Your little sleepy wren?
Feathers as pretty as a snowfall's shirt . . .
O, airfolk at their courtin',
Angelwalkin' on th' sea,
    O my little honey, you wonder me.

Autobiographical Note

My father, Eating Small Boat,
Used to say that this white man business remind me
Of a time there was oh maybe a good fifty or sixty Chiefs
Come into the Council Tent frowning at every blade of grass
Because somebody had been hunting at the wrong time
Or some such earth-rumbling thing
And they're about to shake out the Painted Sticks of Judgment
When somebody notices one of those little buffalo bugs

With a bright wavy cross stamped on his rearend
And he's tugging away like crazy at a ball of birddirt
Trying to drag it up and over the Sacred Moccasin
Of the oldest and most important Chief in all the Sioux Nation.

Well, now, for maybe an oak tree's heartbeat
They just stand gawking at that goofy little bug
Bent down so low their feathers seem to cover a single
    great head.
So then—then that determined little cuss,
With one last wiggle of that gaudy-funny behind,
Succeeds in getting it up and over—
When *bam!* there he is flat on his back!
But still hugging away at that bit of birddirt!
Well, very slowly those Chiefs raised themselves up—and they
    cleared their throats,
As though each has suddenly thought of something very
    important to say.
And then—then they all started to laugh!
And those Chiefs they whooped and they danced around
    in that tent
Until finally the whole damn thing came tumbling down
    on top of them!

"Let Me In!"

Making the Scene the Hard Way

Hell, they'll never let him in
If you're a fake, then shake
But if you're on the level
Brother, you'd better travel
Because this is Fraud's Hall
And they don't want you in no-how

Welcome freaks and rot-mouth yappers
Phony pukes and monkey-slappers
Funny-hat it for the people
Keep it foul O play it safe and simple
There's nothing better for a laugh
Come on, Looney, off with the pants
Jig and dance, let your bottom shine
Show 'em your heart's in the right place
If you want your name in their paper
You'll have to misbehave real nice'n proper

No, they'll never let him in
He might bloody somebody's nose
Oh if you're a fake, buddy, shake
But if you're on the level
You're just asking for trouble
Because this is strictly their dirty lousy show
Only thing to do is tell them No
And go right on traveling alone

"Gentle and Giving" and Other Sayings

Gentle and giving—the rest is nonsense and treason.

No man's life is beautiful except in hurtless work.

The autumn leaf is emblazoned with spring's belief.

He who lives in sin's fear has mistaken eternity's hour for God's year.

It is in the nature of man to expose with laws of doubt and impatience, no feeling of wonder that he should be a participant in such an incredible undertaking; but rather the shameful certainty that what has been willed without him must in some way resemble the productions of his own sand-castle magnificences.

Sin is sin-said.

Truth is always what they don't say.

The concern for "honor" in our dealings, whether with or from another, or filed singly in what may surely be taken to represent the only true and real estate of this flesh, will, I am afraid, like the old use of paupers in ditches to plug up any possible leaks in a one-way economy, fail somewhat of its purpose unless we now consider rather gravely what answer should be given to those who never under any circumstances have any question whatever to ask about anything whatever.

Rathooks and gilly-plasters, my lords! True, it is at best a flea's hole fit, but after all you've only your civilization to bring through it.

Take taking from those who give and nobody anywhere will need any more such gifts.

Since we are not able to do what we should do, perhaps it would be well to consider what we can't do. But since what we can't do is admit that we are not able to do what we should do, we end by finding ourselves somewhat in the position of the fellow who woke up to discover his hands and feet tightly bound and masked maniacs in the act of slaughtering his wife and children and setting fire to the house. In fact, exactly in that position.

"The real truth of the matter" is usually a lie all slicked up to do a spot of their particularly dirty work.

"Mother love"—precisely.

"Modern scientific accomplishments"—a wealth of methods coupled with a poverty of intentions which, having nearly exhausted the hell-potential of the earth, move on now to the first frontier of the heavens.

What shall light us to murder and defile if by some chance the Laws of the State happen to get turned off?

Out of slavery, freedom—yes, and roses from the pig's behind.

Law and order embrace on hate's border.

Knowing you for what you are, Sir, if what you say is not true, I'll have no trouble at all believing it.

Why should anyone be surprised at what the men "in power" are capable of—didn't every mad-Judas one of them begin his career by slowly and brutally strangling an innocent child?

Drugging and rouging the Angel, making him kiss any and every serpent's ass for pay—and there you have the art of our day.

About the poet Legion. Oh yes, I agree with you completely—taste, sensibility, talent, until they come out of his ears; but what a foul shame all that has to be wasted on such an out-and-out, no-good, irresponsible bastard.

Yes, they've dirtied the tree, and dirtied the earth around it, but somehow I feel they won't succeed in keeping much more than the record of their own lack of spirit and humility tethered here.

God must have loved the people in power, for he made them so very like their own image of him.

486

Who setting forth encounters himself has been the world journey.

Where? What place is a child looking at a bird in?

The consciousness of sin is always looking ahead to what has been.

An ear with a hippopotamus attached—what an amazingly unlikely way for the buzz of a tiny fly to get itself heard!

In the love of a man and a woman is the look of God looking.

"Wide, Wide in the Rose's Side"

Wide, wide in the rose's side
Sleeps a child without sin,
And any man who loves in this world
Stands here on guard over him.

INDEX

491

494

497